SPENSER STUDIES

XIX

SPENSER STUDIES

A Renaissance Poetry Annual

XIX

EDITED BY

William A. Oram   *Anne Lake Prescott*
Thomas P. Roche, Jr.

AMS PRESS
NEW YORK

SPENSER STUDIES
A RENAISSANCE POETRY ANNUAL

edited by

Anne Lake Prescott, William A. Oram, and Thomas P. Roche, Jr.

is published annually by AMS Press, Inc. as a forum for Spenser scholarship and criticism and related Renaissance subjects. Manuscripts must be double-spaced, including notes, which should be grouped at the end and should be prepared according to *The Chicago Manual of Style*. Authors of essay-length manuscripts should include an abstract of 100-150 words and provide a disk version of the article, preferably in a Windows-compatible format. One copy of each manuscript should be sent to Thomas P. Roche, Jr., Department of English, Princeton University, Princeton, NJ 08544, one copy to Anne Lake Prescott, Department of English, Barnard College, Columbia University, 3009 Broadway, New York, NY 10027-6598, and one copy to William A. Oram, Department of English, Smith College, Northampton, MA. 01063

Please send inquiries concerning subscriptions or the availability of earlier volumes to AMS Press, Inc., Brooklyn Navy Yard, 63 Flushing Ave., Bldg. 292, Suite 417, Brooklyn, NY 11205, USA.

ISSN 0195-9468
Volume XIX, ISBN 0-404-19219-X

Contents

Illustrations

Index

LAUREN SILBERMAN

The Faerie Queene, Book V, and the Politics of the Text The Kathleen Williams Lecture, 2002

Reductively political criticism can have the effect of "decanonizing" Spenser for what Louis Montrose has termed Spenser's alleged "racist/Misogynist/elitest/imperialist biases." *The Faerie Queene* is far more subtly engaged by politics than straightforward ideological critique generally allows for. As a test case, three stanzas from Book V of *The Faerie Queene* that articulate a fairly blatant misogyny and male supremacy are read with attention to how various textual processes undercut, subvert, or criticize explicit assertions or narrative situations in the text. Poetic context does not so much repudiate the ideological content of the passages as it disparages the explicit politics while letting it stand.

*W*ITH THE NEWNESS OF NEW HISTORICISM mellowing into familiarity, many critics, including me, find themselves taking a second look at the practice of political criticism. It seems to me quite salutary to try to sort out what is of continuing value in a given school of criticism and what might better be dismissed as its early excesses. Parenthetically, I was tempted to say "lasting value" instead of "continuing value," but as Spenser reminds us, apocalyptic Sabaoths sight pronouncements are, by nature, premature. It is too soon to tell what will really last. I should like to begin by making some general comments about the practice of ideological critique, then focus closely on the Radigund episode in Book V of *The Faerie Queene* and then on three particular stanzas, the ideology of which seems clear—and ripe for criticism. The stanzas are what Carol Kaske has termed "red flag stanzas," and, although Professor Kaske is fully capable of speaking for herself on the matter, her felicitous phrase has always called to my mind the delicious image of red flags waving in a field full of bulls. The stanzas I shall be considering articulate fairly blatant misogyny and male supremacy. The first stanza occurs after Artegall has been captured by the Amazon Radigund and forced to wear a dress and spin, and the narrator condemns the cruelty of womenkind when they repudiate their just subjection to men. The second two occur when Britomart has defeated and killed Radigund and describe how Britomart restores rulership to men. Although these three stanzas are often treated as straightforward expressions of Spenser's ideological commitments, I shall argue that the contexts in which these charged stanzas occur—of Book V, of the entire *Faerie Queene*, of literary traditions with which Spenser was familiar and of sixteenth-century political history—complicate and enrich what seems to be ideologically straightforward assertion. I should like to suggest—briefly and by a kind of extrapolation—that if the sexual politics of these stanzas is more complicated than it first seems, then the political commitments of episodes that allegorize near-contemporary events in Ireland and the Low Countries as the rescue of imperilled female figures Irena and Belge are also more complicated than might initially appear. Being a resisting reader—to use feminist critic Judith Fetterly's useful term—is inescapable, given the horrible ideas people have had in the past—and doubtless still have today, although we have much less perspective on our own ideological predilections than on those of other people in other times. Not to register distress at doctrine offensive to modern sensibilities is likely, I think, to entail shutting down one's attention-paying capabilities. If you are not, in some way, disturbed by manifestations in a literary text of what would in other circumstances disturb you, then you might not be taking it all in. Besides, we have some obligation to exercise our moral judgment; the alternative is to let it atrophy.

In this regard, I am reminded of an experience I had as an undergraduate at Smith College in a course on Chaucer. The professor was a marvelous, tweedy gentleman of the old school who managed to teach the entire "Miller's Tale" with great appreciation of the humor but without once uttering the word "fart"—his delicacy was charmingly old-fashioned even then and undoubtedly stands as a reproach to contemporary willingness to use such words just to get a cheap laugh. At any rate, when he turned to "The Reeve's Tale" in the following class, he confidently announced to us that the humor of that tale, in which two itinerant scholars have impromptu and unsolicited sex with the wife and daughter of the miller who has put them up for the night, was nearly as delightful as the humor of "The

Miller's Tale." Well, no. With the wisdom of hindsight that is one of the primary compensations of growing older, I can appreciate how potentially damaging it was for a person of the authority of my Chaucer professor to assure a roomful of young women that a representation of acquaintance rape not so very different from situations with which any number of them might have had to contend in their own lives was all good fun. Such a literary judgment is unseemly in a way that makes all of the merely off-the-wall readings of literary texts one might encounter—or produce—pale into insignificance. But even as a purely literary judgment, my Chaucer professor's decision simply to laugh off the sexual violence of "The Reeve's Tale" does not seem to produce a very satisfying engagement with the text. In his book *Chaucer and the Subject of History*, Lee Patterson argues that "The Reeve's Tale" extends and intensifies the *fabliau* violence that the preceding "Miller's Tale" more successfully contained. I'm not necessarily endorsing his argument, but it seems to me that Patterson's reading allows more of "The Reeve's Tale" to resonate and to be grappled with than a reading that fails to register any moral judgment of what is being represented, if only to decide that that judgment is anachronistic.

Notwithstanding legitimate reasons to be resisting readers, however, it seems to me that the current tendency is to err on the side of resistance to the point that resistance threatens to become reductiveness. Needless to say, all criticism is reductive—supposedly, T.S. Eliot was asked to explain the meaning of *The Wasteland* and, by way of response, read the entire poem back to his interlocutor. Similarly, when in Book I of *The Faerie Queene* Archimago disguised as The Redcrosse Knight asks Una "what the lyon ment"—presumably Archimago wonders whether the lion intends to make lunch of them—Una replies with a full repetition of her adventures. Nevertheless, some criticism is more reductive than other criticism—and more reductive than it needs to be. *Ars longa, vita brevis*—we can never do full justice to any text worth our attention. But we can try to be attentive to the ways we contextualize what we read.

One concern is the problem of anachronism, of assessing the politics of an earlier text on the basis of unexamined contemporary political assumptions and in the context of a twenty-first century range of alternatives. To take one example, in the sixteenth century, the probable alternative to a strong monarchy was not participatory democracy but anarchy, civil war, and the reign of wicked uncles. To take another, in the sixteenth century, Irish home rule was not an option. The available choices apparent in sixteenth-century England would have been rule by an oligarchy holding allegiance to the English crown or rule by an oligarchy having political ties to Spain. This is not to justify England's colonial policy in Ireland in all of its nasty particulars or to naturalize English discourse about Ireland designed to justify English colonial rule. It is rather to suggest some constraining pressures of context.

A further concern in judging the politics of a literary text is the issue of the text's stance to its thematic content, the possibility that various textual processes undercut, subvert, or criticize explicit assertions or narrative situations in the text. This probably seems embarrassingly obvious, but it is amazing how often one encounters critics who function as if assertions in literary text are unproblematic expressions of authorial intent or ideological statement—or how easily one is tempted to do so oneself.

The alternative, an ironic reading, presents its own hazards as the Scylla and Charybdis of the critical enterprise. On the one hand is the risk of neutralizing everything that from a contemporary standpoint is ideologically unpalatable by an ironic reading. I always think, in this regard, of Edmund Kean's performance as Shylock. At the point at which Shylock hears that Jessica has eloped with Lorenzo and a bag of money, Kean would deliver Shylock's lines "I would my daughter were dead at my foot, and the jewels in her ear: would she were hearsed at my foot, and the ducats in her coffin!" and then ad lib "No! No!" That is a histrionic version of something extremely easy to do by subtler means. Unless, however, we are prepared to believe that *The Canterbury Tales* wholeheartedly endorses the monk's rejection of monastic rule or that Swift *really* advocated eating babies as a solution to economic problems in Ireland, we are stuck with ironic readings. No one disputes this in principle. Nevertheless, there remains the possibility, especially when one is in the ideological-critique mode, of shutting one's ears to irony and attacking a text in a crude way for precisely what the text itself attacks in a subtle way. I suppose that if dead poets came back to haunt critics who misrepresented their work, none of us would be getting much sleep.

It might be worth reflecting for a moment on what leads people to focus on the expository aspect of poetry, whether to critique or to affirm. On the one hand, there has been a fairly strong drive among critics, especially of previous generations, to identify their sense of self with the writer's authority, not, however, conceived as authority to question, explore, see things different ways at once, but authority to promulgate doctrine. This has generated pressure to take literary works at face value. More recently, critics seem to be locating a sense of self in a sort of contestatory relationship with the author or text, manifested sometimes by a certain censoriousness of tone as much as by explicit critique of ideological content. This stance affords, I think, a sense of political importance and political agency to the critical enterprise that it might not otherwise be seen as having. Considering both these positions together, one begins to appreciate Charles Kingsley's observation that " a [games]keeper is only a poacher turned outside in, and a poacher a keeper turned inside out." I find any naively expository approach particularly unsatisfactory when reading *The Faerie Queene* because it seems to me that the authoritative narrative voice—what Harry Berger memorably calls the "moralist and oralist"—is one of the least reliable things in the entire poem and that one of the major processes of *The Faerie Queene* in general is to put its own discourse in question.

Politically aware criticism is immensely exciting and allows us to see literature in substantially new ways and see our own political commitments in new ways, but politically reductive criticism has the effect not of changing undergraduates' political ideas but of moving the best minds among them out of the field of English literature. I should say at this point that I have chosen not to offer straw person examples of what might be considered reductive ideological critique of Spenser mostly because I think that the real problem with reductively ideological reading is not what gets published in journals but what gets rejected by journals and what gets filtered down into classrooms—or what doesn't get into classrooms at all when departments of English do not offer graduate courses on Spenser or teach his work to undergraduates.

In his essay "Spenser's Domestic Domain," Louis Montrose articulates a powerful challenge to what he identifies as the "decanonizing" of Spenser on the grounds of Spenser's alleged "racist/misogynist/elitest/imperialist biases," and I'd like to think that Montrose is signaling a trend when he defends Spenser, that the critical *Zeitgeist* is shifting in ways to promote wider engagement with Spenser's work—perhaps if Spenser is sufficiently de-canonized, he can be reintroduced as a noncanonical author. Or perhaps we at Kalamazoo should work to supplant the New Historicism with the New Hedonism, confident that Spenser will be less readily dismissed for alleged political biases when the intellectual pleasure of engagement with a literary text becomes more central to the critical enterprise.

Let's turn, then, to some promising examples of Spenser as sexist and see what kind of fun we can have. First, however, I should briefly like to contextualize the Radigund episode in a broad reading of *The Faerie Queene* and then of Book V. First, I want to have as a working proposition that individual books of *The Faerie Queene* can be seen

as essays—as is signalled by their subtitles: Of Holiness, Of Chastity
as in *De Senectute* or "Of Books"—essays as in attempts at exploring
a given problem. *The Faerie Queene* is in some ways like a series of
projects as each successive book takes up problems that were left out
of previous ones. I am positing here a high degree of intentionality;
these are intellectual projects (among a lot of other things), the product of a powerful, quirky poetic intellect. *The Faerie Queene* can be
seen in the tradition of the Renaissance double book—works such
as *Utopia*, *The Scholemaster*, and *Don Quixote*—which offer contrasting
perspectives on their subject matter. Book I establishes Christian
eschatology as the ultimate context. A standard of truth is established
as the evidence of things unseen. Throughout Book I, the hero, the
Redcrosse Knight, is educated in not trusting his senses. Underlying
this process is a recurring pun on truth/trouthe: trouthe—faith and
loyalty—is shown to be superior to truth conceived as empiricism.
Ultimately, the fallen world is properly seen as a series of signs point-
ing to the higher truth available to faith alone. Book II takes up the
project of coping with, rather than transcending, the fallen world. It
focuses on problems of naively applying Christian allegory to secular
circumstances. Book II demonstrates how faith in methodology ab-
sent a concern for how that methodology functions in context results
in a systematic and dysfunctional defense against, rather than engagement with, the sensual world. Book III shifts the basis of allegory to
something appropriate to making sense of sensual experience, working from within conventional erotic discourse to produce something
new. Book III uses a female hero as a defamiliarization device and
presents the ideal of androgyny as an emblem of the capacity for
change and improvisation. As *The Faerie Queene* continues from
Book III into Book IV in the 1596 installment, the image of the
hermaphrodite with which Book III concluded in 1590 is cancelled
as Book IV shows how the ideals constructed in Book III are destroyed when subjected to the pressure of existing institutions and
ideologies: the Book III ideal of love cannot stand up to hierarchy
and its epistemology of improvisation cannot survive the desire for
security.

For a full discussion of the above, you can buy my book—please.
Let me move on to current speculations about Book V. To do this,
I will need to pick up the pace, but please bear with me. It seems to
me that in Book V we see a shift from the theoretical consideration
in Book IV of existing institutions and ideologies—that is, of how
existing institutions and ideologies ruin beautiful ideals—to a practical consideration of why beautiful ideals have to be sacrificed for
immediate political goals. It is fair to say that Book V displays great

cynicism, but it also demonstrates a clear sense of just what is sacrificed. The sacrifice is considerable but the stakes are high: preventing defeat and conquest by Catholic Spain. Book V provides a critical examination of discourse as agitprop. It registers the need for such manifestly political discourse while at the same time making its operations available for scrutiny. Propagandistic discourse appears, to a great extent, as the manipulation of sexual ideology and images for political ends. Whereas in previous books, erotic discourse was a vehicle for understanding the world, in Book V erotic discourse and images are a means of generating politically useful emotion. In a double figuration, the nation is conceived as the body politic and represented as a lady to be rescued. Ireland is lady Irena, menaced with execution by Grantorto, a wicked giant who stands allegorically for the great, twisted wrong, and political tyranny of Catholic Spain. The Low Countries are presented as Mama Belge and her babies—the seventeen provinces of the Low Countries ruled by Philip II of Spain represented by the seventeen babies slain by the giant Geryoneo— an image that might be translated nearly unchanged to a World War I poster. In the Belge episode, graphic images of sexual violence are shown to be a means of inciting and directing whatever emotional energy is at hand to political goals.

Prince Arthur rides to Belge's rescue and defeats Geryoneo, but Arthur's single combat with this representation of wicked, Catholic Spain as a male knight is followed by a more graphic encounter with a nameless, explicitly female monster who lurks under the altar of an unnamed Idol, a monster whom he kills in a manner that has erotic overtones:

> But then the feend her selfe more fiercely reard
> Vppon her wide greatwings, and strongly flew
> With all her body at his head and beard,
> That had he not foreseene with heedfull vew,
> And thrown his shield atween, she had him done to rew.

> But as she prest on him with heauy sway,
> Vnder her wombe his fatall sword he thrust,
> And for her entrailes made an open way,
> To issue forth; the which once being brust,
> Like to a great Mill damb forth fiercely gusht,
> And powred out of her infernall sinke
> Most vgly filth, and poyson therwith rusht,
> That him nigh choked with the deadly stinke:

Such loathly matter were small lust to speake, or thinke.

(5.11.30–31)

This is properly horrifying, but the equation of sex and violence in the killing of the female monster and the disgust directed at her grotesquely "leaky" body are not, I think, presented as something fundamentally ambiguous. This is in conspicuous contrast to earlier episodes. In Timias's fight with the wonderfully gross personification of Lust over the lady Amoret, Lust holds Amoret in the position of human shield. Timias, intending to pierce Lust with his spear, keeps hitting Amoret, much to the delight of Lust. When is a spear not just a spear? The ambiguity of what is represented when Timias "fights Lust" reflects the complexity of his feelings and intentions towards Amoret, whom he is committed to love from afar. To take another example from Book IV, Britomart recognizes Artegall as the knight whom she loves, and he falls in love with her, after they traverse to and fro, trading strokes in a battle with highly erotic overtones. In those earlier episodes, the registers of sex and violence complicate the action in a way they do not in the fight between Prince Arthur and the nameless female monster. The point is not that Spenser here condones unconditionally and unreflectively the equation of sex and violence, but that he condones it conditionally and reflectively. I doubt that the self-awareness with which Spenser uses images of sexual violence to incite patriotic fervor made him a better man, but it probably made him a better poet.

The episode in which those two passages of apparently clear, but objectionable ideology occur concerns the issue of women's rule presented from what seems like the perspective of John Knox. A monstrous regiment of women, led by the Amazon Radigund, is overthrown by Britomart, who rescues her lover Artegall from the Amazon, returns the women of Radigund's city to their former subjection to men and then disappears from the text unceremoniously. Having been released from Radigund's prison, Artegall leaves Britomart to continue his quest to rescue Irena, the female embodiment of Ireland. Our last sight of Britomart has her riding aimlessly from place to place seeking to ease her sorrow. It seems to me that the disappearance of Britomart from the text is as significant to a reading of the episode as the overtly ideological content. Given the focus throughout Books III and IV on the importance of Britomart's adventures as a goal-directed quest, the description of her random movement for purely anodyne purposes seems to have signifying value: something important in previous books has been given up in pursuit of the more politically and historically determinable quests of Book V.

In a sense, Britomart falls into historical allegory by acting like Elizabeth and never recovers. As Louis Montrose has pointed out in an essay on *Midsummer Night's Dream*, Elizabeth benefited from conventional sexual politics and condoned sexual hierarchy from which she conveniently exempted herself. Similarly, all the inhabitants of Radigund's city adore Britomart as a goddess and "hearkened to her loring" (V.vii.42.9) as they subordinate all other women. Determinate historical allegory in Book V is even harder on other fictional characters. The wicked witch Duessa, who in previous books has demonstrated splendid resilience as she keeps turning up again and again to make trouble, gets beheaded when she comes to look too much like Mary, Queen of Scots. Having experimented with really very radical and utopian images of gender and gender relations in previous books, images that bore precious little relation to late sixteenth-century social practice, Spenser in Book V gets real, while, with a genuinely extraordinary critical intelligence, registers some sense of just what price reality exacts.

The Radigund episode takes the ideal of androgyny figured by Britomart as Martial Maid and affirmed in the image of the hermaphrodite at the conclusion of the 1590 *Faerie Queene* and subjects it to a reality check. An earlier episode—Britomart's encounter with Dolon; or The Night the Bed Fell—sets out the ideal that the Radigund episode sends up. In the House of Dolon, Britomart—wearing her armor all night and accompanied by Artegall's groom, the iron man Talus—is mistaken for Artegall and attacked by his enemies. She has no difficulty supplying the place of Artegall and dispatching his enemies. In contrast, the Radigund episode plays cultural construction of gender against biological gender ascription. The episode contrasts the fluid ease with which cultural constructions of gender may be traded back and forth with the resistance of biological gender to similar reversal. Initially, Radigund's coup seems to affirm the primacy of gender as a cultural construction: her usurpation of male political prerogatives is accompanied by her assignment of female cultural attributes to the men she subdues. Artegall, along with other knights defeated by Radigund, is required to wear female clothing and to sit and spin. Not only is gender construed as a function of social role and artifact—the distaff versus the sword—but the entire situation is conspicuously mediated by the literary and art historical traditions of Hercules and Omphale or Iole.

The most commonly accepted version of the myth, found in the works of Diodorus Siculus, has Hercules sold to Queen Omphale as

a penance for an act of murder committed in a rage. Many versions,
especially in the visual arts, emphasize his having to wear women's
clothing and spinning. Boccaccio conflates Omphale with Iole, one
of Hercules' many love interests, and ascribes the transvestitism to
Hercules' desire to please her. In subduing Artegall, Radigund successfully repeats a very literary model of the reversal of cultural attributes and the effeminization of the male. However, the grotesquely
comic love story that follows Artegall's cross-dressed imprisonment,
as Radigund falls in love with her prisoner, shows how sexual physiology complicates the cultural gender bending upon which Radigund's rule depends. Radigund finds her intended sexual exploitation
of Artegall frustrated, since the more she starves him, the less he is
able to perform sexually. As Talus observes to Britomart, "he is not
the while in state to woo" (V.vi.16). Book V grounds its repudiation
of female rule in physiology as a primary, highly deterministic force,
but, ironically, the specific dynamic used to figure the biological
necessity for male domination and female subservience is the accommodation of male impotence. Accordingly, Britomart's intervention
on behalf of patriarchy proceeds from her disillusionment with a
cross-dressed Artegall:

> Ah my deare Lord, what sight is this (quoth she)
>> What May-game hath misfortune made of you:
>> Where is that dreadfull manly looke? Where be
>> Those mighty palmes, the which ye wont t'embrew
>> In bloud of Kings, and great hoastes to subdew:
>> Could ought on earth so wondrous change haue wrought,
>> As to haue robde you of that manly hew?
>> Could so great courage stouped haue to ought?
>> Then farewell fleshly force; I see thy pride is nought.
>
> (5.7.40)

If Britomart is to get a dynasty out of this man, she is clearly going
to have to make accommodations, and make them she does. The
Radigund episode presents male dominance as naturally, biologically
determined. The text is framed in a way, however, not to subvert
or repudiate male dominance, but to rob determinism of much of
its glamour. Parenthetically, I do not think that my reading of the
Radigund episode recruits Spenser into the ranks of contemporary
feminists. After all, theorists of male backlash make similar arguments
on behalf of male dominance, but their tone seems to be "Easily
threatened and proud of it, man!" Spenser seems to maintain a fairly

strong and ironic sense of the pragmatic politics underlying the ideology of the male rule that he advocates. In this, perhaps, we might see Spenser the colonial administrator, who does what he thinks he has to do without entertaining abundant illusions about it.

With the preceding in mind, let's look at the two red-flags-in-the-bullring passages and see if the explicit politics are not more complicated than first appears. The first follows a description of Artegall, forced to wear a dress and spin flax along with the other male prisoners of Radigund.

> Such is the crueltie of womenkynd,
>   When they haue shaken off the shamefast band,
>   With which wise Nature did them strongly bynd,
>   T'obay the heasts of mans well ruling hand,
>   That then all rule and reason they withstand,
>   To purchase a licentious libertie.
>   But vertuous women wisely understand,
>   That they were borne to base humilitie,
> Vnlesse the heauens them lift to lawfull soueraintie.
>
> (V.v.25)

On the face of it, that is a blatant endorsement of female subordination, uncompromising except as is necessary to accommodate women who actually hold power, namely Elizabeth. The obvious way to neutralize the political content of this passage is to posit an unreliable narrator, and I am about to do something like that, but I should like to locate that ironic reading in the contexts of a theory about how slippery the narrative voice is in this passage and how a network of literary subtexts complicates that voice. I think that the seemingly authoritative—and misogynist—statement in the passage actually inscribes the all-too-human impulse to abstract and universalize personal injury. In her splendid book, *Thinking About Women*, Mary Ellman counters the accusation that women always take things personally with the observation "Men always get *im*personal. If you hurt their feelings, they make Boyle's law out of it" (xiii) The tendency to make a legal case out of injured feelings is not limited to men—Elizabeth did it all the time—but the particular sense of personal injury being projected onto the narrator and ventriloquized in this stanza as authoritative doctrine—in a spectacularly depersonalizing gambit—clearly has its source in Artegall and his fellow male prisoners. This interpretation is suggested by comparing Spenser's treatment with its source in the *Orlando Furioso*. In both works, the Martial

Maid heroine thinks herself deserted by her lover and laments his absence, but where Spenser's Britomart blames Artegall and herself pretty much equally, Ariosto's heroine Bradamante conspicuously blames everyone but herself for her lover's absence. I should argue that in the stanza in which Spenser's narrator castigates women in general, the narrator is not simply a mouthpiece for the poet, but rather Spenser's narrator here echoes Ariosto's character Bradamante and thereby takes Bradamante's strategy of projecting blame outward to a further level of depersonalization. Delegating a personal complaint to the narrative voice itself one-ups Bradamante's practice of blaming her troubles on other characters. Here is Britomart:

> There she began to make her monefull plaint
>   Against her Knight, for being so vntrew;
>   And him to touch with falshoods fowle attaint,
>   Oft did she blame her selfe, and often rew,
>   For yelding to a straungers loue so light,
>   Whose life and manners straunge she neuer knew;
>   And euermore she did him sharpely twight
> For breach of faith to her, which he had firmely plight.
>
>   (V.vi.12)

Here is Bradamante:

> Then, newly giving vent to her distress,
> Repeating her by now familiar wails,
> Calling Ruggiero cruel, pitiless,
> To the full blast of woe she spreads her sails
> And in an anguished voice with bitterness
> Against high Heaven itself she rants and rails,
> Calling it weak, unjust and impotent,
> Since perjury receives no punishment.
>
> She turned against Melissa in her grief,
> The grotto and the oracle she cursed,
> To which she has accorded such belief,
> She'll perish in the sea of love immersed.
> She turned next to Marfisa for relief;
> Her mounting frenzy rising to its worst,
> She cried and shrieked and endless clamour made
> And on her kindness threw herself for aid.
>
>   (O.F. 42.25–26)

I do not think that the misogynist and patriarchal content of what Spenser's narrator says is repudiated by its context as an allusion to the unreliable utterances of Bradamante in the same way that, say, various aspects of Sir Scudamore's sexual politics are repudiated in Book IV, largely by their disastrous consequences. Rather, in the Radigund episode, the ideology of male dominance is disparaged but left to stand.

Add to the mix, just to show you how complicated literary filiations can get, the fact that in addition to the passage from Ariosto just cited, the Alexandretta episode from the *Orlando Furioso*, one of the most brilliant send-ups of utopian thinking I have ever read, figures into the subtext of Artegall's encounter with Radigund. Let's back up all the way to the *Argonautica*, a romance written by Apollonius in the 3rd century B.C.E. In it we read of Lemnos, the island of killer women, who, having dispatched their faithless husbands, establish an all-female community ruled by the queen Hypsipyle. Their experiment in female rule is a resounding success, except for the one problem of producing future generations of Lemnians. Jason and the Argonauts arrive on the scene as a kind of floating sperm bank, and that problem is solved. Hypsipyle says something to the effect of "I'll call you," to Jason as he sails off after the Golden Fleece. In Ariosto's version, the women, abandoned on an island by their lovers, form their own society and establish a policy of killing men on philosophical grounds, because men deserve it. The society constructed by a founder figure keeps having to be reworked in order to accommodate various features of reality. First, all men are killed on principle. Then, a small number of men washed up on their island are spared at random for reproductive purposes, in the ratio of one man for every ten women. Then, because one of the male prisoners is particularly cute and appeals to the founder's daughter, a custom is established by which any given man may be spared if he defeats ten male knights and—the proviso is later added—satisfies ten women in bed. In addition to having a lot of good, dirty fun, Ariosto is showing here, I think, how a utopian society founded on first principles has to compromise its principles in order to survive in the real world. I also think that Spenser might be adapting Ariosto's bawdy female utopia as he shows Radigund's regime giving way to the world as we know it.

As with the first stanza examined, which excoriated the cruelty of womankind, the stanzas detailing Britomart's restoration of male dominance to Radigund's city occur in a context that complicates them as a political statement without actually repudiating the politics. Here are the stanzas:

So there a while they afterwards remained,
    Him to refresh, and her late wounds to heale:
    During which space she there as Princes rained,
    And changing all that forme of common weale,
    The liberty of women did repeale,
    Which they had long vsurpt; and them restoring
    To mens subiection, did true Iustice deale:
    That they as a Goddesse her adoring,
Her wisedome did admire, and hearkened to her loring.

For all those Knights, which long in captiue shade
    Had shrowded bene, she did from thraldome free;
    And magistrates of all that city made,
    And gaue to them great liuing and large fee:
    And that they should for euer faithfull bee,
    Made them sweare fealty to *Artegall.*
    Who when him selfe now well recur'd did see,
    He purposd to proced, what so be fall,
Vppon his first aduenture, which him forth did call.

                                          (V.vii.42–43)

The presence of patriarchal ideology in a sixteenth-century text might be troubling to twenty-first century sensibilities (although I often wonder why, if it *is* so troubling, some critics seem to have such a good time focusing on it), but it is not particularly problematic in the sense of commanding attention by jarring expectations. What does merit special notice, here, is the fact that two stanzas after we hear that Britomart has repealed the liberty of women, we see Artegall ride off to liberate the lady Irena. In the brief space of two stanzas, we see the sexual part of sexual politics disappear from the discourse and then reappear in a kind of return of the repressed, in the form of Irena, female allegorical embodiment of Ireland.

    The political mythology that represents militarily contested territory as a beleaguered romance heroine is a powerful instrument of ideological manipulation. In giving us some critical perspective on that mythology as we see the beleaguered Irena emerging as a literary transformation of the subjugated women of Radigone, Spenser's text opens up the processes of political discourse in ways that, I suspect, will repay careful attention. The sexual politics of repressing the women of Radigone are part of a much larger picture. That larger picture of political discourse is built up, however, through a range of verbal details of sexual politics. Stanza 42 of Book V presents the forced subordination of women to men as Britomart restores them "to mens subiection." The following stanza turns its attention to the newly liberated men, but it does not record Britomart giving them power over the women, but over the city. This subtle—and, to be sure, slight—asymmetry records, I should argue, a shift from one discursive formation to another. The subordination of women in Radigund's city of Radigone and the idealization of woman as a figure for a nation and people conceived as "the body politic" appear as alternative arrangements. The contrast does not invalidate either formation, but it does highlight both the artifice of the figure of Irena—indeed of each formation—and the political and ideological uses to which each formation may be put. Compare the relative ease with which Artegall rescues damsel-in-distress Irena in a storybook single combat to the mess he gets himself into trying to deal with Radigund as a female adversary. One can readily imagine a colonial administrator entertaining fantasies of rescuing a colonized nation without interference from the colonized themselves. The reality was, of course, killing a lot of Irish in the name of liberating Irena.

Even the idealized representation of Irena's rescue, however, is not without countercurrents. Although Artegall defeats and kills Grantorto, the allegorical embodiment of Spanish Catholic mischief who has been threatening to execute Irena, he must leave Irena before he can reform her kingdom thoroughly. Artegall's climactic victory modulates into a much less triumphalist representation of Elizabethan Irish policy. More conspicuously problematic is the way Artegall's victory over Grantorto is compromised when for pragmatic reasons Artegall performs the same act of discarding his shield for which Sir Burbon/Henri of Navarre is criticized at the opening of Canto 12, an episode about which Anne Prescott enlightened us here at Kalamazoo a few years ago. Sir Burbon has shamefully laid aside the shield carrying the emblem of the true faith in hopes of obtaining the love of his lady Flourdelis—in a clear allegorical representation of the infamous bit of sixteenth-century realpolitik whereby Henri of Navarre decided that "Paris is worth a mass" and became Henri IV of France. Artegall gives Burbon a severe talking-to and then helps him despite his shameful actions, much as Elizabeth, for reasons of political expediency, supported Henri IV even after his conversion to Catholicism. Later in the same canto, in his battle with Grantorto, Artegall lets go of his own shield when his opponent's axe is embedded in it, in what seems to be a purely tactical maneuver on the level of simple action narrative: Artegall is never admonished for a breach of chivalric decorum that is comparable to and, indeed, a clear echo of the lapse that brought shame to Sir Burbon.

I don't know—yet—what to make of all of the poetic complications in the way Spenser represents sixteenth-century history in Book V, but I am convinced that the complications are where most of the fun is. Clearly Elizabethan foreign policy and colonial policy figure into Book V in an important way, and we owe a great deal to New Historicism and other politically informed criticism for not letting us forget that. Similarly, the sexual politics underlying representations of male and female figures—of all sorts—do not cease to be relevant simply because feminist criticism has been practiced in the academy long enough to have a track record of achievement. But the politics are only a place to begin. To see as much as we can in reading Book V of *The Faerie Queene*, we need to deploy our critical faculties—in every sense of the term—with care.

Baruch College

JEFF DOLVEN

The Method of Spenser's Stanza

"The Method of Spenser's Stanza" proposes the analogy of method—in its late sixteenth-century sense, particularly as associated with Ramus—as a way of understanding how Spenser's stanza works. That stanza's two most distinctive moments, the medial couplet and its final alexandrine, have the normative (if by no means inevitable) effects of a second thought in the middest and a summary of sententious closure. It is a shape imposed on experience in order to yield, time after time, a particular form of thought, a particular kind of lesson. In this it is like the dream of a universal method which can be applied in order to give the same intelligibility to diverse materials (e.g., the tendency of Ramist analysis to reduce texts to a single "dialectical ratiocination"). Arthur's advice to Una after the defeat of Orgoglio ("Dear lady, then said that victorious knight [I.viii.44]) makes the principal example.

*L*ET ME BEGIN BY quoting from the story of a clownish young man who sets out on a great quest for which he is not very well prepared. You may find that the details come back to you with a certain alienated majesty:

> A Worthy Knight was riding on the Plain,
> In Armour Clad, which richly did Contain
> The Gallant Marks of many Battels fought,
> Tho' he before no Martial Habit sought;
> How Warlike ere his Person seem'd to Sit
> On a Bold Steed, that scarce obey'd the Bit:
> Upon his Breast a Bloody Cross display'd,
> The Precious Drops for him his Saviour paid;
> And on his Mighty Shield the same did bear,
> To shew his Faith was his Valours Care.[1]

I could go on—as Edward Howard did, at length, casting the whole of Book I into heroic couplets and publishing the results in 1687 as *Spenser Redivivus: Containing the First Book of the Faery Queen, His Essential Design preserv'd, but his obsolete Language and manner of Verse totally laid aside.* In his preface Howard declares himself to be especially concerned with saving his readers from what he called Spenser's "tedious stanza" (A3v). The couplet he prefers may be a tacit slape at rhymeless John Milton, whose *Paradise Lost* goes conspicuously unmentioned in the preface's brief history of English poetic ambition.[2] But that couplet is also a means by which Spenser's great matter might be more "genuinely and succinctly convey'd" (A3v), "abreviated and, as I conceive, improv'd" (A4r).

Howard's claims for his chosen form might remind us of those made by another turner of couplets, Alexander Pope, almost fifty years later. Pope prefaced his *Essay on Man* by arguing that couplets allowed him to treat his subject "more *shortly* [. . .] than in prose itself; and nothing is more certain, than that much of the *force* as well as *grace* of arguments or instructions, depends on their *conciseness . . .* " Couplets served him as a compositional method, a way of thinking and presenting his "principles, maxims, or precepts": their "chain of reasoning" is among the chief means by which (to quote now the *Essay on Criticism*) "*Nature*" may be "*Methodiz'd.*"[3] Compared with Pope, Howard's amateur and uncompressed rhymes cannot be said to show a particularly strong methodizing hand. What I want to ask here is whether method might be exactly the word for what is missing in his rewriting of Spenser; whether it might be the best word for one particular kind of work that the stanza he banishes actually does in its nearly four thousand instances over the length of *The Faerie Queene.*

This is a question I will shortly put to one stanza in particular, Arthur's advice to Una after Red Cross has been haled up from Orgoglio's dungeon. But first I want to consider what that word "method" might have meant to Spenser. The idea of a rational program by which unfounded knowledge might be discarded and new learning built from the foundations—something close to what we might now call scientific method—had to wait for the Royal Academy. The authorities behind the word circa 1590 were as various as Aristotle, the Stoics, Galen, and above all the Protestant educational reformer Petrus Ramus; it was most often understood as a means for bringing systematic order and concision to existing fields of study. A method was a *modus operandi*—*via* and *ordo* were common synonyms—by which diffuse materials could be approached, organized,

and conveyed to others. It offered a model of thinking and a procedure for teaching.[4] Spenser himself never used the word in his poetry,
but he lived in the midst of a great fashion for it, and his friend
Gabriel Harvey was among its early English enthusiasts. When both
men were still at Cambridge Harvey wrote an elegy for Ramus called
Ode Natalia in which a heavenly virgin named Method presides over
the goddesses of the arts of grammar, rhetoric, logic, arithmetic, and
geometry, all reformed by Ramus, and offers consolation to their
unmethodized sisters, music, astronomy, theology, jurisprudence,
and medicine. The work is a peculiar and—for a mind like Spenser's—suggestive compound of method and allegory.[5]

The counsel Arthur gives to Una may bias the case that there is
something methodical or methodizing about the Spenserian stanza
itself. It is one of the most concerted instances of instruction between
characters in the poem, and it puts the peculiar pressure on the representation of thinking that teaching always does. Still I hope it will
set some general features in high relief. It comes in the forty-fourth
stanza of canto viii, Book I:

Faire Lady, then said that victorious knight,
   The things, that grieuous were to doe, or beare,
   Them to renew, I wote, breeds no delight;
   Best musicke breeds delight in loathing eare:
   But th'only good, that growes of passed feare,
   Is to be wise, and ware of like agein.
   This daies ensample hath this lesson deare
   Deepe written in my heart with yron pen,
That blisse may not abide in state of mortal men.

                                                (I.viii.44)[6]

The opening lines are highly controlled. The victorious Arthur begins
with the rhetorician's distinction between doing and suffering, a topos of analysis implying that what follows will be carefully structured
argument. "I wote" reinforces this deliberateness. It concedes to Una
her desire to forget, but also asserts that the wisdom Arthur imparts
is already known, already thought or thought out. That wisdom
might be paraphrased roughly as follows: the past is painful; it is hard
(as always in Spenser) to recognize the difference between agent and
victim, particularly in oneself; renewing the past renews its pain and
confusion. The compound of remembering and repeating in that
word "renew" comes from Aeneas' famous renovare, and for a moment it is as though Arthur were giving advice to Virgil's hero

too—the hero who fears, at the beginning of *Aeneid* II, that in retelling the Fall of Troy he will suffer it again.[7] The problem is old and intractable, but at least Spenser's victorious knight speaks with the authority of one who knows his mind.

The fourth line, then, sounds a kind of preliminary closure: it is syntactically autonomous, and finishes the opening ABAB quatrain with a sententious ring. The next two lines would seem to open up a new unit of thought. The "but" of "but th'only good" is not the unsettling double-take of "Yet armes till that time did he neuer wield" (I.i.1); instead it inaugurates a new quatrain, one that will be a room as fit for its own stage of argument as was the last. But this impression depends upon a hasty reading of that decisive-sounding fourth line, "Best musicke breeds delight in loathing eare," one that (as Hamilton's edition testifies) has provoked more than its share of commentary and emendation.[8] I would suggest the paraphrase, "It is music that best restores delight to an ear poisoned by loathing," and argue that part of the line's difficulty is that it does *not* in fact complete the thought of lines 1 to 3. Instead it is part of lasting good that can come of what you have been through is to remember it well enough to recognize its like in the future. Now the stanza seems to have fallen into three groups of three lines each: not an arrangement abetted by the rhyme scheme, though there are plenty of other examples of it in the poem. What is important for my purposes is that the effect of readjustment I have just described is typical of the unstable relations generated by the couplet at the center of the stanza. Because, as Empson observed, this couplet can be troped both as a moment of disruption and of closure, it introduces a regular-as-clockwork schedule for microcosmic reflection on the cosmic problems of the poem's order and ideas of order.[9]

"Ware of like agein" marks the first full stop in the stanza, and the next line takes a still more decisive didactic turn. "This daies ensample hath this lesson deare/Deepe written in my heart with yron pen,/That blisse may not abide in state of mortal men." It is important to remember the visceral horror of the previous stanzas, Orgoglio's castle awash with the blood of innocent babes, and the spectacle of the emaciated and obdurately silent Red Cross, his fresh dried up like withered flowers. Like the description of the disrobed Duessa that will follow, the vividness of the details seems to exceed the requirements of the emblem: this is the grim *experience* that Arthur must transmute to useful knowledge. He works by stages. The first is "ensample," etymologically poised between "sample," a piece of the original experience, and *exemplum*, an epitome of it. The next stage is a "lesson," still more abstract, another insulating remove.

But we have already seen Arthur's concern for the discplacement of
memory by music: music which is the perfect threat, in its resistance
to representation, to being ware of like again. The next line seems
to be driven by the same anxiety. The lesson must be written on the
heart with an iron pen, and the pain lost in translation—the grievous-
ness of what was done and borne—is renewed in the violence of the
act of inscription itself. Arthur is wrestling with the impossible balance between the lesson as comfort and punishment. And for all this
scrupling, still the last word is the maxim of the hexameter, self-
balanced on its medial caesura, ripe for the commonplace book.
"That blisse may not abide in state of mortal men."

How does Howard manage the same stanza?

> Then to Lady gallant Arthur said,
> All grief repeated is more grievous made:
> Nor can the softest sounds delight the Ear
> Of him that loathing does the Musick hear.
> From actions past no Counsel can arise,
> Other than future Care of being more wise.
> And in my heart this Maxim fix'd I find,
> That constant Bliss abides not with Mankind.

> (L4r)

Howard's complaint against Spenser's form is that "the Writing in
Stanza's must render Verse sententious and contrain'd, the most
weighty part of their meaning still being to be expected at the Period
of the Stanza; so, in that consideration, their Composure must needs
be less difficult than where the force of each single Line is to be
weigh'd apart" (A3v). He seems to mean that Spenser's verse is "sententious and contrain'd" because it leaves the last line to do all the
moral work, rather than distributing the burden evenly; there is a
note of self-congratulation in his claim that his couplets—which are
less sententious, one assumes, only because no one sententia particularly stands out from the throng of its neighbors—are more difficult
to write. His own interest in their autonomy (and in their "composure," in a double sense) means that Howard cannot hear the excruci-
ated second-thoughts of Arthur's instruction. He does, however,
recognize the peculiar force and authority of the hexameter. Once
again Empson is the canonical guide to "possible variety" (34) of
effects that this final line achieves, but so often there is something
reflective, summary, or even epigrammatic about it. In a poem so
wary of rest it repeatedly proposes itself as a moment of provisional

rest (even if that rest is only the formulation of a prayer: "God helpe the man so wrapt in *Errours* endlesse traine" [I.i.18]). Arthur's didactic urgency puts a still finer point on this effect than usual, as though the poem has handed its own procedures momentarily over to its duodecimal hero in order to reflect on them with greater detachment.

So: a double-take in the middest; a final, elongated, balanced (or notably unbalanced) *sententia*; a system of rhymes that proposes a variety of relations between them. Is this enough to speak of the stanza as a method? In order to answer this question I want to step a little further back and consider the poem and the stanza in particular as a mimesis of thinking. This is a topic that has long occupied Spenser's critics in one form or another: Isabel MacCaffrey's wonderful book on Spenser's *Allegory* describes *The Faerie Queene* as "a model of the mind's life in the world"; more recently, both Kenneth Gross and Gordon Teskey have been thinking about Spenserian thinking.[10] Angus Fletcher's wrestle in *Colors of the Mind* with what he calls "noetics"—a poetics of thinking—also has Spenser much on its mind.[11] What makes this topic so elusive and compelling is that thinking itself seemed to be, for want of a better word, too *big* to think about: if a given mind were to compass thought in its entirety, what space would be left over for thinking *about* it? Wouldn't that just be more thinking, still to be reflected upon? Reflection is a supplement always being subsumed. One recourse is to admit that when we think about thinking what we imagine are reductions or schemes or, in McCaffrey's phrase, "models" (6), or, in Fletcher's "iconographies of thought" (15–34). And this is precisely what method is. We may take method primarily to be a tool, a cognitive procedure by which some desired order may be brought to new materials. But it is also a picture of the mind at work on those materials: in the ordering of the object we see the order of the mind. This order may be understood as a subset of mental activity, or (by a mistake either consoling or terrifying) as just what the mind does, ideally or actually. Logic and rhetoric are among the Renaissance disciplines that work this way: the five stages of composing an oration, for example, were often taught by schoolmasters as though they might come to be coextensive with the ideal student's mental life. The stanza too has an analogous power to filter and render all experience, imposing on it a particular shape, deriving from it a particular kind of lesson. Certainly *The Faerie Queene* never thinks without it.

At bottom this is only an analogy: I cannot say more than that it might help us understand how the stanza works, and, more tenuously, that the intellectual fashion for the one method might have contributed to Spenser's turn away from the variety of *The Shepherdes Calender* to the unflagging regularity of *The Faerie Queene*. Still I can make the analogy a little more specific. The basic procedure of Ramus's method was to resolve a field of knowledge into its constituent elements by a technique of dichotomizing analysis: this is the operation that yields the ramifying trees of his diagrams, each branch splitting into two and then splitting again. In matters of literary analysis, however, the point was to isolate the "dialectical ratiocination" or maxim at the heart of the discourse; method becomes a matter of stripping away ornament to arrive at essence. So Cicero's *Pro Milo*, for example, can be reduced to the formula "It is permissible to kill a criminal."[12] The application of the method is complete when it yields this fecund minimum; the process has two separate moments, the first unfolding in time, the other finished, timeless. The Spenserian stanza might likewise be understood as an engine for deriving some kind of concrete result in the form of that sententious hexameter: for making, out of thinking, a thought. Gordon Teskey has distinguished broadly between *The Faerie Queene* as a poem in which thinking actually happens and *Paradise Lost* as poem that teaches what has already been thought. I would suggest that a play between thinking and thought is constantly dramatized within *The Faerie Queene* itself, particularly as a problem of teaching; a play, as Arthur defines it, among experience, memory, and maxim. The stanza is built to raise the problem of their relation continually.

This is not to say that the hexameter is inevitably to be identified with fossilized thought. Nor does every stanza work the way I am describing: there are plenty that defy these structural generalizations. But the incidence of conformity is high enough to generate an expectation, and when that expectation is violated—or transcended—the difference is meaningful. On analogy with Teskey's thinking about allegory one might speak of a kind of "stanzaic capture," the fiction that the stanza is imposed upon some antecedent matter that once had a shape of its own. Stanzas that do not fit, particularly those that do not crystallize in their final line, cast doubt on the capacity of the method to process the full range of experience. Such mis-fit is among the stanza's resources, and a measure of how much more capricious it turns out to be than is the methodical promise it encodes. (But then those stanzas that fit too well, as Arthur reminds us, generate their own kind of doubt too.)

I would like to think that Gabriel Harvey could have been persuaded to recognize in Spenser's device the promise of method, though the two men seem to have talked more about lines than about stanzas. It is at all events a more flexible instrument than Ramus ever had, building in as it does a moment of disruption and perhaps of doubt; in this it may even anticipate the programmatic doubt that became essential to the seventeenth century's version of the concept. Spenser applied his method more than thirty-eight hundred times over the course of *The Faerie Queene*, pouring the welter of ideas and events in his massive poem into its idiosyncratic shape again and again; day, we must imagine, after day; year after year. The contest staged there between thinking and thought is parallel to—though it cannot simply be mapped onto—the contest between narrative (or romance) and allegory, forces in the poem that often collaborate but tend fundamentally in different directions. Allegory too might fruitfully be considered under the rubric of method, particularly in those templar moments when it seems most like a mode of analysis. The notorious trick of saving the revelation of a character's name for the end of an episode is a little like the consolidating closure of the hexameter writ large. But none of this is to say that *The Faerie Queene* is a methodical poem: rather, that there is method in it, on a variety of levels: the ambivalent search for a structure of thinking that could be widely and recurrently applied to help us understand and fashion other understanders. In this at least Spenser was a characteristic if ever skeptical citizen of an intellectual moment avid after such reliable, programmatic access to the truth. He may have sleepwalked through the rooms of his accumulating memory palace, and he may have dithered over every threshold, turning forward, then back, but we have to allow that he had the peculiar presence of mind to shut the door behind him, every time.

Princeton University

Notes

1. Subsequent citations by page number in parenthesis in the text. For a much more thoughtful and thorough examination of Howard than I attempt here, see Clare R. Kinney, " 'What s/he ought to have been': Romancing Truth in *Spenser Redivivus*," *Spenser Studies* XVI (2002): 125–38.

2. The book was licensed by Roger L'Estrange, the Surveyor of the Press, on September 21, 1686; author of a broadside against Milton entitled "No Blinde Guides" (1660, L'Estrange presumably would have had no objection to Howard's tactical omission.

3. Alexander Pope, *The Poems of Alexander Pope*, ed. John Butt (New York: Routledge, 1989), 502, 146. On compression, wit, and method in Pope's *Essays*, see Patricia Meyer Spacks, "Imagery and Method in *An Essay on Criticism*," *PMLA* 85 (1970): 97–106.

4. On the range of Renaissance definitions of method and their sources, see Neil W. Gilbert, *Renaissance Concepts of Method* (New York: Columbia University Press, 1960).

5. For an account of the Ode Natalia and Harvey's interest in method generally, see Kendrick W. Prewitt, "Gabriel Harvey and the Practice of Method," *SEL* 31:1 (1990): 19–39.

6. Edmund Spenser, *The Faerie Queene*, ed. Thomas P. Roche (Penguin, 1980), I.viii.44. Subsequent citations in parentheses in the text.

7. Virgil, *Eclogues, Georgics, Aeneid I-VI*, tr. H. Rushton Fairclough (Cambridge: Harvard University Press, 1994), II.3.

8. Hamilton notes eighteenth-century emendations of "delight" to "dislike" or "no delight"; he goes on, "If the text is kept, possible paraphrases are: 'music best breeds delight, not a recital of grievous matters'; or 'only the best music, not a recital etc., may breed delight." Edmund Spenser, *The Faerie Queene*, ed. A. C. Hamilton (Toronto: University of Toronto Press, 2001), 111n.

9. William Empson, *Seven Types of Ambiguity* (New York: New Directions, 1966), 33–34.

10. Isabel McCaffrey, *Spenser's Allegory: The Anatomy of Imagination* (Princeton: Princeton University Press, 1976), 6; Gross and Teskey's work has been presented at recent conferences (e.g., Teskey's " 'And therefore as a stranger give it welcome': Courtesy and Thinking," presented at the conference "The Place of Spenser," Cambridge, England [July 2001]; and Gross's MLA paper reprinted here).

11. Angus Fletcher, *Colors of the Mind* (Cambridge: Harvard University Press, 1991), 169–70.

12. See Walter Ong, *Ramus, Method, and the Decay of Dialogue* (Cambridge: Harvard University Press, 1958) 191. On this double movement in Ramist method—dichotomous exfoliation and analytic reduction—see Martin Elsky, "Reorganizing the Encyclopedia: Vives and Ramus on Aristotle and the Scholastics," *The Cambridge History of Literary Criticism: Volume 3, The Renaissance*, ed. Glyn P. Norton (Cambridge: Cambridge University Press, 1999), 406.

KENNETH GROSS

Shapes of Time: On the Spenserian Stanza

The Spenserian stanza is the poet's chief engine for organizing the ongoing, ever-expanding movement of his allegorical poem, an emblem of his attempt to order time and to discover the emergent orders *of* time, something exemplified in this essay by a crucial stanza from the Garden of Adonis, which shows well the form's intricacy and generosity, its power of continuity and transformation. The essay ends by juxtaposing this stanza form to that of Donne's unfinished satiric poem of 1601, *Metempsychosis*, a work which adapts Spenser's stanza in a way that supports the poem's strange, often grotesque rethinking of the Spenserian vision of life and human creation as they exist in time.

*I*WANT TO FOCUS ON A single stanza from the Garden of Adonis in Book III, canto vi of *The Faerie Queene*—Spenser's great cosmogonic digression, that place of crossings and thresholds, an embryonic space that exists "eterne in mutabilitie," both outside and within the world as we know it. A few stanzas before the one I will examine, a personification of Time emerges as a deathly native of the Garden, beating down plants with his flaggy wings; we see that "all things must decay in time, and to their end do draw." Yet, as if to put off his own dismay, the poet surmises that "were it not, that *Time* their troubler is, / All that in this delightfull Gardin growes, / Should happie be, and have immortall blis" (III.vi.41). He extends this further as he goes on, seeking to answer Time's violence by finding a way to incorporate the threat of time within his vision of the Garden's creative order. Here is the stanza:

> There is continuall spring, and harvest there
>   Continuall, both meeting at one time:
>   For both the boughes doe laughing blossomes beare,
>   And with fresh coloures decke the wanton Prime,
>   And eke attonce the heavy trees they clime,
>   Which seem to labour under their fruits lode:
>   The whilst the ioyous birdes make their pastime
>   Emongst the shadie leaves, their sweet abode,
> And their true loves without suspition tell abrode.

> (III. vi. 42)

This stanza shapes a desired locus that contains and resists the poet's prior fears of temporal calamity, offering not a breach but an expansion of possibility; he finds a possible place of time that is defined by an activity at once human and natural. In this stanza Spenser reframes in cosmic terms a *topos* of the earthly paradise that goes back to Homer's Gardens of Alcinous. We begin with a rare emphatic enjambment, almost Miltonic in its way. We encounter in line 1, that is, a verse of apparent grammatical completeness and formal symmetry, a chiasmus in fact: "There is continuall spring, and harvest there." The two "there's" that bracket this line turn our attention insistently, if elusively, to a sense of place, especially that second locator, at once a concrete and metaphysical "there." The next verse, however, shifts our understanding by pushing beyond the boundary of a phrase we might have thought already complete enough: " . . . continuall spring, and harvest there/Continuall . . . ."[1] The second, surprising "continuall" gains by the enjambment a different urgency. It reminds us more emphatically of the question of time; it reminds us that the Garden is a place made of time, a domain of things continual, also "continuous" and discontinuous. Yet this enjambment ultimately leads us back into the more balanced structural patterns; the slight shock of the breach between lines 1 and 2 is followed by the poet's landing us softly within the mirroring or marrying scheme of a second chiasmus: "continuall spring"/"harvest . . . Continuall." This helps to reinforce Spenser's insistence, rounding out line 2, that in the Garden these opposed earthly seasons are paradoxically "meeting at one time." Especially through this interlocking of chiasmoi, time here becomes an agent of reconciliation rather than destruction. The pair of lines that follow these first two unfold the paradox, playing on the seasonal signs that mark this doubling or compression of opposing times. It is a process in which the dynamic and generative work of nature takes on a completely human character (already suggested in line 1, which speaks of "spring and harvest," rather than "spring and autumn"). Line 3 reads, "For both the boughes doe laughing blossomes beare"—the word "beare" in this context calling up birth as well as mere carrying, but here brought forth in Blakean laughter rather than weeping. Line 4 reads, "And with fresh colours decke the wanton prime"—Autumn seen here as Keats's buxom goddess, painted or decked in color by the leaves of fall, the hues of dead leaves becoming "fresh colors," even as the season of the end becomes "the wanton Prime."

The movement here supports Paul Alpers's account of the peculiar, cumulative independence of lines in the Spenserian stanza, and their way of exerting, despite such independence, a gravitational pull on one another.[2] We can also see clearly the truth of William Empson's insistence on the crucial and continually changing work of the Spenserian stanza's central, fifth line.[3] Here line 5 begins by repeating the opening "And" of line 4–a line that might have seemed sufficiently to cap Spenser's illustration of the opening paradox, and so to complete a self-contained quatrain. This second "And" in line 5 pushes or ekes out our view of the autumnal branches slightly farther, opening up another figure of bearing. Here is the sequence, beginning with line 3: "For both the boughes doe laughing blossomes beare,/And with fresh coloures decke the wanton Prime,/And eke attonce the heavy trees they clime,/Which seem to labour under their fruits lode." From bearing laughter to colorful decking the lines advance to climbing and finally to labor, the note of weight and work, as well as childbirth—these being what distinguish the Garden from the Bower of Bliss. The "they" in line 4 is ambiguous. One wants to know, is it the boughs, the leaves, the colors, or the seasons themselves that "clime" those trees in time? Accompanying this work of nature in the Garden, we see in line 6, is a form of play, a play which is yet also a making—a making *of* play which is a form of time or of being in time, a way of catching at an interval in what is passing: "The whiles the ioyous birdes make their pastime." Here, just before the close of the stanza, we get another enjambment, one that again opens up from what we might have thought a sufficiently closed line. Less dramatic than the first, this enjambment suddenly gives the temporal making of these birds a home: "The whiles the ioyous birdes make their pastime/Emongst the shadie leaves, their sweete abode." But the homing, the innering movement of Spenser's words, is not yet complete. In the hexameter, with another of those striking Spenserian "ands" which so drive the stanza, the poet breaks through with the possibility of a voice that opens up a new dimension in the Garden. The addition of a single letter makes of that protective "abode" a less confined "abrode," a domain at once more free and more worldly: the birds "make their pastime/Emongst the shady leaves, their sweet abode,/And their true loves without suspition tell abrode." The horizon suddenly expands from closed to open. In these last lines of the stanza the repeated adverbial "there's" of line 1 are replaced by the thrice-repeated "their"; the insistent, ambiguous gesture of location yields to a cipher of liberated, unanxious possession of time and space. Note also the internal off-rhyme by which those leaves which have been said to grow, laugh, deck, and shade the Garden suddenly lend their being to those "loves": "Emongst the shadie leaves, their sweet abode,/And their true loves without suspition tell abrode." That telling, that *logos*, is the only music we hear in the Garden.

One need not rehearse at length Spenser's preoccupation with the dangers of envy or the monster-making powers of rumor to catch the force of the wish in that last line. The hexameter here tries to reconcile the innering and outering energy of the Garden, as the Garden as a whole tries to reconcile spring and harvest. Unusual in not breaking into two half-lines, as Spenser's hexameters so often do, this closing verse is yet typical of the eerie, heartbreaking, and breathtaking ease with which a closing hexameter in Spenser can nudge us gently towards a new dimension, open up a broader frame of consciousness, or give us a different set of ears and eyes—the dream of a space beyond that marked by the more normative measure of the pentameter.[4] This is a small example of the hexameter's flexible capacity to call up or call out, to remind, complete, reduce, clear away, disenchant, apologize, or provoke a delicate wonder, its trick of returning us to a condition at once earlier and later, or of giving the scene described an unexpected genealogy, marking an alternative sovereignty or emblematic frame. Spurred by an And or a Yet, a Thus, So, While, As, As if, Lo or O, the hexameter acts as a minimal conceptual refrain, gathering half-remembered gestures from earlier stanzas, prophesying the energies of those which come later.[5] The hexameter always holds us with a slight breathlessness, leads us to that silence which follows the close of each stanza—for we must always remember that it is a temporal space and silence between the stanzas, as this is continually recharged and made strange by the recurrent hexameter, that as much as anything keeps the poem alive, lends the unfolding cantos their particular lightness and confidence in confronting shifted possibilities, unexpected contingencies of order and change. To go further: in the case of the stanza I have been discussing, one feels that the thing whose meaning is unfolded in the course of the stanza, that image of dynamic conflict and artful freedom, becomes an implicit trope of the stanza form itself. The Garden of Adonis, that is, offers a mythic emblem of the stanza's life, its paradoxical motion, the kind of order and freedom it creates. The Spenserian stanza becomes here a creature of the garden, the sign of its lucid spell, one form in which we see the inter-animations of the temporal and the eternal, death and life, of going on and holding back, the poem's gathering and intertwining of its radically disparate materials within an emergent structure of life.[6] For a moment, the stanza is the Garden. Other cantos ask the stanza to mirror states of existence that are more hieratic, ironic, solemn, playful, enervating, stifling, chaotic, intrusive, or mournful. Here it is as if the stanza itself reinforced within its own formal dimensions this canto's supreme fiction, its intimations of a source of temporal order neither wholly transcendent nor wholly bound to dying nature, a timelessness that holds onto time, contingency, and chance, putting off illusions of cosmic or apocalyptic fixity—a non-hieratic, dynamic tool for mastering the poem's tendency to disperse its energies. It offers itself to us as a fact of mind and a fact of nature, a cosmos and a theater.

We need to find the meaning of such stanzas, but also the meaning of their meaning. This sort of analysis is only a start. It's still not an easy thing to articulate the broader resonance of this stanza form for this poet. There is no space here to speculate in detail on the mystery of how Spenser invented the form. (I like to imagine that the stanza came to him in a dream—say, an image of nine nymphs moving through a maze-like dance figure, as in Colin Clout's vision on Mount Acidale—something like Friedrich Kekule's famous dream of 1867, a vision of intertwining snakes biting their own tails that gave this great scientist, the inventor of modern organic chemistry, a clue to the arrangement of carbon atoms in the benzene molecule.) Still, we can ask in regard to the stanza, how did it dispose his attention while he wrote? How did it compel his word choice, syntax, and grammar? Where did its greatest delight lie? What does the stanza form have in it of dream, prayer, and chart, to use Kenneth Burke's three metaphors for the forms of literary action?[7] As much as anything, we need to reflect on what it meant for the poet to have a thing like this on which he could depend, a form to which he could commit himself and his writing day after day, year after year, as he struggled with what Angus Fletcher has described as the evolving, knowingly inefficient system of his poem.[8] We should consider what he gained from the stanza's generosity and intricacy, its implicit refusal of both discursive chaos and sharp, epigrammatic closure, its power of continuity and transformation, able to renew the organizing

energy of a narrative mode which can tend toward the aleatory and
the dispersed, threatening merely to decompose or deliquesce (to
borrow G. Wilson Knight's characterization of the Spenserian
mode).[9] The stanza is both the ground and the figure; it is both seed
and seed-bed, the atomic fuel or genetic code of the poem's unfolding
structure, the analogy of analogies that shapes the motion of Spenser's
romance.[10] It is crucial to creating the sort of poem which Wallace
Stevens describes so well in his essay, "The Figure of the Youth as
Virile Poet": "Anyone who has read a long poem day after day as,
for example, *The Faerie Queene*, knows how the poem comes to
possess the reader and how it naturalizes him in its own imagination
and liberates him there."[11]

I end with a text by a younger contemporary of Spenser's, John
Donne, an author who did as much as anyone to un-write the Spenserian mode in English poetry, but who nevertheless had an acute ear
for the formal and mythopoetic ambitions of Spenser's poetry. Donne's unfinished satiric poem of 1601, *The Progress of the Soule*, or
Metempsychosis, is in its own way a universalizing epic myth of time,
though a myth more ferocious, even Gnostic in its bent than Spenser's. It recounts in 500 or so lines the bizarre life-history of a nameless
and "deathless" soul, its passage through multiple bodies from the
beginning of time to the present. This soul has little distinct character
of its own, no face or voice. Far from being a principle of orderly
continuity through change, it is rather a kind of blank spirit of heresy
and subversion, a cosmic *picaro* or a minim of the power of *fortuna*.
Its homes are myriad. Beginning inside the fruit of the forbidden tree
in Eden, the soul passes (or rather finds itself thrown) into various
violent and insidiously treacherous beings—an obscenely anthropo-
morphic mandrake root, a lustful sparrow, a ponderous and tyrannical
whale, a machiavellian mouse, a rapine ape, and a vicious woman,
the bride of Cain; the soul ends up inside heretics like Mohammed
or Luther, even, it is hinted, inside the poet himself. Through a
welter of material and historical crises, this soul remains, in a nominal
sense, "eterne in mutabilitie": no final catastrophe looms, and its
survival in time is all but guaranteed by something in its creation.
But each rebirth leaves the soul at the mercy of new chances, a prey
to its own desires and to the desires of others, both devoured and
devouring. Donne gives us an image of archaic origins more pitiless,
more unforgiving, than any we find in Spenser. The soul never ripens,
it has no inborn entelechy in Aristotle's sense, nor is it one of the
seminal reasons or *logoi spermatakoi*—the divine causes hidden within
the changing forms of the created world—such as James Nohrnberg
has seen breeding in Spenser's Garden.[12] All changes come to this

soul violently from without. Its rebirths leave as little room for hope, reparation, and blessing as they do for mourning. The scenes of insemination, of passage from body to body, are especially bizarre and abrupt, and the soul seems hardly begotten or born than it is killed. The satirical energy of the poem has more in common with Thomas Nashe or Rabelais than Spenser; yet it also takes aim at the vision of continuous life that Spenser entertains a text like the Garden of Adonis—the vision of a world sustained by change, eternal *in* change, despite the violences built into time, nature, and human work.[13] The key to Donne's dialogue with Spenser is the stanza form which he invented for *Metempsychosis,* a stanza that is, like Spenser's, made up of rhyming pentameters with a closing hexameter, but ten lines long rather than nine, and rhyming *aabccbbddd*. Studying this form, one feels the impertinent power of the single added line to ruin the subtle mathematics of Spenser's form. Donne has also contrived a rhyme pattern that makes of Spenser's flowing, interwoven harmonies something more abrupt and disjunctive in structure. It is a pattern that piles rhymes up together rather than allowing them subtly to reach across space; it pointedly refuses the spell of the Spenserian stanza. Donne's stanza thus embeds in itself his poem's broader challenge to a Spenserian metaphysic; Donne exacts from his altered form a darker, even an antithetical vitality. Listen to the following:

Just in that instant when the serpent's gripe,
Broke the slight veins, and tender conduit-pipe,
Through which this soul from the tree's root did draw
Life, and growth to this apple, fled away
This loose soul, old, one and another day.
As lightning, which one scarce dares say, he saw
'Tis so soon gone, (and better proof the law
Of sense, than faith requires) swiftly she flew
To a dark and foggy plot; her, her fate threw
   There through th'earth's pores, and in a plant housed her anew.[14]
                      (stanza 13)

Donne's stanza form itself, with its consecutive rhymes all balled up together, gives us a sort of picture of the soul's life, alighting on one rhyme and sticking to it until it is reborn in another's syllable.

    Like all poets of his generation—including the slightly older Shakespeare, Marlowe, and Jonson—Donne must have been in awe of *The Faerie Queene.* His very need to wrench Spenser's vision so violently shows the quality of its force for him. The lines I have quoted indeed suggest by contrast just how powerfully Spenser links together his vision of life in time with the movement of his stanza. Yet Donne's verses, in this strange combination of homage and parody, also remind us of just how delicate and how contingent a contrivance the Spenserian stanza is, how much of desire and will are wrapped up in the power of that form to keep at bay the disjunctions of time, and also how subtly the form lets Spenser hug the coast of chaos. *Metempsychosis* shows us something of that vision of time that the Spenserian stanza helps its inventor to critique and against which his poem offers a defense.

University of Rochester

NOTES

1. See John Hollander's account of the revisionary drama of Miltonic enjambment in his essay, " 'Sense Variously Drawn Out': on English Enjambment," in *Vision and Resonance: Two senses of Poetic Form.* (New York: Oxford University Press, 1975), 91–116.

2. See Paul Alpers, *The Poetry of "The Faerie Queene"* (Princeton: Princeton University Press, 1967), 36–69.

3. See William Empson, *Seven Types of Ambiguity: A Study of its Effects in English Verse* (3rd ed., revised, London: Chatto and Windus, 1953), 33–34.

4. In his *Summa Lyrica,* Allen Grossman describes the effects of lines which measure less or more than the "common ground" of the ten-syllable iambic line in English poetry in ways that are suggestive for an understanding of the movement of Spenser's hexameter (though Grossman does not address the Spenserian Stanza directly). "In the line of less than ten syllables the silence around the precinct is like a vacuum. Something has been taken away, and what is within presses outward against radical emptiness. The line of ten floats in a social space managing its boundedness by stratagems of reciprocity. The line of more than ten is sinking into the ground of selfhood. In it is portended the dissolution of the self in the ground, a version of the apocalypse. Less than ten speaks of change in the mode of changelessness. Ten speaks of mutuality. More than ten indicates the troubling of form by inner possibility." *Summa Lyrica,* section 29.4. in *The Sighted Singer: Two Works on Poetry for Readers and Writers,* Allen Grossman with Mark Halliday (Baltimore: Johns Hopkins University Press, 1992), 280. See also 279–84 more generally.

5. See the more extended account of the energies of closure in the Spenserian stanza, and of their influence on Milton's early stanzaic poetry, in my " 'Each Heav'nly Close': Mythology and Metrics in Spenser and the Early Poetry of Milton." *PMLA* 98, no. 1 (1983): 21–36.

6. See Justus George Lawler, *Celestial Pantomime: Poetic Structures of Transcendence* (New Haven: Yale University Press, 1979), passim, for a remarkable account of how

formal devices in English poetry—rhyme, enjambment, caesura, refrain, chiasmus, etc.—give form to the basic antimonies of human experience and to our wish for their resolution by some higher mode of knowledge and relation. Lawler does not speak about the Spenserian stanza per se, but his arguments can help us find the right angle of view for understanding what is at stake for a poet like Spenser in his particular formal choices.

7.   See Kenneth Burke, *The Philosophy of Literary Form: Studies in Symbolic Action* (3rd ed., Berkeley: University of California Press, 1973), 5–6.

8.   On the "inefficiency" of Spenser's poem, see Angus Fletcher, "Complexity and the Spenserian Myth of Mutability," forthcoming in *Literary Imagination*. Fletcher's recent study, *A New Theory for American Poetry: Democracy, the Environment, and the Future of Imagination* (Cambridge, MA: Harvard University Press, 2003), suggests how the expansive, wave-like movement of Spenser's poetry, its investment in endlessly shifting shapes of time, finds its later development in Romantic and modern poetry, from John Clare and Walt Whitman to John Ashbery.

9.   See Knight, "The Spenserian Fluidity," in *The Burning Oracle: Studies in the Poetry of Action* (London: Oxford University Press, 1939), 1–18.

10.   See, for example, Angus Fletcher's account of how the stanza embodies the archetypal forms of quest-romance and prophecy, the temple and the labyrinth, in *The Prophetic Moment: An Essay on Spenser* (Chicago: University of Chicago Press, 1971), 130–32.

11.   Wallace Stevens, "The Figure of the Youth as Virile Poet," in *The Necessary Angel: Essays on Reality and the Imagination* (New York: Alfred A. Knopf, 1951), 50.

12.   See James C. Nohrnberg, *The Analogy of "The Faerie Queene"* (Princeton: Princeton University Press, 1975), 534–68.

13.   I like to imagine that Donne, when he wrote his poem in 1601, had caught a glimpse of the manuscript of "Two Cantos of Mutabilitie," which Spenser most likely brought back with him to London after his flight from his Irish home in late 1598 on account of the Tyrone rebellion. The parodic cosmogony of *Metempsychosis* comments on the vision of time unfolded in the last book of *The Faerie Queene* as much as on the Garden of Adonis. We, of course, have no information about the origin and fate of the manuscript, who kept it safe after Spenser's death in 1599, or how it came to be published in 1609. Yet there must have been much curiosity among London poets about the last writings of the late author of the great master-work of the previous decade of Elizabethan poetry, and Donne and others might have sought out unpublished material immediately after he died ("for lack of bread," wrote Ben Jonson, though not so obscurely that Spenser failed to be buried in Westminster Abbey at the expense of the Earl of Essex, interred near Chaucer, "his hearse being attended by poets, and mournful elegies and poems, with the pens that wrote them thrown into the tomb," according to William Camden). See *The Faerie Queene*, ed. A.C. Hamilton (London: Longman, 1977), xii.

14.   Quoted from *John Donne: Selected Poetry*, ed. John Carey (Oxford: Oxford University Press, 1996), 67.

SHOHACHI FUKUDA

The Numerological Patterning of *The Faerie Queene* I-III

Each canto of *The Faerie Queene* normally tells two episodes, or is written in two sections. Counting the number of stanzas of each section of the thirty-six cantos of the first three books shows that Spenser almost always tells his episodes in patterns that reveal numbers of significance, often using symmetry or the 2:1 ratio. Most notably, triple use of the number 27 in the first two consecutive cantos is brought into the second and third books at the major turning points, indicating structural contrasts. Thematic contrasts observed between the first two books are even reflected to some extent in numerical patterns. The fact that the numbers found in the canto patterns are all symbolic makes it possible to assume that Spenser premeditated this specific detail of each canto before writing it.

O F ALL THE POEMS PUBLISHED in Spenser's lifetime, *Amoretti* and *Prothalamion* are the only ones that appeared with stanza numbers throughout. Even *The Faerie Queene* was not numbered in the 1590 and 1596 editions; it is only in the 1609 edition that the poem was first published as we now see it. This does not mean that numbers are of no importance to him; on the contrary, a close look at the structure of any of his poems will reveal that some numbers of significance are used throughout with great care. After compiling a list of characters of *The Faerie Queene*[1] and counting the number of stanzas allocated for each part of the cantos, I have come to be convinced that Spenser firmly believed in numbers and that he devised not only each canto but also the whole book in symbolic numbers.

With our still Romantic assumptions of spontaneous and unpremeditated poetic inspiration, it may be difficult for modern readers to allow that Spenser laid out his poem, stanza by stanza, before writing it. But Spenser simply followed the common practice of his age, and it seems quite likely that his first readers, at least some of them, loved to decode his messages hidden in numbers. Spenser will certainly be better understood and appreciated if taken not merely as the bricklayer of individual words, lines, and stanzas, but also as the architect of his faerie land, the one who, by using symbolic numbers, designed each episode in symmetrical or proportional patterns that are ultimately meant to glorify the grandeur of God and to reveal his beautiful mind.

By the simple method of counting the number of stanzas of each part of his episodes, I shall attempt to show that Spenser is no less concerned in what patterns to tell as what words to use. As the four-line argument states, each canto normally tells two episodes, or is divided into two sections. Taking descriptions mainly from my entries in "The Characters of The Faerie Queene," I shall show each part of the episode in the order it is narrated, indicating in parentheses the starting and ending stanza numbers. I shall then show the arrangement of each part of the sections, and finally the overall pattern of the canto. Some cantos can be divided into two or more patterns, making it difficult to decide on one; all I can do is to present a pattern for each canto as I see it.

I. Canto Patterns in Book I

The first canto tells two episodes that are central to the book of holiness: first, killing of the monster, Errour, which foretells the slaying of the dragon (in xi)—Errour here is a serpent in whose form Satan caused Adam and Eve to fall from heavenly grace; and second, encounter with the great magician, Archimago (called "Hypocrisie" at I.i Argument), the greatest enemy of the Red Cross Knight who has been assigned by the Faerie Queene to slay the dragon that besieges Una's parents. Since the dragon is Satan, and Una's parents are Adam and Eve, the allegory of man's fall is clearly presented in the opening episodes.

The knight travels with Una and her dwarf (1–6) and wanders into the Wandering Wood where he approaches Errour's den (7–11). Una advises caution (12–13) but he encounters and kills the monster (14–27). He leaves the Wood and goes on with God as a friend (28). Archimago, disguised as a hermit, hosts the knight and Una (29–35) and sends one of his spirits to Morpheus (36–44) and provokes the knight to leave Una with a dream of her lust for him (45–55).

The symmetrical structure of this canto has been well recognized: A.C. Hamilton, in his 1977 edition of the poem, wrote of stanza 28: "Rose (1975) 14 observes that this central stanza divides the canto into two balancing episodes of twenty-seven stanzas each." Røstvig[2] further sees in it a still more elaborate pattern: the Red Cross Knight approaches Errour's den in 11 stanzas, and kills him in the next 16; in the second section, Archimago hosts him and contrives to betray him in the same 16, but fails to provoke him in the subsequent 11. Thus, the structure is symmetrical: 11 + 16/1/16 + 11. The overall pattern is: 27 + 1 + 27.

The numbers in this canto are all symbolic: 55, the total count, is gained by adding the numbers 1 to 10 (such numbers are called perfect numbers, all signifying a pyramid, the symbol of eternity); 28 is gained by adding 1 to 7 and means eternal life; 27, the cube of 3 (the number of divine completeness and perfection), signifies the three-fold structure of the world and therefore stability; 16 is the number of virtues; and 11 is one of the numbers that symbolize Christ's life and salvation.[3]

The second canto tells of Archimago's success in separating the knight from Una, and introduces his partner, Duessa. Archimago betrays the knight by the false vision of Una in bed with a squire (1–6), and she searches for her knight after he flees from her (7–8), as Archimago then disguises himself as the Red Cross Knight (9–11). The knight meets and kills Sansfoy (12–19), and thereby wins his companion, Duessa (20–27). He fails to hear the warning of Fradubio who tells how he and his lady, Fralissa, were transformed by Duessa into trees after he had left Fralissa for Duessa and saw the witch in her naked ugliness (28–45).

The first section of this canto (1–27) is divided into the same pattern as that of the first half of canto i: 11 + 16. The second, told in 18 stanzas, can be divided into two: 2 (rest under the trees) + 16 (Fradubio's story). The overall pattern is: 27 + 18.

By telling how the Red Cross Knight is deceived, first by Archimago in canto i and then by Duessa in ii, Spenser establishes his scheme of temptation in this book: the two magicians lead the knight into miseries that he must endure before he can attain his final victory and union with Truth. This is revealed, or supported, in the use of specific numbers arranged in a rhythmical pattern: (11 + 16) + 1 + (16 + 11)/(11 + 16) + (2 + 16). It is easy to see here that the numbers 11 and 16 are deliberately arranged, that 27 is in the 2:1 ratio (27 + 1 + 27/27 + 18), that 16 is used four times, weaving the four sections together, and finally that 100, the number of stanza total, indicates the two cantos are conceived as a unit.[4]

The third canto tells of Una. Her misfortune is first lamented (1–2). She is befriended by a lion (3–8), and sees Abessa, the deaf and mute daughter of Corceca, who flees from her (9–12). While she spends the night in their cottage, her lion kills Kirkrapine who robs churches to support Abessa (13–20). When she leaves the cottage (21) she is pursued and cursed by Corceca and Abessa (22–23). The disguised Archimago deludes Una (24–32). Sansjoy wounds Archimago and kills her lion (33–42), and seizes Una (43–44).

This canto is well balanced with two stanzas at the center (22–23) depicting Una who is pursued and cursed by Corceca and Abessa. The first section is: 2 (lament) + 10 (Lion and Abessa) + 9 (Corceca and Kirkrapine), and the second: 9 (Archimago) + 10 (Sansjoy) + 2 (Una seized). The whole structure is symmetrical: $2 + 10 + 9/2/ 9 + 10 + 2$, or in a compressed form: $2 + 19/2/19 + 2$. The overall pattern is: $21 + 2 + 21$. The number 19 is the one Spenser uses, like Tasso, mostly for "events associated with evil powers,"[5] and 21 is the sum of numbers up to 6 (also, 21 is three-fold 7, both symbolizing divine completion).

The fourth canto tells the Lucifera episode. Led by Duessa, the knight comes to the house of Pride (2–5) and is admitted by its porter, Maluenue (6) and taken to the audience chamber where he makes obeisance to Lucifera (7–15). With Duessa, Lucifera heads the procession of the seven deadly sins driven by Satan (16–37): she stands up and orders her coach (16–17); each of her six counselors is mentioned in 3 stanzas (18–35), followed by Satan (36) and Duessa (37). Sansjoy challenges the knight for Sansfoy's shield, and Lucifera arranges the joust between them (38–43). That night Duessa visits Sansjoy's bedroom and counsels him in his forthcoming battle (44–51).

The first section tells of the Red Cross Knight in 15 stanzas, or the sum of the numbers up to 5. The middle section ($2 + 3 + 3 + 3 + 3 + 3 + 3 + 2$) is symmetrical ($2 + 18 + 2$), and properly told in 22 stanzas because 22, the number of letters in Hebrew, connotes completion. The last section on Sansjoy ($6 + 8$) is in 14 stanzas, which do not balance the first, perhaps hinting that the pagan knight does not equal the "faithfull" knight.

The Lucifera episode is continued to the fifth canto. The structural imbalance is brought into its first section (told in 19 stanzas) composed of three parts in an imbalanced pattern ($5 + 8 + 6$): the Red Cross Knight comes out and swears an oath over wine, and Lucifera is seated (1–5); Sansjoy is defeated (6–13); Duessa intercedes, triumph is sounded, the knight is feted as Lucifera's knight, and then his wounds are attended (14–17) while Duessa weeps (18–19).[6] The second section is told in a symmetrical pattern: Duessa visits Night (20–28); she descends into hell in Night's chariot (29–36); at her request, the dead Sansjoy is restored by Æsculapius (37–44); Una's dwarf sees the victims in Lucifera's dungeon and the Red Cross Knight flees on hearing it (45–53).

The structure of this canto is: 5 + 8 + 6/9 + 8 + 8 + 9. The overall pattern is: 19 + 34.

According to the argument, the sixth canto tells of Una's release from Sansloy by the satyrs and their blind worship of her. All this, however, refers only to the first episode: Sansloy attempts to rape Una but flees when the fawns and satyrs appear (2–8), and rescued and adored, Una teaches them truth (9–19). Satyrane, who was nurtured by satyrs and visited by his mother (20–29), befriends Una and helps her escape the satyrs (30–33). Archimago deceives Una by saying that Sansloy killed her knight (34–39) and provokes Satyrane to fight Sansloy while Una escapes pursued by Archimago (40–48).

This canto can be variously divided. First, if the episode of the satyrs is separated from the rest, the overall pattern is: 19 (satyrs) + 29 (Satyrane). Second, if the episode of Satyrane's birth and nurture is grouped at the center, the canto reveals a symmetrical pattern: 19 (satyrs) + 10 (Satyrane) + 19 (Una with Satyrane). Third, if Archimago's plot is singled out, the pattern is: 33 (Satyrane) + 15 (Sansloy). Of the three possible patterns the last one seems more plausible to me because the canto is primarily, as the argument says, about Sansloy from whose "lawlesse lust by wondrous grace/fayre Vna is releast." Though placed at the center in symmetry, Satyrane is simply, as his name indicates, a character devised to save her from the satyrs, or the blind worshipers of Truth. As far as the scheme of the book goes, therefore, Archimago's plot to destroy her is of primary importance and the canto should be taken as such. The point is clearly stated in the last action told in the canto: "[Archimago] . . . her pursewd apace,/In hope to bring her to her last decay."

The seventh canto, introducing Orgoglio and Arthur, tells of the knight's imprisonment in Orgoglio's dungeon, or the fall of man. The Red Cross Knight yields to Duessa and drinks from the fountain whose nymph Diana had cursed (1–6). When he is thus enfeebled, Orgoglio appears to defeat and imprison the knight in his dungeon (7–15) and takes Duessa as his mistress, placing her on his dragon (16–18). Una's dwarf carries the knight's armor, shield, and spear to her and tells her of her knight's capture by Orgoglio (19–27). Guided by him, she sets out and meets Arthur and his beloved squire who carries his spear (28–37). She tells her story to Arthur (38–51) who promises to rescue her knight (52).

In this canto on Prince Arthur, the number 9, which symbolizes prime virtue, is repeatedly used: 9 (joined by Duessa) + 9 (imprisoned) + 9 (Dwarf's report)/1 (Una's departure)/9 (Arthur and Timias) + 5 (Arthur's request) + 9 (Una's story) + 1 (Arthur's promise). The central 19 stanzas (19–37) have a symmetrical pattern: 1 + 8/ 1/8 + 1. The overall pattern of this canto is: 27 + 1 + 24. The number 27 certainly refers us back to the first three sections told in the same number (Errour, Archimago, and Sansfoy), while 24, the number of the hours of a day, is used again in the next canto, for the killing of Orgoglio, indicating continuity of the story.

The eighth canto tells of Arthur's killing of Orgoglio and his rescue of the Red Cross Knight. Approaching Orgoglio's castle, Timias blows his horn that opens its doors (2–5); Arthur fights against Orgoglio (6–11) and Timias defends him against Duessa's dragon but, weakened by her magic potion, is almost overcome until rescued by his master (12–16); and Orgoglio is killed after Arthur's shield is uncovered (17–24). This section is concluded with Una's congratulations: Timias captures the fleeing Duessa and guards her (25) while Una congratulates Arthur and Timias on their victory (26–28). Arthur's rescue of the knight is told in the next 16 stanzas: Arthur enters the castle to confront Ignaro, who is the foster-father of Orgoglio and porter of his castle but lacks the key to unlock the door that imprisons the knight (29–36), and frees the knight and Una welcomes him (37–44). Una asks that Duessa be stripped of her robe to expose her ugliness and let go, and she is expelled (45–50).

It is observed that the three major episodes here (Orgoglio's death, 17–24; Ignaro, 29–36; Arthur's rescue, 37–44) are all told in 8 stanzas each, placed in the 2:1 ratio. It is also seen that the whole of Arthur's fight is told in 19 stanzas (6–24). The overall pattern is: 28 + 22 (or, if the continuity from vii is to be shown: 24 + 4 + 22).

The ninth canto tells of Arthur's dream and of Despaire. At Una's request, Arthur relates his birth, and nurture by Timon through Merlin (2–5), and he goes on to relate his youth (6–12), and his dream of the Faerie Queene's love for him that has occasioned his quest for her (13–15). They exchange gifts (18–19) and each leaves on his quest (20). The Red Cross Knight meets Trevisan fleeing from Despaire who had persuaded Terwin to take his own life (21–32) and visits the cave of Despaire (33–36); and overcome by his arguments to despair (37–47), he is about to take his own life (48–51) but is saved by Una (52–53). Seeing him depart safely, Despaire tries to take his own life but forever fails (54).

The most obvious feature of this canto is contrast: Arthur's past which culminates in his dream vision of the Faerie Queene's love for him is set against the knight's despair symbolized in Despaire himself attempting to take his own life. The first section (1–19) can be divided: 1 (eulogy on the golden chains) + 11 (Arthur's birth, nurture, and youth) + 3 (his dream and quest) + 2 (response of Una and her knight) + 2 (exchange of gifts). Stanza 20 functions as the connecting one. The second section (21–54) is divided: 12 (Trevisan) + 4 (Despaire) + 11 (arguments) + 4 (attempted suicide) + 2 (Una) + 1 (Despaire). In a larger grouping, the pattern is: 19/1/12 + 19 + 3. It is interesting to see here that the two contrasting episodes (dream vision and despair) are both told in 19 stanzas. The overall pattern is: 19 + 1 + 34. (It is seen that 19, used for Arthur's killing of Orgoglio in ix, is used here again. This is an instance of how difficult it is to decide on the "right" pattern, the one Spenser had in mind; we should be aware that in some cantos two or more patterns coexist.)

The tenth canto tells of the house of Holinesse. Una takes her knight to the house of Holinesse where they are admitted by Humilta and Reverence and received by Cælia (2–11). Fidelia and Speranza greet Una and the knight is taken to a bedroom by Obedience (12–17). At Una's request, Fidelia teaches doctrine in her schoolhouse and Speranza teaches hope for salvation (18–22). Una asks Cælia to comfort her knight, and he is instructed by Patience who takes him to the house of Penance to be purged of sin (23–28). Una shares his anguish and welcomes him on his recovery (29). At Una's request, Charissa teaches him to live righteously (30–33). At Una's request, Mercie guides him to the holy Hospital with its seven Bead-men and instructs him in the charitable life (34–45). Mercie leads him to the hill of Contemplation who receives him in his hermitage (46–52), and leads him to the highest mount and shows him the way to the New Jerusalem (53–59). Contemplation reveals the future role of the knight among the saints as "Saint George of mery England" and counsels him to serve the Faerie Queene (60–63) and reveals his Saxon ancestry and his name, Georgos (65–66). The knight thanks him and returns to Una (67–68).

This canto is divided into two well-proportioned halves. Stanza 33 clearly indicates the end of the first phase of his instruction, which is completed with Charissa's teaching, as its last line declares: "From thence to heauen she teacheth him the ready path." The first section of 33 stanzas is equally divided into three parts of 11 stanzas each: 11 (Cælia) + 11 (Fidelia and Speranza) + 11 (Patience and Charissa). Now he leaves the house of Holinesse with Mercie guiding "his weak wandering steps" (the phrase which Milton is later to recall at the close of his epic) and after going "by a narrow way" he is brought to the holy Hospital, at stanza 35, where the second phase of his teaching begins. The second half can be divided: 10 (holy Hospital) + 7 (Contemplation) + 7 (New Jerusalem) + 7 (St. George) + 2 (Una). It is observed here that three parts, all told in 7 stanzas, follow the account of the holy Hospital with "seven" Bead-men. The whole structure is framed in fearfully symbolic numbers, most fittingly with Mercie at the center: 11 + 11 + 11/2/10 + 7 + 7 + 7 + 2. We can now see that the overall pattern of the "core" canto of the book of holiness reveals the most divine number on both sides: 33 + 2 + 33.[7]

The eleventh canto tells the dragon episode. The Red Cross Knight is led by Una to her native land and he tells her to watch from afar (1–4.5) and, invoking the help of Clio and Phœbus (4.6–7), Spenser describes how the dragon looks (8–14). The knight is beaten and falls into the well of Life (15–30); the dragon claps his wings as victor (31) and Una prays for her knight without sleeping (32). The second day's fight ends with the knight's fall under the tree of Life (33–48) from which the dragon stays away (49) and Una prays again for her knight without sleeping (50). Early on the third day the knight slays the dragon and Una congratulates him on his victory (51–55).

This canto is told in a succession of symbolic numbers: 7 (arrival and invocation) + 7 (dragon) + 18 (first day)/18 (second day) + 5 (third day). As is seen here, for both the first day and the second, Spenser tells the fight in 18 stanzas. He depicts the scenes before the fight in double 7 stanzas and concludes the fight in 5, the number of justice. The overall pattern is 32 + 23.[8] The former is the number of the Covenant and the latter that of vengeance on sinners. This canto shares the stanza count of 55 with the first, which also tells the killing of a serpentine monster. The number 23 is used again in the final canto.

The final canto tells of Una's betrothal. Learning of the death of the dragon, Una's father announces peace to his people of Eden and comes out of his castle (2–5). Young men honor the knight with laurel branches, virgins crown Una as a maiden Queen, and everyone marvels at the dead body of the dragon (6–11). The king welcomes the knight and greets Una, and entertains them in his palace (12–15); the knight tells his adventures (16–17), the king offers him his daughter and kingdom (18–20) and Una appears unveiled to become the knight's bride (21–23). Archimago, disguised as Duessa's messenger, delivers her letter to the king claiming that the knight is betrothed to Duessa (24–28). While the magician is explaining (29–32), Una discloses Duessa's and Archimago's deception (33–34) and he is imprisoned (35–36). They are betrothed (37–41) and the book is concluded in a pastoral mood (42).

This canto can be variously divided, but stanza 24 seems to be the dividing one. The first section is, then, taking over the same number from xi, in 23 stanzas—stanza 23, which states "The blazing brightnesse of her beauties beame," is the fitting culmination of the section that begins with the joys of all the people of the land of Eden. This upward movement of joy is interrupted, at stanza 24, by the arrival of a messenger forbidding the banns. (Interestingly, Spenser mentions this change of action in the last three lines of this connecting stanza, reminiscent of a similar change of scenes at I.i.28.) Thus prepared, Spenser begins the second section by saying, "All in the open hall amazed stood,/At suddeinnesse of that vnwary sight," to conclude his tale of victory in all the more festive a mood for this interruption. Spenser's favorite term of joy at 40.6 highlights the extent of the knight's bliss: "Thrice happy man the knight himselfe did hold,/Possessed of his Ladies hart and hand," - indeed, in some years he is to use the same phrase again, this time in telling of his own betrothal at the central fifty-ninth stanza of the *Amoretti* and *Epithalamion* volume, which he begins by saying "Thrice happie she" but it only serves to mention his own bliss: "but he most happy who such one loues best." This canto is divided: 1 + 10 + 12/1/12 + 5 + 1. The overall pattern is: 23 + 1 + 18.

Diagram 1 indicates the stanza count of each canto, that of each section, and its main character or event. It is clearly seen that only the numbers of significance are used. Spenser begins his poem with 27, using it for three consecutive episodes, and again for the first episode of vii, which is the the first canto in the second half of the book. It is easy to see that the four episodes told in 27 stanzas are all about the knight's fall (first into the Wandering Wood; second, into the magician's hand; third, into the witch's hand; and finally, into Orgoglio's dungeon). As has already been seen, the first three episodes in 27 stanzas are arranged in a rhythmical pattern (11 + 16/1/16 + 11 // 11 + 16), and the fourth one is in a different pattern with the number 9 repeated three times, in which the imprisonment of the knight is preceded by the joining of Duessa and followed by the report of Una's dwarf on this event which leads to his rescue.

Three cantos of Book I are formed in symmetry. First, the opening canto: 27 + 1 + 27; second, iii: 21 + 2 + 21; and third, x: 33 + 2 + 33. This last number of Christ's life is found again at vi in telling of the "wondrous grace" granted to Una.

The number 19 is used for two episodes: in telling Sansjoy's defeat (v) and Arthur's story (ix). Though not shown in the diagram, it is used for four more events: for the two main parts of canto iii; for Una among the satyrs (vi); and for Arthur's killing of Orgoglio (viii).

Other numbers repeatedly used are 18, 22, 23, and 34. The number 18, which signifies water, is used for Fradubio's episode (ii) and for the concluding story of the book. The number 22 (completion) is used for Lucifera's procession (iv) and for the knight's rescue and Duessa's expulsion (viii). The number 23 (vengeance on sinners) is used consecutively, as is the case with the opening cantos, for the victory over the Dragon (xi) and for the union of Faith and Truth (xii). The number 34 is used for Duessa's visit with Night (v) and for Despaire (ix). Furthermore, the number 24, which is used for Arthur in vii, is used again for Arthur's victory over Orgoglio in the first section in viii.

Diagram 1 also shows the contrasting canto structure of Book I as I see it: the first two cantos (the fall of man to Errour and to False-hood) are contrasted with the last two (the victory over Satan and the union of Faith and Truth); iii (Truth separated from Faith) is singly contrasted with x (virtues perfected); iv and v (Pride and Night) are set against ix (Despaire); and contrasted at the center are vi (Truth blindly worshipped) and the combined cantos vii and viii (Faith imprisoned and restored to Truth).

Spenser's concern with symmetry is also seen in the structural resemblances, most obviously in the consecutive use of 27 for i–ii, and 23 for xi–xii (and 18 for the second section of both ii and xii). Cantos iii and x, two contrasting cantos in the diagram, both have a symmetrical pattern with the number 2 at the center ($21 + 2 + 21$; $33 + 2 + 33$). The numbers 19 and 34 are used for the contrasting cantos v and ix. Røstvig, in her diagram on page 303, sees one-to-one canto contrasts (i–xii, ii–xi, etc.). In her analysis, the central cantos are in 100 stanzas, which seems to indicate that these are paired, and therefore contrasted at the center—Una's involvement with the satyrs which leads to her escape with Satyrane is in contrast to her knight's imprisonment and her meeting with Arthur. It seems more likely to me, however, that Spenser considers vii and viii together because the two tell the one story of the fall and rescue of the Red Cross Knight by Arthur. This is numerically hinted, as has been noted, by the use of 24 at the end of vii and at the beginning of viii.

II. CANTO PATTERNS IN BOOK II

It has been observed that the first two books of the poem are parallel in structure.[9] We will now see if any of the thematic parallels are reflected in stanza numbers. First I shall show the pattern of each canto as I see it and then compare it with the corresponding canto of Book I.

The first canto is uniquely Spenserian in that it reveals simultaneously two patterns, both in his favorite numbers. Archimago escapes from his shackles (1) and seeks revenge on the Red Cross Knight (2–4), but instead finds Guyon riding, guided by the Palmer (5–7). Archimago complains to Guyon that the Red Cross Knight sexually abused his lady, Duessa (8–11) and shows her to him (12–23); and then guides him to the knight (24–25) but Guyon recognizes him and they are reconciled (26–33). They shake hands and are parted and Guyon travels on guided by the Palmer (34). The episode of Amavia and Mordant is told in the remaining 27 stanzas (35–61): Guyon succours the dying Amavia (35–45) who tells him how Acrasia poisoned her husband and dies (46–56) and Guyon and the Palmer bury the couple (57–61).[10]

Thus divided, this canto reveals two symbolic numbers: 33 + 1 + 27. This pattern corresponds with that of the first canto of Book I in that a transitional stanza divides the canto connecting the episodes. In addition to this obvious pattern, however, it is possible to see a different one similar to that of the opening canto. If the first 7 stanzas are taken to be introductory and if stanza 34 is added to the first section, the overall pattern is: 7 + 27 + 27. The parallel structure is seen in the arrangement of the numbers: 7/16 + 11/11 + 16. Although the order of the numbers 11 and 16 is reversed from that of I i (11 + 16/1/16 + 11), the symmetrical arrangement of the same numbers makes the parallel unmistakable, as will further be strengthened by the use of 27 in the next canto. We must admit, however, that the double use of 27 is discernible only by those who are well aware of that in the opening canto. It is interesting that doubly (and "darkly") hinting at the pattern of the corresponding canto of Book I, Spenser begins the book of temperance with 33, the number so importantly used for the book of holiness.

The second canto first tells the story of Ruddymane's bloody hands which Guyon fails to cleanse (1–10). Guyon bears Mordant's arms (11) and finding his horse stolen, journeys on foot to Medina's castle (12) where she lives with her elder sister, Elissa, and her younger sister, Perissa (13–19). Guyon fights Hudibras and Sansjoy until they are reconciled by Medina (20–33) who persuades them all to feast together (34–38) and at her request Guyon tells them that the Faerie Queene has appointed him to capture Acrasia (39–44) who caused the deaths of Mordant and Amavia (45–46).

The first section of this canto tells of the babe's bloody hands, in 10 stanzas, and then of Medina's castle, in 9; while the second relates the fight and reconciliation, in 19, and then Guyon's task and the story of Amavia and Mordant, in 8.[11] The canto is divided: 10 + 9/ 19 + 8. The overall pattern is: 19 + 27.

The first section of the third canto introduces Braggadocchio who steals Guyon's horse and his spear (4–5), dubs Trompart his liegeman (6–10), and meets Archimago who promises to bring him Arthur's sword to defeat the Red Cross Knight and Guyon (11–19). He flees in fright when the magician disappears and hides from the approach of Belphœbe (20). The second section introduces Belphœbe who is seen first by Trompart (21–33) and then by Braggadocchio who attempts to embrace her (34–42). The last line of stanza 26 is a rare half line in the poem. If we hold that in Spenser nothing is done without an apparent reason (as in Amoretti the last line of Sonnet 45 is in alexandrine, indicating its centrality in the sequence of 89 sonnets), the half line here is a definite marker calling attention to the fact that it stands at the center of the blazon in 11 stanzas that describe Belphœbe (21–31). The same number of stanzas follows, depicting her encounter with Trompart and Braggadocchio (32–42) who stand awe-struck at her angelic figure (43–46). The 26 stanzas are thus in the pattern: 11 + 11 + 4. Stanza 20, which depicts the approach of Belphœbe, can be added to the second section, gaining the total number of 27. The overall pattern of this canto is then the same as that of ii: 19 + 27.

The fourth canto, after moralizing on birth, horsemanship, and temperance (1–2), tells the Phaon episode. Guyon rescues Phaon from Occasion and Furor (3–15) and comforted by Guyon, Phaon tells him how his friend, Philemon, tricked him into believing that he saw his lady, Claribell, having an affair with Philemon—but what he saw was her maid, Pryene, in Claribell's clothes (16–28). Phaon goes on to explain that he killed Claribell (29) and on learning the truth from Pryene, poisoned Philemon (30), and while he was seeking to kill Pryene, he was tormented by Occasion and Furor (31–33). Guyon and the Palmer advise him not to be intemperate (34–36). Atin, Pyrochles's squire, confronts Guyon and warns him of Pyrochles's approach and rails at him (37–46).

This canto can be divided into two sections: one of 28 (Phaon trapped) and the other of 18 (his revenge). It is observed that three parts of this canto are all told in 13 stanzas each: first, the story of Guyon who rescues Phaon (3–15); second, how Phaon was trapped by his friend (16–28); and finally, advice in 3 (34–36) and Atin's warning in 10 (37–46). In the pattern of 2 + 13 + 13/5 + 13, the number 13 is placed in the 2:1 ratio.

The fifth canto introduces Pyrochles and Cymochles. First, Pyrochles, the symbol of anger, is told in 24 stanzas: he attacks Guyon but is subdued by him (1–12) and counseled in temperance (13–16); he is then allowed by Guyon to unbind Occasion and Furor only to be abused by them (17–23), but the Palmer advises Guyon not to intercede (24). In the second section, Atin, Pyrochles's squire, reports to Cymochles of his brother's apparent death, who then leaves Acrasia's Bower of Bliss (25–38).

The first section is told in two parts of 16 (Pyrochles) and 8 (Occasion-Furor), in the 2:1 ratio, while the second is in two parts of 10 (Bower of Bliss) and 4 (Atin's message and Cymochles's departure). The structure of this canto is: 16 + 8/10 + 4. The overall pattern is: 24 + 14.

The sixth canto first tells the Phædria episode: she ferries Cymochles to her island on the Idle Lake (1–10) where he lapses into lust (11–18); then she brings Guyon there but he resists her (19–26); when the two fight, she pacifies them (27–36). The second section tells about Guyon after he is ferried back (37–51): Guyon is ferried back and railed at by Atin (37–40); Pyrochles seeks to quench his inner flames in the Idle Lake but is saved by Atin from drowning (41–47); and is healed by Archimago (48–51). This canto is told in a pattern of symmetry, in each section: 10 + 8 + 8 + 10/4 + 7 + 4. The overall pattern reveals two perfect numbers (i.e., sum of numbers up to 8 and 5 respectively): 36 + 15. This pattern hints at the sixth canto of Book I, which has a similar pattern (33 + 15).

The seventh canto tells Mammon's episode. Guyon meets Mammon (3–6) and debates with him over the need of wealth (7–19), and then descends into Mammon's house of Richness (20–25). He is tempted by wealth (26–34) and by the source of all wealth (35–39). He is then confronted by Disdain (40–42) and refuses worldly advancement through marriage to Mammon's daughter, Philotime (43–50). He enters the Garden of Proserpina where he meets Tantalus and Pilate (51–62), refuses to eat the fruit of gold and sit on its silver stool (63–64), and requests Mammon to return him to the world, where he faints (65–66).

In this canto of temptation, told in 66 stanzas, or in the sum of numbers up to 11, the temptation itself is fitly told in 40 stanzas, as noted by Hamilton in his comment on 26.5: "The forty stanzas that describe Guyon's three temptations in Mammon's house—from here to 66.4—correspond to the forty days of Christ's temptations in the wilderness, as Hieatt 1973:51 has noted." The stanza total from 26 to 66 is 41, and not 40, but this makes stanza 46 the central stanza of the temptation scene. Indeed, it describes Philotime, daughter of Mammon, "in glistring glory" holding "a great gold chaine ylincked well,/Whose vpper end to highest heuen was knitt,/And lower part did reach to lowest Hell." This also makes it clear that "Ambition, rash desire to sty" (i.e., to mount up) is what money leads people to, the chief enemy of human mind. That can be assumed simply because it is stated at the central stanza. Thus, this canto on Mammon, though not told in any symmetry (19 + 6/9 + 5 + 3 + 8 + 12 + 2 + 2), has its central thought stated at the midpoint. The overall pattern is: 25 + 41.[12]

The eighth canto tells of Arthur's rescue of Guyon. After marveling at "care in heaven" (1–2) Spenser tells how the angel sent by God summons the Palmer to save the unconscious Guyon (3–9) whom Pyrochles and Cymochles seek to disarm (10–16), but Arthur arrives to save him (17–29). Pyrochles attacks Arthur by wielding Arthur's sword and defending himself with Guyon's shield but is wounded (30–32) and Cymochles unseats and wounds Arthur (33–39). Wielding Guyon's sword given him by the Palmer, Arthur kills Cymochles (40–45) and Pyrochles (46–52), and pledges friendship with Guyon (53–56).

The first section of this canto tells what leads to the fight and the second depicts the fight itself: 29 + 27. (Behind this, double use of 27 is clearly hinted: 2 + 27 + 27.) This pattern is obvious enough, but we cannot ignore the fact that stanza 29 has a rare unrhymed line. Hamilton's comment on it reads: "The failure to rhyme may mark the perversity of the act, as Røstvig 1994:313 suggests." Revenge on a seemingly dead body is certainly perverse, but it is easier to think that it simply marks its central position; with this stanza at the center, the canto divides into a pattern in perfectly Spenserian numbers: 28 + 1 + 27. I think this is more likely because, if perversity is the point, the marker should then be at stanza 13, the center of the act. Since other unrhymed lines are all found at the center of the topic (II.ii.7 on Faunus; II.ii.42 on Guyon's talk; and II.iii.28 on Belphœbe), it is natural to assume that this marker of Spenser's indicates its centrality. If this is so, it means further that number symbolism is as much important to him as other factors.

The ninth canto tells of the house of Temperance. After talking about the Faerie Queene (2–9) Arthur and Guyon disperse Malengin's villains who assault Alma's castle (10–16) and are welcomed and entertained in the castle hall (17–20). At their request Alma takes them on a guided tour through the castle (21–60).

This episode of the well-proportioned human body is aptly told in the 2:1 ratio, in the overall pattern: 20 + 40.

The tenth canto, following a four-stanza invocation, recounts what the two knights read separately in Eumnestes's chamber. Arthur reads Briton moniments ("A chronicle of Briton kings, from Brute to Vthers rayne"). The chronicle, told in 64 stanzas (5–68), can be divided into four parts: 4 (prehistory, 5–8) + 28 (first dynasty, 9–36) + 4 (Donwallo, first British king, 37–40) + 28 (all the rest, 41–68). The four parts are thus told rhythmically in two significant numbers, 4 and 28, signifying harmony and stability respectively. The chronicle ends abruptly at 68.2, and so stanza 68 is often omitted from the total number, and the number 63 thus gained (the product of 7 by 9, used in II.ix as the ratios of body and mind in the temperate body) is made much of, as summarized in Hamilton 2001: "The 63 stanzas name 62 kings from Brute to Uther, making Arthur the 63rd, a number that marks the 'Grand Climacteric' of human life." It seems to me, however, that rather than such an evil, sinister number as 63, the number 64 simply fits Arthur better; 64 is most obviously 8 by 8, which is Spenser's number for Arthur: it is in the 8th canto that he kills Orgoglio, in Book I, and Pyrochles and Cymochles, in II. After the chronicle, Spenser has one stanza on his delight. In the meantime Guyon reads *Antiquitie of Faerie lond* ("rolls of Elfin Emperors, till time of Gloriane"), in 7 stanzas (70–76). This part ends with a stanza on Alma inviting them to dinner (77). The whole structure is: 4/4 + 28 + 4 + 28 + 1/7 + 1, and the overall pattern is: 4 + 65 + 8.

The eleventh canto tells Arthur's conquest of Maleger. Beginning with two moralizing stanzas followed by two about Guyon who leaves for Acrasia's island, the main story is told in 45 stanzas (the sum of numbers up to 9). Maleger's twelve troops besiege Alma's castle (5–15) and Arthur offers to fight for her and rides out (16–19) and chases Maleger, but is held down by Malecasta's two hags, Impatience and Impotence (20–28). Timias comes to his rescue (29–31) and Arthur kills Maleger by crushing and throwing him into a standing lake (32–46). The two hags kill themselves (47) and the fainting Arthur is succoured by Timias (48) and cured by Alma (49).

This canto can thus be divided: 4 + 15 + 9/3 + 15 + 3. Only one episode is told here without any obvious division. The movement, however, changes from downward to upward at stanza 29 when

Timias comes to rescue Arthur. Both the number 28 in the first section and the symmetry in the second seem to support this assumption. The overall pattern is: 28 + 21.

The final canto is divided into two sections of 1–41 and 42–87. The theme of the first is temptation and is properly told in 40 stanzas. Thus, after the first introductory stanza, the 40 stanzas depict the temptations, which Guyon must go through on the third day of his voyage to Acrasia's island. This part is constituted of encounters with various dangers in the stanza count of either 8 or 12—the Gulfe of Greedinesse, in 8 (2–9); the wandering Islands, Phædria's floating island, and the quicksand of Vnthrifthed, in 12 (4 each, 10–21); deformed sea-monsters and the weeping Maid, in 8 (22–29); and mermaids, harmful fowls in the fog, and the beasts on Acrasia's island which the Palmer tames with his staff, in 12 (30–41). The rhythmical pattern (8 + 12 + 8 + 12) is appropriate to the triumph of the knight of temperance, and prepares the reader for the story of the Bower itself in which the dominant number is 12. Guyon approaches the gate of the Bower, in 4 stanzas (42–45) and rejects the wine offered by Genius and then by Excesse, in 12 (46–57). He enters the Bower and falters momentarily on seeing the antics of two naked maidens wrestling in a fountain, in 12 (58–69). And finally, after hearing a melodious sound, in 2 (70–71), he sees Acrasia with Verdant, binds her, releases him, and destroys the Bower, in 12 (72–83). Moralizing on her deformed lovers concludes the episode, in 4 (84–87). Thus the structure of the conquest scene (4 + 12 + 12 + 2 + 12 + 4) reveals three 12s in the 2:1 ratio, and is surrounded by 4, the number of unity. The overall pattern is: 41 + 46.

Of the 683-stanza book, the central, 342nd stanza is vii 54, which tells of the fruit of golden apples in the garden of Proserpina. It suggests, as noted by Hamilton, the forbidden fruit of the tree of knowledge of good and evil; as the cause of man's fall, it is the most appropriate object to mention at the center of the book of temptation. Thus, with its central thought expressed at the center, the book is presented in symmetry. The first two cantos telling the deaths of Mordant and Amavia are clearly contrasted with the last one telling the revenge by Guyon on their behalf. In the next inner circle Belphœbe astonishing Braggadocchio (iii) is in contrast to Arthur killing Maleger (xi). Phaon's revenge (iv) and the British history (x) may look, at first sight, quite ill-matched, but the structure thus contrasted, whether personal or national, seems to suggest Spenser's conviction that history is after all a succession of revenges. Since it is quite difficult to find any nation whose history is free from blood-shed, we must admit with Shakespeare that: "Uneasy lies the head that wears a crown."[13] The disturbed emotions of the mind depicted in Pyrochles and Cymochles (v–vi) make a sharp contrast to the perfectly controlled body shown in Alma's castle (ix). The two great enemies of the human mind are brought into the next pair: Mammon's temptation (vii) contrasts with Arthur's victory that brings death to the two brothers (viii). Unlike Book I, this book has its central pair placed at the beginning of the second half of the book, and yet recessed symmetry, either in one-to-one or one-to-two pairing, does exist. As Diagram 2 indicates, the second half of Book II begins with the eighth canto. This explains why in the second book Arthur appears in canto viii rather than vii as in the first. We may now say that in each of the first two books Arthur appears only in the second half of the book, at its beginning.

We can see in Diagram 2 that some numbers repeatedly used in Book I are also used. Suggesting its continuity from the previous book, it properly begins with 33, but as the emphasis shifts from grace to nature, this number of Christ's life ceases to be used in this book. The number 27 is used for four cantos (i, ii, and iii; and viii, the first to begin the second half) and remains to be the most important number. The number 28 is used for three cantos (iv, viii and xi), and we know it is used two more times in the chronicle section in x. Quite aptly for the book of temperance, 40, the number of temptation, is used, including those hinted at by 41, for 3 sections, in cantos vii, ix, and xii. The number for negative events, 19, is used twice, for ii and iii. Unlike Book I, no canto is told in symmetry and the ninth is the only one told in the 2:1 ratio, although we have already observed this ratio within sections. Thus the thematic correspondences between the first two books are most definitely reflected in the parallel use of 27 at the beginning of both the first and second halves of each book. The close relationship will be made more distinct as we examine the structure of the third book.

III. CANTO PATTERNS IN BOOK III

The book of chastity differs from the first two in seeing Arthur from the beginning. In fact, it begins by mentioning "The famous Briton Prince," linking him with Britomart. In the first two books he appears after the midpoint and achieves major undertakings, whereas in the third there is no comparable task that requires his superhuman power. This may be due to the virtue of chastity, one that is hard, as personified in Britomart, to be fatally endangered. Let us now see how much, if any, such a new type of book differs from the first two in the use of numbers and patterns.

The first canto tells the episode of Castle Joyous. Traveling with Arthur, Guyon fights Britomart and is unhorsed by her, but the Palmer and Arthur reconcile them (1–12). Riding in the forest, they see Florimell fleeing from the Foster, and Arthur and Guyon seek to pursue her (13–18). Britomart comes to Malecasta's castle and before the gate saves the Red Cross Knight from Malecasta's six knights (19–30) and is entertained in her Castle Joyeous (31–46). Malecasta lusts after Britomart believing her to be a man and steals into her bed but is rebuffed (47–62), and although her knights defend her, Britomart and the Red Cross Knight force them to flee (63–67).

The introductory section of this canto is told in 18 stanzas: the reconciliation of Guyon and Britomart, in 12; and the beginning of Florimell's pursuit, in 6. The remaining 49 stanzas can be divided into two sections of two parts each: Britomart's rescue of the Red Cross Knight, in 12, and entertainment in the castle, in 16; Malecasta's lust, in 16, and the defeat of her knights, in 5. The pattern is: 12 + 6/12 + 16/16 + 5. The overall pattern of this canto is in symbolic numbers: 18 + 28 + 21. It is seen that Britomart's face is aptly compared to the moon at stanza 43, the 25th or center of the main episode of this canto narrated in 49 stanzas.

The second canto tells of Britomart's past. It begins with praise of women, represented, in warlike power, by Britomart and, in wisdom, by Queen Elizabeth (1–3). It tells how Britomart hears of Artegall from the Red Cross Knight (4–16) and how, earlier, she saw Artegall in Merlin's magic mirror (17–26). Since then she has been overcome by an uncontrollable love for Artegall (27–52): she falls in love with him (27–29), and her aged nurse, Glauce, counsels her in her love-sickness (30–47) but fails to cure her by charms and herbal medicines (48–52).

This canto is divided into two sections of 26 stanzas each: 3 (praise of women) + 13 (hearing of Artegall) + 10 (seeing Artegall in the mirror)/3 (Britomart's love-sickness) + 18 (Glauce's counsel) + 5 (charms and herbs). The pattern is proportional: 26 + 26.

The third canto further tells of Britomart's past as she learns from Merlin. After appealing to Love and invoking Clio (1–4), Spenser tells how Britomart seeks Merlin to help find out about Artegall (5–28): led by Glauce, she visits Merlin in his underground dwelling (5–14); he hears Glauce's complaint (15–20) and tells Britomart of Artegall's birth, upbringing, his marriage to her, and death (21–28).

Last of all, he reveals their descendants (29–50). Coming home, she disguises herself as a Saxon knight and goes to faery land as directed by Merlin (51–62).

This canto can thus be divided into four parts: 14 + 14 + 22 + 12. If we divide this canto noting the full stop at the end of the second line of the argument ("Merlin bewrayes to Britomart,/The state of Arthegall./And shews the famous Progeny . . . "), the overall pattern of this canto is: 28 + 34.[14]

The fourth canto, after eulogizing on Britomart's valor (1–3), tells of Marinell's defeat and Arthur's pursuit of Florimell, Marinell's love. Britomart leaves the Red Cross Knight and, coming to the rich strand, laments her love (4–11), and wounds Marinell (12–18). He was conceived when his mother, Cymodoce, was raped by Dumarin (19–20), and given wealth by his grandfather, Nereus (21–23), and Cymodoce had warned him to avoid women's love because of Proteus's prophecy that he would be overthrown by a virgin (24–28). He is carried to Cymodoce's bower to be attended by Liagore (29–44). In the meantime, Archimago pursues Britomart (45), the Red Cross Knight takes the other way (46) and Timias pursues the Foster (47), while Arthur pursues Florimell, but night falls and he lies down on the ground (48–54), complains against night and leaves before daybreak (55–61). Arthur's pursuit of Florimell, mentioned only briefly in the first canto, is told here in the last 14 stanzas where his own love-sickness is fully described.

The canto is divided: 3 (valor) + 8 (rich strand) + 7 (Marinell wounded) + 10 (prophecy)/16 (cure) + 17 (Arthur). The overall pattern is: 28 + 33.

The fifth canto relates Timias's episode, which actually tells of Belphœbe's chastity. In seeking Florimell, Arthur meets her dwarf who tells him that Florimell left the court four days before, vowing never to return until she found Marinell dead or alive, and Arthur promises to help him find her and looks for his squire, Timias (3–12) who kills the Foster and his two brothers (13–25). Belphœbe finds Timias in a swoon and binds his wounds (26–36) and then takes him to her bower where she heals his wounds (37–41) only to wound his heart by loving her, leaving him in despair (42–50). The canto ends with praise of her virginity (51–55).

This canto is divided: 2 (love) + 10 (Florimell) + 13 (Foster killed by Timias)/11 (Timias tended by Belphœbe) + 5 (Timias healed) + 9 (Timias pining in love) + 5 (Belphœbe, example of chastity). The overall pattern is: 25 + 30.

The sixth canto tells of the birth and upbringing of the twins, Belphœbe and Amoret. The twins are born to Chrysogone, daughter of Amphisa (2–4) who conceived them while asleep through the effect of the sun's rays (5–10). Venus in her search for Cupid (11–16) meets Diana, and both search for him (17–25) and come to the place where Chrysogone lies still in a trance with her newborn babes by her side (26–27). The goddesses agree to take the babes: Diana/ Phœbe adopts Belphœbe to be brought up by a nymph while Venus adopts Amoret in Cupid's place and nurtures her in the Garden of Adonis (28–29). It is a paradise on earth (30–45) where Adonis enjoys his life with Venus and sports with Cupid (46–50). Amoret is raised here by Cupid's wife, Psyche (51–52) and then taken to the court of the Faerie Queene where she loves Scudamour (53). The canto ends with a transitional stanza on Florimell (54) making this canto equally divided into two sections of 27 stanzas each: the birth of the twins and their upbringing. As far as space is concerned, however, Amoret is the central figure: although in the birth scene she is mentioned only at one line (4.5), in the rest of the canto she is predominant except for the two lines on Belphœbe (28.4–5).

As is well known,[15] the Garden of Adonis is placed at the center of the book. Beginning with the phrase "Right in the middst of that Paradise," stanza 43, the 340th of 679 stanzas of Book III as it first appeared in 1590, indicates the exact midpoint of the book. The Garden itself is told in 16 stanzas from 30 to 45, and the last of it lacks line 4 (supplied in half-line in the 1609 edition). Clearly, the 8–line stanza signals the central position of the Garden. This canto is thus given a well-balanced pattern: 27 + 27.

The seventh canto is about Florimell and Satyrane. Her palfrey collapses and she walks and finds refuge in the Witch's cottage (1–11). But she must flee from her son (12–19) and chased by a hyena sent by the Witch, she escapes in a fisher's boat (20–27). The hyena kills her palfrey and is about to devour her when Satyrane comes and finding Florimell's girdle, fears her dead and binds her palfrey with her girdle (28–36). Satyrane allows the hyena to escape in order to rescue the Squire of Dames from Argante, but is himself seized by Argante and freed when she sees Palladine (37–44). Recovering from a swoon, Satyrane finds the Squire who tells him about Argante (45–52). He is amused by the Squire's story of how he tried to find chaste women while in the meantime the hyena goes back to the Witch (53–61).

The first section is told in Spenser's favorite pattern: 11 (Florimell) + 16 (Witch). The second, divided in two numbers (9 + 8 + 8 + 9), is in symmetry: 9 (girdle) + 16 (Satyrane) + 9 (Argante). The overall pattern is: 27 + 34.

The eighth canto tells of the False Florimell and Florimell. In order to console her son, the Witch fashions the False Florimell (1–10) who is first taken by Braggadocchio (11–13) and then by Ferraugh (14–19). In the meantime, Florimell is harassed by the Fisher (20–27). She is saved by Proteus (29–36) but harassed by him and cast into his dungeon (37–43). She is sought by all the knights of the court, notably by Satyrane who tells Paridell about her girdle and the hyena devouring her palfrey (44–50). At the Squire's suggestion, they approach the nearby castle, but their entry is refused (51–52).

The first 19 stanzas are about the False Florimell, and the rest are all about Florimell. Each Florimell is thus told in a number that symbolizes the nature of each person: 19 + 33.

The ninth canto tells the first half of the Malbecco episode. Satyrane and Paridell hear from the Squire why Malbecco will not accept guests (3–6), and after failing to be accepted, they shelter in a shed by the gate (7–11). Britomart comes and fights Paridell but Satyrane reconciles them, and they enter the castle (12–18). They are brought into a room where Britomart doffs her guise (19–24). In the dining room, Paridell seduces Hellenore (25–31) and recounts his Trojan lineage from Paris, and Britomart joins him to discuss the Trojan ancestry of the Britons (32–53).

This canto can be divided into two sections: entry into Malbecco's castle (1–24) and the dining room scene (26–53). Stanza 25 functions like I i 28: it first describes how Paridell feels after finding Britomart to be a woman and then how they beg Malbecco of his wife's company. Paridell seduces Hellenore at dinner table and primarily to impress her, discusses his ancestry with Britomart, but all this can be grouped as an after-dinner talk or entertainment. What seems important is that their discussion is delivered, as is Merlin's prophecy, in 22 stanzas in all. The overall pattern is: 24 + 1 + 28.

The tenth canto tells of the outcome of Malbecco's jealousy. The next morning Britomart and Satyrane leave the castle (1) but Paridell stays to persuade Hellenore to elope with him (2–11). She sets fire to her husband's castle and escapes with Paridell (12–16). Malbecco searches for her and engages Braggadocchio and Trompart to find her (17–33). As they travel together, they meet Paridell who tells him that he has abandoned her (34–38). At Trompart's advice, Malbecco buries his wealth (39–42) and finally finds his wife among the satyrs, but she refuses to go home with him (43–52). He finds his money stolen and is transformed into Jealousy (53–60).

Hellenore's elopement is told in 33 stanzas and Malbecco's transformation in 27. Perhaps some irony is intended in framing the most human, uniquely unholy episode in the most sublime of Spenser's numbers: 33 + 27.

The eleventh canto depicts Britomart in Busirane's house until she comes to the second room. With Satyrane, Britomart pursues Ollyphant (3–6) and while alone in the woods, she finds Scudamour, hears him complain that Busirane has imprisoned Amoret, and promises him to free her (7–20). She passes through the flame at the porch to Busirane's castle but Scudamour is forced to retreat (21–27). In the first room, Britomart sees tapestries of the loves of the gods (28–46), the statue of Cupid (47–48) and the motto over the door, "Be bold" (49–50). In the second room, she wonders at the bas-relief, the spoils of war, and the same motto on the other side of the door, and on the far door, "Be not too bold" (51–54). She waits until dark, but no creature appears (55).

This canto is told in two scenes of before and after her entrance into the house: 27 + 28.

The last canto recounts Amoret's rescue. At about 10 o'clock a shrill trumpet is heard, followed by thunder, lightning, earthquake, smoke and sulfur, and at midnight a stormy wind blows open the iron gate, and Britomart sees Cupid's masque led by Ease (1–26) in which Britomart sees Amoret led by Despite and Cruelty (19–21) followed by Cupid (22–23). The door is shut and Britomart must wait until the midnight of the second day to enter the third room (27–29), where she sees Busirane torturing Amoret (30–31). Britomart is wounded, but overturns Busirane's power and releases Amoret (32–40), binds him with Amoret's chains (41), and restores her to Scudamour (42–47). But in the second edition, with Scudamour gone, she keeps her (42–45).

The first section of this canto ends with the closure of the door at 27. The door opens for Britomart to enter at 29, and so stanza 28 can be taken as the transitional one. The overall pattern of this canto is: 27 + 1 + 19. In the second edition, it is: 27 + 1 + 17.

Since the last two cantos tell one episode of Busirane, the two can be treated as a unit. Then the last stanza of canto xi becomes the transitional one, and the combined pattern has the 2:1 ratio: 27 + 27 + 1 + 27 + 1 + 19. The last number is 17 in the second edition. The change from 19 to 17 may well be intentional: if we add xii.28 to the second section, the pattern for the last canto is: 27 + 18, the same as that of I.ii. We now find that the last two cantos of Book III are numerically matched to the first two of Book I. The parallel structure is clear enough in the first edition, and clearer in the second. Indeed, the first and last two cantos of the first part of *The Faerie Queene* are framed in unmistakably similar pattern—most notably in the use of 27 in the 2:1 ratio. This distinct feature is supported in the 1596 edition, in the total number of 100 and the combined use of the numbers 27 and 18 that symbolize earth and water respectively.

From Diagram 3 we find that in Book III Spenser uses the numbers 27 and 28 most often. Repeated use of 27, seen in the first two books at the beginning, is here seen twice: at the center (vi–vii) and at the end (xi–xii). Including the second section of canto x, 27 is used six times in this book. The number 28 is used for five sections: in cantos i and xi, for Britomart; in iii, for Merlin; in iv, for Marinell; and in ix, for Paridell. The number 33 is used for three sections: in cantos iv and viii, for Florimell; and in x, for Hellenore. The number 26 is used in canto ii for both sections, forming symmetry. The number 34, used twice in Book I, is also used twice here: for prophecy, in in iii; and for Satyrane, in vii. The number 19 is used in viii for False Florimell (and again for Amoret's rescue, in the 1590 edition). Though not shown in the diagram, also noteworthy is 22, the number of completion, used for two history parts in the contrasting cantos: for Merlin's prophecy, in iii; and for Trojan ancestry, in ix.

   Diagram 3 further shows that the stories in Book III are arranged in contrasts: Britomart's friendship with the Red Cross Knight, Guyon, and Arthur (i) is in contrast to her rescue of Amoret from Busirane (xi–xii); Britomart's love of Artegall (ii–iii) is set against Malbecco's jealousy of Hellenore (ix–x); Marinell wounded by Britomart (iv) and Timias's pain of love for Belphœbe (v) contrast with Florimell harassed by the Fisher and Proteus (viii); and centrally contrasted is the idyllic birth and nurture of Amoret and Belphœbe (vi) against the inhumane suffering and imprisonment of Florimell (vii). Thus, the symmetry and numerology observed in the first two books of *The Faerie Queene* are observed in the third in such a way that the whole arrangement of the cantos also suggests Spenser's favorite 2:1 ratio. From the diagram we also find that the first two books are contrasted in five pairings while this one is contrasted in four.

As I have argued elsewhere,[16] Spenser uses the number 27 even in the *Cantos of Mutabilitie*. The use of 27 at the major points of the poem is obvious enough to say that Spenser devised his poem upon numerical patterns. It seems very likely to me that he uses this number as a kind of marker. Whenever he has it, something of prime importance is being said. As shown in the three diagrams printed on one page, we see it first at the beginning of the poem, then at the midpoint where Orgoglio makes his first appearance; in the second book, it is used again at the beginning, and in the eighth canto where

Arthur kills the two brothers; and in the third, the triple use of 27 at the two centrally contrasting cantos highlights the three chaste ladies, and the final heavy use of it in the closing cantos suggests circular return to the opening episodes of the poem, from the magician's house back again to Errour's den and the great magician's house.

Since in some cases just adding or deducting a stanza gains another number/pattern, the numbers shown in my diagrams may not exactly be what Spenser had in mind. And it is not always easy to find a definite pattern for each canto. Yet it seems to me that enough has been found to show that Spenser is at least a deeply number-conscious poet. All the episodes are in fact carefully and deliberately structured in patterns that reveal numbers of significance. Gerard Manley Hopkins is later to write: "The world is charged with the grandeur of God." I am tempted to think that this is what Spenser had in mind when he was writing about his faerie land; he needed divine numbers to reveal divine order of the world. Following in the footsteps of his predecessors, Spenser designed each of his episodes before writing them so that they would look beautiful, as any architect would want. Living in difficult circumstances at a time when people did not live long, creating beautiful patterns in his poetry must have been his daily joy and sole consolation. He certainly is, in Milton's words,[17] "sage and serious" in the head, but at heart he is almost always playful, genuinely playful, in his use of words. This explains why he liked to write in alliteration so much; he enjoyed creating joyful sounds. He is even kind to his readers and spared no pains in directing them when to stop and think, where to look, and what to see. Making up his own patterns constituted much of his pleasure. He loved to read, and above all, as Røstvig says,[18] he loved Tasso and endeavored to go beyond him by making up even more elaborate patterns on more sublime subjects. We can imagine him first assigning an appropriate number to each part of his story and finally "tailoring" its length to achieve the effects he wanted. We may now conclude that relating his tale in symbolic, beautiful numbers was his way of revealing his beautiful mind.

Kumamoto, Japan

NOTES

1. This article is indebted to "The Characters of *The Faerie Queene*" in A.C. Hamilton ed., *The Faerie Queene* (Harlow: Pearson Education, 2001), 775–87. Quotations refer to this edition. An earlier version of the first chapter appeared, in

Japanese, in Kyushu Lutheran College *VISIO* 27 (2000): 97–106, as a review of Maren-Sofie Røstvig's analysis of canto patterns of *The Faerie Queene* I in her *Configurations: A Topomorphical Approach to Renaissance Poetry* (Oslo, 1994), 267–312, and that of the second chapter, in *VISIO* 28 (2001), 153–58. In my numerological thinking I owe much to this great book. I am also indebted to A. Kent Hieatt's review of Røstvig's book in *English Language Notes* 34 (December 1996): 79–83.

2.   Røstvig, 274–75.

3.   For meanings of symbolic numbers I am indebted to Alastair Fowler, *Spenser and the Numbers of Time* (London, 1964); Alastair Fowler, *Triumphal Forms: Structural Patterns in Elizabethan Poetry* (Cambridge, 1970); and Røstvig, *Configurations*.

4.   It may be useful to know that the numbers 27 and 18 signify earth and water respectively. According to Fowler's note (1964:188), each of the four numbers 8, 12, 18, and 27 is gained by adding half of its preceding one to itself (8 + 4 = 12; 12 + 6 = 18; 18 + 9 = 27), and these were regarded as numbers of harmony symbolizing the four elements: 8 assigned to Fire, 12 to Air, 18 to Water, and 27 to Earth.

5.   For the number 19, see Røstvig 260 and 269.

6.   Røstvig, at 282–83, sees that two stanzas on Duessa's crocodile tears divide the canto into the 1:2 ratio: 17 + 2 + 34. She also sees that adding the two stanzas, the first section is balanced: 2 + 4 + 7 + 4 + 2. This is misleading because the fight begins at stanza 6 and the pattern must be: 2 + 3 + 8 + 4 + 2.

7.   Along with this pattern, Røstvig, at 287–89, sees another pattern, which is obtained by adding the holy Hospital episode to the first section: 1 + 44 + 22 + 1. Although it yields the 2:1 ratio, it seems more fitting to me to divide the instruction into inside and outside of the house of Holinesse.

8.   My analysis of I.xi. is based on the assumption that stanza 3 was, as Hamilton 2001 notes, "Omitted 1590 by the printer; or, less likely, added by S. *1596*." It is supported by the important reference to the brazen tower with the watchman waiting for "tydings glad" (which suggests an Old Testament prophet awaiting to announce the gospel, as Kaske 1969 notes). The numbers employed seem further to strengthen this assumption: the double use of 7 makes a perfect beginning; and the stanza total, 55, connects this canto with the first. Røstvig, without commenting on the added stanza, divides this canto into a pattern of 33 + 22 stanzas, but stanza 33, in my view, belongs to the second day.

9.   See A.C. Hamilton, *The Structure of Allegory in "The Faerie Queene"* (Oxford, 1961), 89–123.

10.   Røstvig's elaborate analysis of this canto, pp. 314–20, is based on symmetries she finds (8 + 15 + 8/2/5 + 8 + 2 + 8 + 5; overall pattern: 31 + 2 + 28), which disagrees with mine. This is misleading because in my view stanza 8 belongs to the next part.

11.   Røstvig, at 320–23, sees the 2:1 ratio in her pattern (2 + 14 + 14/1/7 + 7 + 1; the overall pattern: 2 + 28 + 1 + 14 + 1).

12.   Røstvig, at 328–31, sees a different pattern: Guyon's rejection of wealth in the centrally placed stanzas 33–34 is flanked by 30 stanzas on each side, in each of which a pattern of recessed symmetry is incorporated with each halfway point (17 and 50) at the center, forming the overall structure: 2 + 30 + 2 + 30 + 2.

13.   *Henry IV*, Part 2 (1597), III.i.31.

14.   If Merlin's chronicle (26–50) is grouped together at the center, the structure is: 25 + 25 + 12. Merlin's chronicle in 25 stanzas can be divided, as suggested by Berger (in Hamilton's note for 26–50), into the first cycle of 16 stanzas (25–41) and the second cycle of 8 (43–50), with one transitional stanza, forming the pattern in the 2:1 ratio thus: 16 + 1 + 8.

15.   See Hamilton's note on III.vi.43.

16.   In "The Numerological Patterning of the *Mutabilitie Cantos*" in *Notes and Queries* 248:1 (March 2003): 18–20, I argue that interposed over the obvious pattern on *Mutabilitie* (39 + 19/13 + 33 + 13) is another one that is discernible only by those who know Spenser's use of this number: 27 + 1 + 27/27 + 32.

17.   From *Areopagitica* (1644) quoted in R. M. Cummings, ed., *Spenser: The Critical Heritage* (London, 1971), 163–64.

18.   See *Configurations*, 203–64.

Diagram 1 *The Faerie Queene* I: Canto Patterns and Contrasts

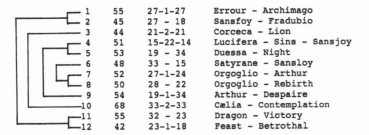

1	55	27-1-27	Errour - Archimago
2	45	27 - 18	Sansfoy - Fradubio
3	44	21-2-21	Corceca - Lion
4	51	15-22-14	Lucifera - Sins - Sansjoy
5	53	19 - 34	Duessa - Night
6	48	33 - 15	Satyrane - Sansloy
7	52	27-1-24	Orgoglio - Arthur
8	50	28 - 22	Orgoglio - Rebirth
9	54	19-1-34	Arthur - Despaire
10	68	33-2-33	Cælia - Contemplation
11	55	32 - 23	Dragon - Victory
12	42	23-1-18	Feast - Betrothal

Diagram 2 *The Faerie Queene* II: Canto Patterns and Contrasts

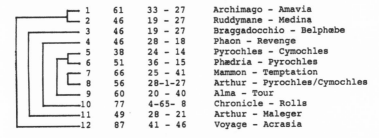

1	61	33 - 27	Archimago - Amavia
2	46	19 - 27	Ruddymane - Medina
3	46	19 - 27	Braggadocchio - Belphœbe
4	46	28 - 18	Phaon - Revenge
5	38	24 - 14	Pyrochles - Cymochles
6	51	36 - 15	Phædria - Pyrochles
7	66	25 - 41	Mammon - Temptation
8	56	28-1-27	Arthur - Pyrochles/Cymochles
9	60	20 - 40	Alma - Tour
10	77	4-65- 8	Chronicle - Rolls
11	49	28 - 21	Arthur - Maleger
12	87	41 - 46	Voyage - Acrasia

Diagram 3 *The Faerie Queene* III: Canto Patterns and Contrasts

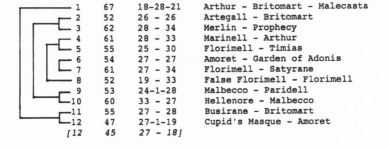

1	67	18-28-21	Arthur - Britomart - Malecasta
2	52	26 - 26	Artegall - Britomart
3	62	28 - 34	Merlin - Prophecy
4	61	28 - 33	Marinell - Arthur
5	55	25 - 30	Florimell - Timias
6	54	27 - 27	Amoret - Garden of Adonis
7	61	27 - 34	Florimell - Satyrane
8	52	19 - 33	False Florimell - Florimell
9	53	24-1-28	Malbecco - Paridell
10	60	33 - 27	Hellenore - Malbecco
11	55	27 - 28	Busirane - Britomart
12	47	27-1-19	Cupid's Masque - Amoret
[12	45	27 - 18]	

ANDREW WALLACE

"Noursled up in life and manners wilde": Spenser's Georgic Educations

Spenser's didactic ambitions for *The Faerie Queene* are directly implicated in the variety and complexity of the poem's narratives of education. The essay argues that georgic metaphors and practices establish a specific vocabulary for the educational problems in which Spenser's poem is so deeply interested. It argues, further, that the georgic strain in *The Faerie Queene* is not restricted to a specifically Virgilian context, and that Spenser is engaging with the georgic metaphors that humanist educators adduced as explanatory fictions for instruction. Spenser's interest in Virgil is indeed one part of this story, but *The Faerie Queene*'s pedagogical georgic is also prominent in texts ranging from Xenophon's *Cyropaedia* to educational treatises by Erasmus, Richard Mulcaster, and others. Especially in his accounts of the educations of Red Cross and Satyrane, Spenser uses georgic to understand the process by which the pupil extrapolates from a set of specialized practices a pattern for more ambitious conduct in the world.

A NUMBER OF SCHOLARS HAVE ARGUED that Spenser was a canny interpreter of Virgil's poem on agricultural management. Reading the georgic strain in *The Faerie Queene* as a critique of the ubiquitous pastoralism of Elizabethan court culture, or as the residue of Spenser's brief sojourn at an undervisited vocational checkpoint on the Virgilian *rota*, scholars have usually treated georgic as a position from which the poet passes judgment on pastoral and heroic.[1] These arguments, however, tend to ignore any interest Spenser might have had in the explicit didacticism of the *Georgics*. They also ignore the educational implications of georgic metaphors generally. The georgic strain in *The Faerie Queene* is not restricted to Spenser's brief borrowings from Virgil's middle poem. Instead, a range of georgic metaphors and practices combine to establish a vocabulary for the problem of education in *The Faerie Queene*. Spenser's interest in Virgil is indeed one part of this story, but *The Faerie Queene*'s pedagogical georgic is prominent in texts ranging from Xenophon's *Cyropaedia* to educational treatises by Erasmus, Richard Mulcaster, and others. In Spenser's accounts of the educations of Red Cross, Satyrane, Belphoebe, and Amoret, and even in the narrator's self-presentation as plowman at the end of the first edition of *The Faerie Queene*, georgic practices ranging from plowing and pruning to animal husbandry and hunting are treated as the primal scene of education. Spenser was not alone in exploiting a connection between georgic and education, and this essay attempts to reimagine georgic as the capacious thing it seems to have been for sixteenth-century poets and pedagogues.

1. "BUT NOW MY TEME BEGINS TO FAINT AND FAYLE"

What kind of technology for fashioning gentlemen is *The Faerie Queene*?[2] Richard Waswo underscores the workmanlike character of a verb that has occasioned much scholarly commentary: "to 'fashion' (*facere*) is to do what a blacksmith does with iron."[3] Waswo's formulation points to one of the possible ways in which Spenser might be said to have metaphorized the elusive aspirations of his didactic project. The blacksmith's forge provides a vivid metaphor for the methodical process by which Spenser claims that he and his text will remake his Elizabethan readers. A different category of labor, however, is invoked in the final stanza of the 1590 *Faerie Queene*. When Amoret and Scudamour are reunited at the end of the original version of Book III, Spenser's narrator is plowing rather than hammering[4]:

> Thus doe those lovers with sweet countervayle,
>   Each other of love's bitter fruit despoile.
>   But now my teme begins to faint and fayle,
>   All woxen weary of their journall toyle:
>   Therefore I will their sweatie yokes assoyle
>   At this same furrowes end, till a new day:
>   And ye faire Swayns, after your long turmoyle,
>   Now cease your worke, and at your pleasure play;
> Now cease your worke; to morrow is an holy day.
>
>   (III.xii.47)[5]

Juxtaposing his own arduous labors with the promise of rest (and, for Amoret and Scudamour, sexual consummation), Spenser's poetic field work makes the most of its ancient etymological pedigree. The Latin word *versus* refers both to plowed furrows and to the poet's turn from the end of one line of verse to the beginning of the next. In ancient Greek the same semantic range is governed by the word *boustrophedon*, which describes the "ox-like-turn" of poet and plowman, plow and pen.[6] In addition to the etymological game it plays, this georgic stanza also serves as a reminder that the poet of *The Faerie Queene* is laboring in an explicitly didactic vocation.[7]

In the last stanza of the 1590 version of his poem Spenser engages in a kind of wish-fulfillment fantasy. By taking to the plow at the end of his volume the poet metaphorically puts himself in command of a technology which, unlike poetry, generates visible proof of its efficiency and integrity as a cultural practice. The plowman produces evidence of the success of his labors in a way that the poet cannot. Pausing at the end of his text Spenser transforms his solitary poetic vocation into a cooperative agricultural project. He suggests that he and his fainting and failing team have earned their "holy day," but the intensely physical experience of cultivation—an experience to which the poet's weary and sweaty team bears witness—is at best a provisional account of instruction.[8] The tone of this terminal georgic stanza is almost unabashedly optimistic, but the poet's desire "to fashion a gentleman or noble person"[9] implicates him in labors that leave behind no trace of their success—no trace, that is, of a causal relationship between *The Faerie Queene* and any virtues that might be espoused at court by its readers. Spenser's grand didactic ambitions remain, as they must, curiously intractable; as didactic poet and self-styled plowman, he harvests an invisible crop. Spenser does not, however, invoke the georgic topos merely to suggest its inadequacy. His version of georgic is supple enough to make visible the problems that vex the didactic enterprise in which he is engaged without invalidating the metaphors and practices in which he frames those problems.

This georgic stanza is Spenser's last word as didactic poet and narrator in the 1590 *Faerie Queene*, and much of its ability to shed light on Spenser's didacticism is derived from its structural apposition to the *Letter to Ralegh*. The stanza marks a specific point of entry into the didactic poetics expounded in the *Letter*: first, because sixteenth-century educators seem to have prized Virgil's didactic poem as a statement about the mechanics of instruction[10]; second, because educators habitually adduced georgic metaphors and analogies in order to describe their theories and justify their practices. The *Letter to*

Ralegh is not, of course, secretly concerned with georgic, and the *Georgics* itself possesses no monopoly on the didactic function that humanist poetics ascribed to literary production generally. Spenser is, after all, clearly willing to associate the didactic instrumentality of poetry with heroic texts by the usual suspects—Homer, Virgil, Ariosto, Tasso. It is significant, however, that a connection between georgic and education is established long before Spenser or, for that matter, Virgil. Xenophon's *Cyropaedia*, for which the *Letter to Ralegh* reserves special praise, repeatedly exploits the educational implications of georgic practices in order to account for the fashioning of Cyrus as a martial paragon.[11]

Humanistic pedagogy was deeply invested in a model of exemplary and imitative learning, but educators also brought the vast resources of figurative language to bear on the operation of instruction. Educators collapsed these discourses by employing georgic metaphors as explanatory fictions for the teacher's task. Insofar as these metaphors strive to conceptualize the way instruction operates on students, they often mount an acutely self-conscious inquiry into the ethics and mechanics of instruction. Georgic metaphors are among the most pervasive figurative resources of treatises ranging from pseudo-Plutarch's "The Education of Children" and the writings of early continental humanists, to Elyot's *Governour*, Mulcaster's *Positions Concerning the Training Up of Children*, and most famously, Bacon's "Georgickes of the mind concerning the husbandry & tillage therof" in *The Advancement of Learning*.[12] The wide semantic field of the Latin word *cultus*, which ranges from cultivation to culture and teaching, establishes an etymological foundation for the insistence with which educators mapped agriculture on to education. Pruning, grafting, tilling, and, unfortunately for students, manuring—these are resilient tropes for what Mulcaster calls the "training-up" process. In the hands of educational theorists these georgic metaphors and analogies are used to posit, however cautiously and provisionally, a model for the process by which information is imparted to and internalized by students.

Georgic supplies one of the most sophisticated figurative resources of educational writing. Although the *Georgics* has always been the least famous of Virgil's three canonical poems, it is nevertheless repeatedly quoted and alluded to in humanist educational treatises. Individual verses and passages are transformed into educational precepts by continental authorities such as Pier Paolo Vergerio, Aeneas Silvius Piccolomini, and Erasmus, all of whom quote directly from Virgil's poem in order to claim an ancient pedigree for their own prescriptive statements of method.[13] Arguing that the education of youth should begin early, Vergerio quotes Virgil's assertion that farm animals must be trained almost from birth to perform their agricultural tasks: " 'Dum faciles animi iuvenum, dum mobilis aetas,' ut est Maronis versus" ("while young minds are malleable, while they are young enough to change," as Virgil's verse goes).[14] Piccolomini (later Pope Pius II) quotes the *Georgics* in support of the argument that teachers must prevent their charges from associating with pernicious influences: " 'Multum est in teneris consuescere,' sicut Vergilius ait" ("Habit is strong in tender years," as Vergil says).[15] In defense of his own minute attention to orthographical problems in *De liberorum educatione* (1450), Piccolomini quotes from the *Georgics* again, this time borrowing a famous phrase in which Virgil trumpets the glory that will accrue to his account of the beekeeper's arts in the Fourth Georgic: " 'In tenui labor est,' ut Vergilius ait, 'at tenuis non gloria" ("The labor is small," as Vergil says, "but not the glory").[16]

If these tags seem merely symptomatic of the eclectic marshalling of aphorisms that humanist educators encouraged, georgic also supplied a bursting storehouse of analogies with which theorists might gloss and account for the operation of instruction on students. These metaphors and analogies make compelling objects of study because it is often difficult to gauge exactly where and how oversimplifications of the educational process grade into more speculative and ambitious inquiries. Erasmus, for instance, is characteristically sensitive to the promise and limitations of humanism's rhetoric of cultivation. His pedagogical georgic offers an important precedent for the flexibility with which Spenser explores this vocabulary in *The Faerie Queene*. Erasmus is keenly aware that georgic metaphors seem to invite ruthlessness on the part of literal-minded educators. At times he devotes himself without qualification to a vision of education as an almost physical engagement with the young scholar. Throughout the *De pueris* he repeatedly figures pedagogy as a version of cultivation grounded in discourse. Able pedagogues, he insists, are like those efficient farmers who

> train seedlings when they are still tender to lose their wild nature before the process of hardening sets in. They watch that their saplings do not grow crooked or suffer any other kind of harm; in fact, even if something has already gone wrong, they act quickly to rectify the damage while the trees are still pliant and responsive to a guiding hand. Can any animal or plant serve our will and convenience unless our own efforts come to the aid of nature? The sooner this is done, the more successful will be the results.[17]

The notion of the student's physical responsiveness to "a guiding hand" is introduced as a gloss on the discursive exchange of knowledge and expertise. But Erasmus—a keen opponent of corporal punishment in the classroom—also cautions against the temptation to literalize the metaphors that proliferate in the rhetoric of education. His remarks begin as an attack on metaphor and Old Testament wisdom, but he gradually works his way back to specifically georgic projects. Those projects are derided as crude accounts of the relationship between preceptor and student. Georgic metaphors become repugnant precisely when Erasmus passes from images of cultivation to the more onerous projects of animal husbandry. He views the urge to practice these metaphors in the classroom as a dark statement about the plight of young scholars and the brutality of the schoolmasters who would train and subdue them:

> At this point someone may din into our ears such Old Testament proverbs as, 'He that spareth his rod hateth his son: but he that loveth him chasteneth him betimes,' or 'Bend your son's neck in his youth, and bruise his sides when he is a child.' Perhaps for the Jews of a long time ago this sort of discipline was appropriate, but nowadays we must interpret these sayings from the Old Testament more liberally. However, if you wish to follow scripture literally, can you imagine a more ridiculous method for imparting the elements of language to children than to bend their necks and to bruise their sides? Would you not think that an ox was in training for the plough or an ass for the pack-saddle, but hardly that a human being was receiving instruction towards good behaviour?[18]

Physical intervention is robbed of its promise as an explanatory fiction, and Old Testament proverbs are attacked as ruthless and misplaced provisions appropriate only for the training of livestock or "for the Jews of a long time ago." Paradoxically, this negative view of georgic metaphors is a clue to the sophistication with which they are adduced in educational treatises. Immediately following the passage quoted above, Erasmus returns to the text of the *Georgics*, this time in search of an aphoristic attack on the impulsive analogizing of physical and georgic projects in educational discourse: "As for the stick with which you are supposed to bruise your child's sides, even here I might make a suggestion, if you wish: 'Relentless toil overcomes all,' as the supreme poet Virgil expresses it."[19] This maxim from the *Georgics* ("labor omnia vicit[20]/improbus" [1.145–46]) has been viewed as a key to the poem by modern scholars who have seen in it an ethics of diligent toil as well as a more pessimistic account of the relationship between humanity and the natural world.[21] In the *De pueris*, however, it marks just one of many intersections between the *Georgics* and the schoolroom.[22] Erasmus' use of the tag serves as a reminder that the poem could provide its own refutations to the analogies and aphorisms culled from it.

This is an important point because it helps account for the curious fact that within educational discourse negative perspectives on the explanatory function of georgic coexist alongside a more positive view of its fitness. To Erasmus, at least, it is readily apparent that georgic metaphors are both helpful and troublesome as explanatory fictions for the teacher's task. This is more than a deconstructive game with metaphors because the problem at hand is disciplinary rather than psychological. That is, the problem centers on Erasmus' desire to make intelligible the pedagogical practices—rather than the psychological processes—that make learning possible.[23] Negative and positive assessments of georgic metaphors contribute equally to this project.

As Erasmus evaluates the rhetoric of cultivation, Old Testament educational precepts, and the connection between the education of young schoolboys and the taming of animals, he turns his eye to the primal scene of education and educational discourse. His preoccupation with these topics suggests that georgic projects are in some sense the original act of education. As Erasmus suggests, these georgic metaphors are ripe for a critique of the violence that is so often implicit in them. Mary Thomas Crane and Rebecca Bushnell have examined this problem from the perspective of the teacher's potentially violent ascendancy over the student, and for what georgic metaphors reveal about conflicting attitudes to childhood and subjectivity during the Renaissance.[24] Crane and Bushnell read this classroom georgic as a test case in the ethics of instruction, but educational metaphors must also be explored from the perspective of the student—that is, from the perspective of the student who is expected to extrapolate from specialized practices courses of action that are at once more general and more ambitious. Georgic metaphors and analogies are often used to describe the project in which educators are engaged—this is where Crane's and Bushnell's arguments are most illuminating. Students, however, are implicitly challenged to decide how to accept and when to refuse this invitation to view human attainments in direct relation to incremental victories over the recalcitrant savagery of the natural world.

It is in this educational context that the georgic strain in *The Faerie Queene* should be understood. Spenser treats the student's involvement in an epistemological task of inference and extension as the foundation for a series of sophisticated narratives of education in *The Faerie Queene*. The education of Red Cross is an illuminating example because it establishes a paradigm for Spenser's use of the *Georgics*. Virgil provides one context for Spenser's interest in education without exhausting the resources of a pedagogical georgic that is never merely Virgilian.

2. "In Ploughmans State to Byde"

The birth and discovery of the young changeling who becomes Red Cross marks a collision between Spenser's allusive engagement with the *Georgics*, on the one hand, and his interest in a more expansive pedagogical georgic, on the other. Red Cross is a student in the schoolroom of Heavenly Contemplation when he learns for the first time of his descent "from an ancient race/Of *Saxon* kings" (I.x.65.1–2), and of his abduction at birth by a faery:

Thence she thee brought into this Faery lond,
  And in an heaped furrow did thee hyde,
  Where thee a Ploughman all unweeting fond,
  As he his toylesome teme that way did guyde,
  And brought thee up in ploughmans state to byde,
  Whereof *Georgos* he thee gave to name;
  Till prickt with courage, and thy forces pryde,
  To Fary court thou cam'st to seeke for fame,
And prove thy puissant armes, as seemes thee best became.

                                      (I.x.66)

The stanza crafts a narrative for *The Golden Legend*'s hypotheses about St. George: *Georgos* is Greek for "farmer" (or literally, "earth-worker"), an apt name for the Christian hero who succeeds and sanctifies the "red earth" of the Hebrew Adam.[25] But Spenser's young foundling also derives his name from the husbandry of the plowman who discovers and raises him. He is thus labeled or claimed as the product of a specific class of vocational training. The episode seems to reflect on an enigmatic passage near the end of Virgil's First Georgic. After a harrowing description of the wars that followed the assassination of Julius Caesar, Virgil imagines a future Roman laborer baffled by his encounter with the artifacts of forgotten wars. The living child dug up by Spenser's plowman brings new life to the bones that are unearthed in Virgil's poem:

> Scilicet et tempus veniet, cum finibus illis
> agricola incurvo terram molitus aratro
> exesa inveniet scabra robigine pila,
> aut gravibus rastris galeas pulsabit inanis,
> grandiaque effossis mirabitur ossa sepulcris.

(1.493–97)

(Yes, and a time will come when in those lands the farmer, as he cleaves the soil with his curved plough, will find javelins corroded with rusty mould, or with his heavy hoe will strike empty helmets, and marvel at gigantic bones in the upturned graves.)

Adding a healthy dose of Reformation apocalyptics to Virgil's interest in a record of warfare, Spenser's plowman digs up neither bones nor helmets but rather the agent by and through whom the future battles of England's church will be waged.[26] Contemplation's tale is a condensed argument about the role of unflagging diligence in George's quest for salvation,[27] and Spenser's interest in George's "educational profile" may also be treading carefully along the battle lines of Protestant controversies about the role of effort and works in salvation.[28]

If Virgil's plowman is invited to reflect on Rome's violent heritage, Spenser's is assigned a crucial role in the future religious conflicts of the True Church and its nation. This exposed child, so utterly bereft of historical self-consciousness, will be called upon to redeem English history and the English church, a project that William A. Sessions has placed at the center of Spenser's interest in the *Georgics*.[29] Sessions's influential argument for an historically redemptive georgic provides a useful reminder that the question of historical education runs deep in the *Georgics*, as it might be expected to do in a poem that is keenly interested in what gets dug up.[30]

These issues serve the allegorical temper of Book I, but as is often the case in *The Faerie Queene*, the scene's implications are not restricted to Spenser's allegory. Indeed, the discovery of Red Cross seems to codify at the level of narrative Spenser's interest in the specifically educational resonance of Virgil's text. In both Virgil and Spenser these unsettling discoveries are implicitly framed as educational problems. The chief challenge for both plowmen is to make something of what their plows have turned up. Virgil's plowman is invited to accommodate Rome's violent past to what the georgic poet seems to hope will be a peaceful (but perhaps dangerously ignorant and therefore vulnerable) future. Spenser's laborer, however, is granted a surprisingly active role in the fashioning of Holiness. His plowman makes a plowman of the child—a logical response both to the circumstances of the child's discovery and the demands of his discoverer's career. The child's later career as Red Cross suggests that the narrative of Book I can be viewed as a protracted correction of that original act of instruction. Book I recounts a complex educational problem as Spenser narrates the training and the retraining of the foundling—first as a plowboy and then as the Knight of Holiness.

The scene of the child's discovery insists on the absence of any discernible causal link between the plowman's labors and their shocking product. Unlike the plowman we find laboring in the final stanza of the 1590 *Faerie Queene*, the plowman described by Contemplation does indeed fashion a human agent with the blade of his plow. Spenser seems to hold in suspension the rival claims of made (i.e., fashioned) and ready-made (i.e., found) virtue in the education of his hero. The conflict between these two categories of virtue plays out in the first half of the stanza. If Contemplation's account looks like a witty variation on the topos of the hero's humble beginnings, it can also be seen as metaphorical foreshortening of the child's education. Contemplation tells Red Cross: "thee a Ploughman all unweeting fond,/As he his toylesome teme that way did guyde,/And brought thee up in ploughmans state to byde" (I.x.66.3–5). One possible reading of these lines might see the moment of discovery as somehow precluding the possibility of educating this changeling, as if the child were somehow already a plowman when he is unearthed. However, what is surely the primary reading of these lines offers a chronological account of the child's training as a plowman. These two readings generate a productive tension as Spenser weighs the highly condensed conceptual play of metaphor (and allegory's sweet-tooth for shortcuts) against the protracted education that narrative accommodates. The child thus passes from the hands of a strict georgic pedagogy—in which education is delivered as a revelation on the edge of a plow blade—into the hands of the poet and the host of narrative exigencies that fashion Red Cross in Book I.

The discovery of Red Cross instigates his first education in Faery Land—an education that in no way prepares the "clownish person," as he is called in the *Letter to Ralegh*, for the chivalric dimension of Una's quest. Contemplation somewhat optimistically describes Red Cross's life as a seamless progression from exposed child to plowboy to questing knight. The narrative of Book I, however, gives a far more skeptical and fractured account of Red Cross's various attempts to "prove" his "puissant armes and forces pryde" by extending his agricultural attainments into martial exploits. "Prove" is perhaps the most slippery of Spenser's slippery verbs: it can mean "to test or try or make trial" of something one already possesses, but it can also mean "to acquire or learn or find out" by experience.[31] The chronological temper of Contemplation's account suggests that this foundling-cum-plowboy was born equipped for his quest, and that each new experience has successfully prepared him for his next challenge. Readers, however, see him educated and repeatedly reeducated throughout Book I, learning as much from failure as from success. Red Cross's career as plowboy is in a sense utterly discontinuous with his career as questing knight, thus requiring the lengthy and almost always painful retraining to which he is subjected. Metaphorically, however, it is entirely appropriate to his allegorical quest and to his status as a theological argument. His ability to carry out the acts of inference and extension required of him—an ability which the chivalric narrative sometimes threatens to deny to him in his moments of defeat—is built into the proper name (*Georgos*) that enables this earth-working Second Adam to sanctify the "red earth" of his Hebrew original. Narrative and metaphor make strange bedfellows, but they do cooperate in this educational fantasy.

It is tempting to guess that Spenser's georgic pedagogy advances a critique (from the inside, as it were) of the explanatory power of georgic metaphors in educational discourse. The discovery of Red Cross does, after all, offer readers a glimpse at the outlandish extreme of the rhetoric of cultivation. His more troubled education by chivalric narrative could thus be read as an antidote to crude or naïve metaphors that seek to disguise a collection of highly contingent exchanges as a closed system of physical interventions on passive material. However, it would be more true to the sophistication of this scene to suggest that Spenser finds in georgic practices a metaphorical vocabulary for the educational issues in which his didactic poem is so deeply invested.

Not all of *The Faerie Queene*'s georgic touches are engaged in this searching inquiry, and Spenser seems to have exploited georgic for different ends as his poem evolved. The 1596 revisions to the original ending of Book III, for instance, excised the georgic stanza that I have interpreted as a vocational shorthand for Spenser's own didactic labors. In 1596 that stanza is scattered and dispersed throughout Books IV, V, and VI, all of which contain brief accounts of the poet's field work. At the end of Book IV, Canto v, readers encounter a georgic flourish that reclaims the Virgilian brevity of the topos of conclusion Spenser had echoed more expansively in 1590: "But here my wearie teeme nigh over spent/Shall breath it selfe awhile, after so long a went" (IV.v.46.8–9). At the end of Book V, Canto iii, georgic supplies another conventional conclusion and transition: "And turne we here to this faire furrowes end/Our wearie yokes, to gather fresher sprights,/That when as time to *Artegall* shall tend,/We on his first adventure may him forward send" (V.iii.40.6–9). There is little interpretative work to do here—certainly, nothing like the complexity of Red Cross's discovery or of the stanza that concludes the 1590 edition. These georgic flourishes are simultaneously diminished and amplified in 1596, both abandoned and reaffirmed as a valuable characterization of Spenser's literary labors. Georgic motifs assume a more regular place among Spenser's strategies for closure in Books IV–VI, but not all of them invite readers to explore the relationship between Spenser's didactic project and the educational implications of georgic metaphors.[32]

Spenser's redaction of georgic is not limited to a few Virgilian set-pieces or, say, to the narrator's pregnant remarks about "salvage nations" who refuse to drive the "painefull plough, or cattell for to breed," and who choose instead "on the labours of poore men to feed,/And serve their owne necessities with others need" (VI.v-iii.35.6–9). In his accounts of Satyrane's education at the hands of his father, of Belphoebe's "ripening" in the woods, and of the highly-attenuated arts of cultivation practiced in the Garden of Adonis, Spenser engages in a series of protracted reformulations of this pedagogical georgic. These episodes press the implications of georgic beyond the Virgilian context explored in Contemplation's account of the discovery of Red Cross. Instead, these episodes are in league with the precedents offered by Erasmus and guided by interest among educators in what Spenser refers to in the *Letter to Ralegh* as Xenophon's "doctrine by ensample." This movement from the text of the *Georgics* to a pedagogical georgic derived from other authors and discourses does not pass judgment on Virgil. Instead, it ties Virgil's didactic poem on agricultural management to sixteenth-century pedagogical discourse and, in the case of Satyrane, to the student's role as an interpreter of metaphor.

3. "Noursled Up in Life and Manners Wilde"

Satyrane's education engages georgic as a means of testing the boundaries of analogy and gauging what might be learned from the act of subduing the wild intractability of natural savagery. This is one of the central projects of a pedagogical georgic in which cultivating programs—from grafting and animal husbandry to the domestication of wild trees in the name of improvement—are consistently used to reflect on the relationship between culture and cultivation. In Spenser's account of Satyrane's education in the forest, animal husbandry and hunting are reimagined under the aspect of the explanatory function accorded to them in educational discourse. Erasmus' self-consciousness about this issue is again pertinent here, as are his apprehensions that the relentless physicality of georgic metaphors and practices might encourage ruthlessness on the part of the literal-minded preceptor. Spenser's account of Satyrane's training calls to mind another kind of ruthlessness: this time on the part of the student who is invited to extrapolate from a set of discrete disciplinary practices a general pattern for action in the world.

The child of a union between a satyr and a woman, Satyrane is "noursled up in life and manners wilde,/Emongst wild beastes and woods, from lawes of men exilde" (I.vi.23.8–9). The satyr, like the centaur, is a conventional emblem for the uneasy yoking of bestial and rational impulses. A dual susceptibility to savage and civilized appetites grants these creatures a prominent position in the discourse of education in poetry—Homer's Achilles, for instance, is tutored by the centaur Chiron. Spenser has his eye on this tradition in his account of Satyrane's education at the hands of his father. Satyrane is in a sense the definitive marginal character in *The Faerie Queene*. Forever on the margins of the poem's main quest narratives, he is also marginal in the sense that he is traditionally viewed as an allegory of a divided loyalty to bestial and human impulses. He is conventionally read as a site of contestation between the world in which he is formed and educated and the world in which he seeks to act. Maurice Evans, for instance, argues that Satyrane strives throughout the poem to outgrow "the bestiality of his parent satyr."[33] Somewhat more optimistically, Donald Cheney describes Satyrane as "a positive aspect of the satyr's world, as a training ground for the human hero who learns to control and hence to use his natural origins."[34] Satyrane, however, seems to embody a slightly different conceptual struggle, a struggle waged at the primal scene of georgic education. This struggle renders problematic the notion that Satyrane seeks or needs to outgrow "the bestiality of his father" and challenges the view that there is any easy intercourse between Satyrane's education and its potential "as a training ground for the human hero." Spenser stages a confrontation between an ethically sophisticated georgic pedagogy and a student incapable of absorbing the complexity of its lessons.

Narratives of education and instruction pervade Book I—consider, for instance, Arthur's account of his education at the hands of Timon (I.ix.3–6), and Red Cross's visit to the House of Holiness (I.x). Canto vi represents a particularly dense and complex study of the training-up process. The canto, which is bracketed by Una's unsuccessful attempts to instruct the satyrs and Sansloy's desire to correct some unspecified "errour" (I.vi.42.9) in his battle with Satyrane, is structured as a series of educational scenes. Tucked between the Una and Sansloy episodes is a series of stanzas describing the apparently flawed education of Satyrane. Spenser's account of his training examines the impulsive analogizing required of students by the pedagogical habit of holding up georgic practices as spurs to other kinds of action. Satyrane's education is retrospectively described from the perspective of his father's role as instructor:

> For all he taught the tender ymp was but
>   To banish cowardize and bastard feare;
>   His trembling hand he would him force to put
>   Upon the Lyon and the rugged Beare,
>   And from the she Beares teats her whelps to teare;
>   And eke wyld roring Buls he would him make
>   To tame, and ryde their backes not made to beare;
>   And the Roebuckes in flight to overtake,
> That everie beast for feare of him did fly and quake.
>
> Thereby so feareless, and so fell he grew,
>   That his owne syre and maister of his guise
>   Did often tremble at his horrid vew,
>   And oft for dread of hurt would him advise,
>   The angry beastes not rashly to despise,
>   Nor too much to provoke: for he would learne
>   The Lyon stoup to him in lowly wise,
>   (A lesson hard) and make the Libbard sterne,
> Leave roaring, when in rage he for revenge did earne.
>
> And for to make his powre approved more,
>   Wyld beasts in yron yokes he would compell;
>   The spotted Panther, and the tusked Bore,
>   The Pardale swift, and the Tigre cruell;
>   The Antelope, and Wolfe both fierce and fell;
>   And them constraine in equall teme to draw.

> Such joy he had, their stubborne harts to quell,
> And sturdie courage tame with dreadfull aw,
> That his beheast they feared, as a tyrans law.
>
> (I.vi.24–26)

Satyrane's tyranny over the animals explodes from a single lesson ("all he taught the tender ymp was but/To banish cowardize and bastard feare") and a set of attendant practical exercises. His knowledge is distilled from a set of regulated actions imposed on him by his father, who compels him to lay his "trembling hand" on the resistant bodies of wild animals. There is more than a hint of the magical about the transfer of knowledge in this emphatically physical pedagogy, as the satyr's (presumably calm) hand forces his son's trembling hand first to touch and then to overwhelm the wild animals of the forest. Satyrane rids himself of that trembling as a visible measure of his own growing mastery, and soon the beasts themselves have learned to "fly and quake." The transfer of knowledge from father to son is in one sense ruthlessly complete, but this is only true insofar as it pertains to that part of the training that demands ruthlessness of the student. Far from struggling to outgrow the bestiality of his father, Satyrane must learn to grow into the full complexity of the lessons imposed on him. He is, after all, only half a creature of the woods by birth, and he is called upon to exercise a more sophisticated ethical awareness than can be extrapolated on the basis of raw analogy from this brand of animal husbandry. Satyrane's father confronts that limitation when he exhorts his son to cease despising and provoking the beasts, but Satyrane seems to absorb nothing of his father's lesson in tempering ruthlessness with restraint. It is not the rigor with which he subdues the animals that is flawed, but rather his tendency rashly to despise the proud beasts he is subduing.

Satyrane's mother, Thyamis, initiates a second phase of her son's career as he undertakes to extend his attainments beyond the narrow sphere in which he acts in the forest. She offers no remedy, however, for his incomplete absorption of his father's lessons. Happening upon her son one day in the woods while he is tormenting a lioness and her whelps, Thyamis instructs him to "leave off this dreadfull play" (I.vi.28.7). Spenser withholds any sign of a direct causal link between her pleas and the course of action her son pursues in the next stanza, but those pleas seem to play a significant role in making Satyrane perceive at least one aspect of the limitations under which he labors:

> In these and like delightes of bloody game

> He trayned was, till ryper yeares he raught,
> And there abode, whylst any beast of name
> Walkt in that forrest, whom he had not taught
> To feare his force: and then his courage haught
> Desyrd of forreine foemen to be knowne,
> And far abroad for straunge adventures sought:
> In which his might was never overthrowne,
> But through al Faery lond his famous worth was blown.
>
> (I.vi.29)

Satyrane extends the geographical reach of his expertise, but there is
no suggestion that he has in any way complicated his grasp of the
responsibilities that attend that mastery. Spenser seems to outline in
this stanza a pair of strategies for reading georgic. He simultaneously
describes a set of ethical demands that might be grafted on to the
physical skills Satyrane acquires, and gestures towards the potentially
reductive readings that are produced merely on the basis of raw analogy. What might otherwise serve as an argument for extending georgic's explicit interest in the management of plants and animals to
more complex ethical and pedagogical registers finishes instead as an
argument about Satyrane's inability to perform that extension. Satyrane is perhaps best seen as a recalcitrant pupil, the skilful student
who will not learn.[35] What is at stake here is not the crudity or
naïveté of his father's lessons or of georgic itself, but rather the sheer
complexity of the act of inference and extension in which the young
Satyrane is engaged.

It is significant that although the other knights in Spenser's poem
are renowned for overcoming men, Satyrane is extolled chiefly for
his ability to overcome animals.[36] If he has been trained for any single
exploit in the poem, it is for his encounter with the hyena that
devours Florimell's horse. The sixteenth-century classroom supplies
a suggestive context for Satyrane's training. Richard Mulcaster, who
taught Spenser at the Merchant Taylor School in London, raised the
stakes on purely metaphorical invocations of cultivation and animal
husbandry. He suggested that standard curricula should be expanded
to include physical exercises such as the hunt, which he described
as a multi-faceted education. Citing Xenophon's authority in the
Cyropaedia, Mulcaster insists that hunting provides "a proper elementarie to warlike uses, and *Mars* his schoole, whether for valiaun-
tnes or for pollicy, because the resemblaunces of the chiefe warlike
executions do fall out in hunting, as the qualitie or courage of the
game offereth cause, either to use force and manhoode, or to flie

to devise and suttletie."[37] Mulcaster seems to possess an optimistic conviction that the practical requirements of hunting can easily be mapped on to "warlike uses." (Note, for instance, that he elides any suggestion that the ethical stakes of war are different than those of the hunt, even though he does go on to acknowledge distinctions between different kinds of hunting.) Mulcaster's former pupil subjects this premise to careful scrutiny in his account of Satyrane's education. If Mulcaster could confidently gloss the hunt as "*Mars* his schoole," his student shows how fearfully limited and problematic is the assumption that there is any kind of transparent passage from specialized practice to general principle.[38] Spenser unfolds in detail a problem that Mulcaster sidesteps—namely, that the student who labors in these metaphorical practices must learn how to accept and when to refuse the invitation to view human attainments as incremental victories over the recalcitrant savagery of the natural world.

If Satyrane's training is bound up in the problem of how the woods stand in relation to principles of civilized self-regulation and governance, the story of Belphoebe is structured as an argument that those same wild territories can produce principles exceeding the standards of the civilized world. In telling Belphoebe's story Spenser seems at first glance to turn his back on the physical georgic pedagogy that shaped Satyrane. The construction and representation of Belphoebe's natural grace is subject to a different set of representational exigencies than the ones that shaped his account of Satyrane's education. Even so, Spenser's account of her training is another clue to the capaciousness of a pedagogical georgic in *The Faerie Queene*.

Spenser readily admits that his portrait of Belphoebe will raise questions in the minds of at least one kind of reader:

> Well may I weene, faire Ladies, all this while
>   Ye wonder, how this noble Damozell
>   So great perfections did in her compile,
>   Sith that in salvage forests she did dwell,
>   So farre from court and royall Citadell,
>   The great schoolmaistresse of all courtesy:
>   Seemeth that such wilde woodes should far expell
>   All civile usage and gentility,
> And gentle sprite deforme with rude rusticity.
>
> (III.vi.1)

He refuses, however, to answer this question at any length, and readers are offered only the briefest and most perfunctory of summaries.

Having "poured forth" on Belphoebe "all the gifts of grace and
chastitee" (III.vi.2.5–6), the "*Graces* rockt her cradle being borne"
(III.vi.2.9):

> So was she trayned up from time to time,
> In all chaste vertue, and true bounti-hed
> Till to her dew perfection she was ripened.
>
> (III.vi.3.7–9)

If the first line of this passage invites readers to imagine Belphoebe's
perfection as the product of a protracted (though intermittent and
unmethodical) act of instruction, the final line suggests that she displays an inborn perfection. There are no trembling hands to train
here: Belphoebe has merely "ripened" in these "salvage parts." If
this is husbandry or cultivation (her "ripening" suggests it may be)
then Spenser has formulated a highly attenuated and impersonal (one
might say, immaculate) conception of the cultivator's arts. Having
crafted this idealized account of Belphoebe's education, Spenser turns
to the technologies of the Garden of Adonis, where Belphoebe's
sister Amoret is "upbrought in goodly womanhed" (III.vi.28.7):

> Ne needs there Gardiner to sett, or sow,
> To plant or prune: for of their owne accord
> All things, as they created were doe grow.
>
> (III.vi.34.1–3)

There is, of course, no gardener in the Garden of Adonis: the absence
of a cultivator's hand is the defining element of "cultivation" in the
Garden of Adonis. Spenser, however, smuggles into these lines a
spectral gardener who neither sets nor sows nor prunes—if only as a
means of making intelligible by way of negation the process by which
Amoret is "upbrought" and by which the Garden's plants have come
to be arranged in perfect rows. In the Garden of Adonis, and indeed,
in his attempt to liken Belphoebe's education in courtesy to the
ripening of some rare fruit, Spenser hovers on the brink of a conventional georgic pedagogy. But his refusal to admit a gardener who
might plant and prune holds at bay the version of georgic that governs
Satyrane's education, as if the mediator were a threat rather than a
facilitator. Amoret is educated by Psyche and Cupid in the Garden of
Adonis, but they are—at least in narrative terms—absentee instructors
whose methods we never see.[39] This secret instruction is an apt education for Amoret, over whom the threat of physical horrors and the

mechanized tropes of love poetry hang like a threatening cloud in the house of Busirane. Busirane's plots look like a crazed inversion of Psyche and Cupid's instruction. The physical threats he poses respond precisely to the absence of a shaping hand in the Garden of Adonis. Practical georgic is banished from the Garden but its vocabulary labors on.

With no narrative account of Belphoebe's education, readers are left instead with her pronouncements on the subject of honor and ethical action. Belphoebe propounds an ethics of continuous toil— "Before her gate high God did Sweate ordaine, / And wakefull watches ever to abide" (II.iii.41.5–6)—in terms that call to mind more conventional assumptions about georgic than the pedagogical version I have described. Ideologies of labor are central to most conceptions of georgic in the *Faerie Queene*, and Spenser consistently characterizes the projects of his heroes and heroines as labors.[40] But the perpetual labor advocated by Belphoebe, which weds the choice of Hercules to a Protestant espousal of labor, is also a terrifying underworld curse in Books I, II, and III (see, for example, Sisyphus at I.v.35; Mammon's laborers at II.vii.35–36; the interminable labor of Merlin's abandoned sprites at III.iii.9–10). Just as georgic motifs are tangled up in a series of erotic, didactic, and metapoetic conceits in the final stanza of the 1590 Book III, so too is the ethical labor to which Belphoebe aspires periodically haunted by its hellish and potentially unredeemable negative image. An "emphasis on disciplined effort"[41] will not account for the range of Spenser's interest in georgic.

Throughout these acts of instruction Spenser explores a tension between competing visions of education as a protracted process and education as revelation. In their most condensed form georgic metaphors aspire to the latter by figuring the exchange of knowledge as a spontaneous fruition of innate principles. In Spenser's account of the discovery and training of Red Cross, for instance, georgic is enlisted in this project. However, Spenser's georgic strain can also mount a more ambitious inquiry into the student's responsibilities as an interpreter of metaphors. There is a sense in which pupils such as Satyrane must strive (with limited success, in his case) to decode metaphors that their instructors have transformed into practices. Satyrane's fate is to master those practices without fully comprehending their metaphoricity. If in some contexts georgic metaphors look like alternately naïve and violent attempts to account for the operation of instruction (because they proceed by objectifying and then subduing violently the "uncultivated" student), a more expansive assessment of the mode's resources, such as the one undertaken by Satyrane's father, can culminate in an attempt to wed ethical principles to the most basic human projects. At this extreme georgic is already sensitive to the ethics of its engagement with the materials upon which it works, just as Satyrane's father immediately perceives the limitations of the lesson he first imposes on his son.

4. SPENSER'S GEORGICS

Framed in the language of cultivation and agricultural management, these acts of instruction bring into relief issues not usually associated with Spenser's handling of the *Georgics*. By assessing these acts of instruction under the aspect of a pedagogical georgic Spenser is also attempting to account for the cultural work performed by his own poetry. The famous Orpheus myth with which the *Georgics* concludes gives one obvious—and perhaps too pessimistic—view of this educative project. Repining at his failures, the singer is dismembered and his limbs scattered even as he continues to sing. When Spenser republished *The Faerie Queene* in 1596 without its paratexts and without the georgic stanza that concluded the volume, he severed his georgic imitations and metaphors from this educational context, and tied them instead to a more limited conception of the mode's resources. In 1596, without the didactic theoretical foundation articulated in the *Letter to Ralegh*, there is no explicit didactic program to underscore the connection between Spenser's georgic imitations and educational discourse. In Books IV, V, and VI Spenser's georgic imitations look increasingly like local touches, like conventional topoi echoed at arm's length from Virgil. This reformulation of what Spenser expects of georgic seems to be linked to an altered sense of what he expects from poetry itself.

A diminished claim for poetry as a teaching instrument is nowhere more evident than on Mount Acidale. In the first stanza of the first canto of Calidore's pastoral interlude, Spenser returns to his plow and promises to dig up one of Calidore's adventures. Georgic and heroic collided at the end of the 1590 volume when Spenser moved from the georgic imitation that closed the original version of Book III to the *Letter to Ralegh*. Pastoral and georgic collide when Calidore chases the Blatant Beast into the pastoral world:[42]

> Now turne againe my teme thou jolly swayne,
>> Backe to the furrow which I lately left;
>> I lately left a furrow, one or twayne

Unplough'd, the which my coulter hath not cleft:
Yet seem'd the soyle both fayre and frutefull eft,
As I it past, that were too great a shame,
That so rich frute should be from us bereft;
Besides the great dishonour and defame,
Which should befall to Calidores immortall name.

(VI.ix.1)

This georgic flourish is a fitting introduction to the episodes in which Spenser crafts (on Mount Acidale, in Book VI, Canto x) his most ambitious account of the powers of poetry. The poet who speaks on Mount Acidale, however, is not the plowman-narrator who had asserted such control over his material at the end of the 1590 volume. It is Colin Clout, whose piping has set in motion a chorus of nymphs and Graces. When Calidore, overeager as always, steps out from the trees "resolving, what it was, to know" (VI.x.17.8), the nymphs and Graces flee and Colin furiously smashes his pipe. Colin can name his dancers and enumerate their virtues, but he admits that he has no power to make them return, no power to restage their dance for his intrusive pupil. Setting aside his anger, Colin attempts very patiently to teach Calidore about the dance he has witnessed, but he confesses himself to be at the whim of his dancers, and Colin lays claim to nothing more than the ability to narrate and anatomize the mystery in which he had appeared to be playing such an instrumental role. Colin is left, moreover, with no claim to vatic authority, and with a student whose ability to learn is continually in question throughout Spenser's Legend of Courtesy. By 1596, it seems, Spenser's claim to didactic authority was yielding diminishing returns.

The scene on Mount Acidale seems to craft an extremely cautious statement about poetry's promise as a teaching instrument. Colin's piping on Mount Acidale hints that the true work of poetry is at once more and less ambitious than the instrumental claims humanist poetics had accorded to literary production. As a work of the imagination, the work of poetry is to imagine complexity. Where complexity already exists—that is, everywhere an eye as generous as Spenser's looks—the work of poetry is to reimagine that complexity, to test it, to stand it on its end. Spenser's various encounters with georgic in *The Faerie Queene* bear the marks of this project as he credits the mode with a sophistication lacking in most accounts of its resources, and mines it for implications it is seldom held to contain. It is too tempting to read Spenser's intermittent georgic strain as a specifically Virgilian phenomenon, and, in those terms, to view georgic merely as a way-station between pastoral and heroic modes about

which scholars are more ready to speak. This temptation ought to
be resisted: a wider frame of reference does better justice to both
poets and to georgic itself.

Carleton University

NOTES

1.   William A. Sessions's essay "Spenser's *Georgics*," *ELR* 10 (1980): 202–38, remains the most ambitious and influential study of the relevance of the *Georgics* to
The Faerie Queene. He argues that Spenser re-imagines georgic labor as a heroic
cultivation of time and a renovation of English history. Andrew V. Ettin argues
that Virgil and Spenser are committed to an ethics of constant and diligent toil ("The
Georgics in *The Faerie Queene*," *Spenser Studies* 3 [1982]: 57–71). For the view that
Spenser explores in *The Faerie Queene* the ethical implications of the passage from
pastoral to georgic to heroic, and that georgic motifs in the poem offer a critique
of pastoral and heroic, see A. Leigh DeNeef, "Ploughing Virgilian Furrows: The
Genres of *Faerie Queene* IV," *John Donne Journal* 1 (1982): 151–66. Anthony Low
argues that Spenser exalts labor and engages georgic in a committed critique of the
Elizabethan court (*The Georgic Revolution* [Princeton: Princeton University Press,
1985] 35–70). See also Joseph Loewenstein, "Spenser's Retrography: Two Episodes
in Post-Petrarchan Bibliography," *Spenser's Life and the Subject of Biography*, eds.
Judith Anderson, Donald Cheney, David A. Richardson (Amherst, MA: University
of Massachusetts Press, 1996) 190: "It might be said that Book I of *The Faerie Queene*
should be read as a St. Georgic; one might also argue that the emphasis on disciplined
effort suffuses the epic—from below, as it were—with the ethos of georgic."
2.   A. C. Hamilton is right to insist that Spenser's intention "to fashion a gentleman or noble person in vertuous and gentle discipline" signifies "something more
than that his work has a didactic bent"(*The Structure of Allegory in* The Faerie Queene
[Oxford: Clarendon, 1961] 54). I do, however, take the phrase to be Spenser's most
explicit codification of that didactic bent. Louis Adrian Montrose helpfully suggests
that "This process of fashioning is at once the book's subject and its object" ("The
Elizabethan Subject and the Spenserian Text," *Literary Theory/Renaissance Texts*, eds.
Patricia Parker and David Quint [Baltimore: Johns Hopkins University Press, 1986]
318). For a survey of the verb's place in Spenser scholarship, see Wayne Erickson,
"Spenser's *Letter to Ralegh* and the Literary Politics of *The Faerie Queene's* 1590
Publication," *Spenser Studies* 10 (1992): 156–58.
3.   Richard Waswo, *Language and Meaning in the Renaissance* (Princeton: Princeton
University Press, 1987), 54.
4.   Abraham Fleming, the first English translator of the *Georgics*, uses "fashion" to
translate Virgil's lines on training calves for farm duties: "Embolden now thy bul-
locks, those which thou wilt fashion to/Th'exercise and occupation of good husbandry." Fleming deems the verb worthy of further definition and offers his own

marginal gloss: "Traine up, enure, or enable" (*The Bucoliks of Publius Virgilius Maro, Prince of All Latine Poets; otherwise called his Pastorals, or shepherds meetings. Together with his Georgiks or Ruralls, otherwise called his husbandrie, conteyning foure books. All newly translated into English verse by A.F.* [London, 1589] F3v). Fleming's lines translate the following passage from the Third Georgic: "tu quos ad studium atque usum formabis agrestem" (3.163).

5.　Edmund Spenser, *The Faerie Queene*, ed. A.C. Hamilton with text by Hiroshi Yamashita and Toshiyuki Suzuki, 2nd ed. (Harlow: Longman, 2001). All quotations from Spenser's poem will be made parenthetically. I have modernized i/j and u/v. Spenser's terminal stanza echoes the last lines of Virgil's Second Georgic: "Sed nos immensum spatiis confecimus aequor,/et iam tempus equum fumantia solvere colla" (2.541–42; But in our course we have traversed a mighty plain, and now it is time to unyoke the necks of our smoking steeds). Quotations and translations from Virgil are taken from the Loeb edition: Virgil, [*Works*], trans. H. Rushton Fairclough, rev. G.P. Goold, vol. 1 (Cambridge, MA: Harvard University Press, 1999). Subsequent references to the *Georgics* are noted parenthetically. In addition to this Virgilian model Spenser would have known at least one famous English analogue to these lines. Chaucer may be echoing Virgil at the beginning of "The Knight's Tale": "I have, God woot, a large feeld to ere,/And wayke been the oxen in my plough" (*The Riverside Chaucer*, ed. Larry D. Benson, 3rd ed. [Boston: Houghton Mifflin, 1987] 1[A] 886–87).

6.　On *boustrophedon* and the 1590 *Faerie Queene* see John Mulryan, " 'Is my team ploughing?': The Struggle for Closure in *The Faerie Queene* 1590," *Ben Jonson Journal* 3 (1996): 145–46.

7.　Here and throughout, I intend "vocational" to be taken as a reflection of Spenser's interest in his aims as a didactic poet rather than as a reference to his putative adherence to the career path described by the Virgilian *rota*. Spenser's adherence to the Virgilian career pattern has occasioned much dispute. Loewenstein, 115, suggests that "career criticism" elides the "the uncertainties of composition, the mystery of the next thing." The most extended critique of this line of criticism is Richard Rambuss, *Spenser's Secret Career* (Cambridge: Cambridge University Press, 1993). For an overview of these disputes and an argument about Spenser's possible interest in the Virgilian bibliographical tradition, see M.L. Donnelly, "The Life of Vergil and the Aspirations of the 'New Poet,' " *Spenser Studies* 17 (2003): 1–35. For a rethinking of the traditional *rota* see Patrick Cheney, *Spenser's Famous Flight: A Renaissance Idea of a Literary Career* (Toronto: University of Toronto Press, 1993).

8.　Spenser, too, knows very well that this sweaty plowing is at best a provisional account of his poetic toils. Anne Lake Prescott suggests that the pervasiveness of such complaints about backbreaking poetic labor may well constitute "a *translatio doloris*." She cites Ronsard's contribution to the poetics of discontented plowing in a poem appended to the 1587 edition of his *Franciade* ("The Laurel and the Myrtle: Spenser and Ronsard," *Worldmaking Spenser: Explorations in the Early Modern Age*, eds. Patrick Cheney and Lauren Silberman [Lexington: University Press of Kentucky, 2000] n.24).

9.　Because of its brevity I do not note page numbers for quotations from the *Letter to Ralegh*.

10.   See, for instance, Roland MacIlmaine's *The Logike of the Moste Excellent Philoso-pher P. Ramus Martyr* (1574). In a chapter treating "Of the illustration of the methode by examples, of Poetes, Orators, and Historiographers," MacIlmaine asserts that the Ramist method is perfectly observed in all effective didactic utterances. Taking the *Georgics* as his chief example, he asserts that "the poetes, orators & all sort of writers how oft soeuer they purpose to teach there auditor, doo alwayes follow this order of methode" (Roland MacIlmaine, *The Logike of the Moste Excellent Philosopher P. Ramus Martyr* [1574; Menston, Eng.: Scolar Press, 1970] 97). MacIlmaine's text translates Ramus' *Dialecticae Partitiones* (1543). On Ramus' commentary on the *Georgics* see Peter Mack, "Ramus Reading: The Commentaries on Cicero's *Consular Orations* and Vergil's *Eclogues* and *Georgics*," *JWCI* 61 (1998) 111–41. Mack observes that Ramus' commentary "aims not only to comment on the words and sentences but to demonstrate the methodical structure of Vergil's treatment of agriculture" (133). Ramus views the *Georgics* as a poem about "physica" (natural science). In Mack's words, "Ramus recognises limits to the extent to which the *Georgics* is a textbook, but thinks that as far as those limits allow, the work can be made methodical" (135).

11.   See below, n.38.

12.   Francis Bacon, *The Advancement of Learning. The Oxford Francis Bacon*, ed. Michael Kiernan, vol. 4 (Oxford: Clarendon, 2000), 135. On Bacon's use of Virgil in *The Advancement of Learning* see Annabel Patterson, "Pastoral versus Georgic: The Politics of Virgilian Quotation," *Renaissance Genres: Essays on Theory, History, and Interpretation*, ed. Barbara Kiefer Lewalski (Cambridge, MA: Harvard University Press, 1986), 241–67.

13.   The *Aeneid* and the *Eclogues*, of course, are also quoted. So, for that matter, are texts by authors as varied as Hesiod, Statius, Valerius Maximus, and Seneca. The *Georgics*, however, assumed a prominence in these treatises that belies the decidedly more modest interest in the poem outside educational discourse during the Renaissance.

14.   Pier Paolo Vergerio, "De ingenuis moribus et liberalibus adulescentiae studiis liber," *Humanist Educational Treatises*, ed. and trans. Craig Kallendorf, I Tatti Renaissance Library (Cambridge, MA: Harvard University Press, 2002), 30–31. Cf. *Georgics* 3.165.

15.   Aeneas Silvius Piccolomini, "De liberorum educatione," *Humanist Educational Treatises*, ed. and trans. Craig Kallendorf, 168–69. Cf. *Georgics* 2.272. Virgil's observation appears in a passage on transplanting trees.

16.   Piccolomini, 226–27. Cf. *Georgics* 4.6. Piccolomini, 228–29, quotes the *Georgics* again in a discussion of prosody. Cf. *Georgics* 2.156.

17.   Erasmus, "A Declamation on the Subject of Early Liberal Education for Children: *De pueris statim ac liberaliter instituendis declamatio*," *The Collected Works of Erasmus*, trans. Beert C. Verstraete (Toronto: University of Toronto Press, 1974–) 25: 300.

18.   Erasmus, 25: 332.

19.   Erasmus, 25: 332.

20.   I cite the modern reading. Renaissance editions give "labor omnia vincit." R.A.B. Mynors notes that by the end of the fourth century the reading adopted by

modern editors of the Georgics ("labor omnia vicit") had become, probably by
analogy with Virgil's "omnia vincit amor" (*Eclogues* 10.69), "labor omnia vincit." It
appears thus in Jerome's preface to his translation of the Book of Daniel. See Virgil,
Georgics, ed. R.A.B. Mynors (Oxford: Oxford University Press, 1990), 29–30.

21.   See, for example, Richard F. Thomas's commentary on the lines (Virgil, *Georgics*, ed. Richard F. Thomas [1988; Cambridge: Cambridge University Press,
1997–1998] 1:92–93).

22.   Erasmus quotes the maxim twice in his *Adagia*: once in support of the adage that
wisdom accompanies poverty; once in support of the conventional and unabashedly
optimistic pedagogical precept "Exercitatio potest omnia" (Practice can do everything) (*The Collected Works of Erasmus*, trans. Margaret Mann Phillips and R.A.B.
Mynors [Toronto: University of Toronto Press, 1974–], 31:I.v.22, 32:II.2.53).

23.   I borrow this distinction from Hugh G. Petrie and Rebecca Oshlag, "Metaphor and Learning," *Metaphor and Thought*, ed. Andrew Ortony, 2nd ed. (1993;
Cambridge: Cambridge University Press, 1998), 578–609: "the question is 'how is
one to make intelligible the acquisition of new knowledge?' not 'what are the
processes involved?' (584)." The problem of metaphor continues to be the subject
of much discussion for modern writers on pedagogy. Petrie and Oshlag admit that
metaphors have been said by some commentators to "have all the advantages over
explicit language as does theft over honest toil" (580). See, for example, R.M.
Miller, "The Dubious Case for Metaphors in Educational Writing," *Educational
Theory* 26 (1976): 174–81; S.I. Miller, "Some Comments on the Utility of Metaphors
for Educational Theory and Practice," *Educational Theory* 37 (1987): 219–27; P.S.
Williams, "Going West to Get East: Using Metaphors as Instructional Tools," *Journal
of Children in Contemporary Society* 20 (1988): 79–98.

24.   See Mary Thomas Crane, *Framing Authority: Sayings, Self, and Society in Sixteenth-Century England* (Princeton: Princeton University Press, 1993), 53–92; Rebecca W. Bushnell, *A Culture of Teaching: Early Modern Humanism in Theory and Practice*
(Ithaca: Cornell University Press, 1996), 73–116.

25.   *The Golden Legend* derives its etymologies for "George" from tillage, earth,
and wrestling: "George is sayd of geos/whiche is as moche to saye as erthe and
orge/that is tilyenge/so george is to say as tilyenge the erthe/that is his flesshe/
and saynt Austyn sayth in libro de trinitate that good erthe is in the heyght of the
mountaynes in the temporaunce of the valeyes/and in the playne of the feldes. The
fyrst is good for herbes beynge grene the .ij. to vynes and the thyrde to whete and
corne. Thus the blessyd george was hyghe in despysynge lowe thynges and therfore
he had verdeur in hymselfe. He was attemporate by discrecion and therfore he had
wyne of gladnes/and within he was playne of humylyte/and therby put he for the
whete of good werke. Or George may be sayd of gera: that is holy/and of gyon
that is a wrasteler. For he wrasteled with the dragon." "The lyfe of saynt George"
from Wynkyn de Worde's 1512 printing of *The Golden Legend* [STC 24879] is
printed as an appendix to Alexander Barclay, *The Life of St. George*, ed. William
Nelson (London: Oxford University Press for the Early English Text Society,
1955), 112–18.

26.   The religious and historical allegory of Red Cross's quest to "repayre" the
"forwasted kingdom" (I.xi.1.3) of Una's parents suggestively accommodates the
prophetic tone ("scilicet et tempus veniet") of Virgil's lines.

27. Red Cross assures his preceptor that he has learned his lesson well: "O holy Sire (quoth he) how shall I quight/The many favours I with thee have fownd,/That hast my name and nation redd aright,/And taught the way that does to heaven bownd?" (I.x.67.1–4).

28. I am indebted to Anne Lake Prescott for this suggestion.

29. See Sessions, "Spenser's *Georgics*," on the "human cultivation of the processes of time" (203).

30. A connection might be drawn between the resources of georgic and the persistently archaeological instinct of Renaissance poetics and aesthetics. See, for example, Thomas M. Greene, *The Light in Troy*, (New Haven: Yale University Press, 1982), 92, 220–41; Leonard Barkan, *Unearthing the Past: Archaeology and Aesthetics in the Making of Renaissance Culture* (New Haven: Yale University Press, 1999); Philip Jacks, *The Antiquarian and the Myth of Antiquity: The Origins of Rome in Renaissance Thought* (Cambridge: Cambridge University Press, 1993); David Galbraith, "Petrarch and the Broken City," *Antiquity and Its Interpreters*, eds. Alina Payne, Anne Kuttner, and Rebekah Smick (Cambridge: Cambridge University Press, 2000) 17–26.

31. The verb has a similar function when Red Cross is said to "earne/To prove his puissance in battell brave/Upon his foe, and his new force to learne;/upon his foe" (I.i.3.6–9), and also when Una explains to Arthur that she found in Red Cross "a fresh unproved knight" (I.vii.47.2). Britomart desires "to prove her utmost might" (III.xi.25.1) when she braves the fiery porch of the house of Busirane.

32. The georgic stanza that introduces Calidore's pastoral career in Book VI is an important exception to which I turn in my conclusion.

33. Maurice Evans, *Spenser's Anatomy of Heroism: A Commentary on* The Faerie Queene (Cambridge: Cambridge University Press, 1970), 45.

34. Donald Cheney, *Spenser's Image of Nature: Wild Man and Shepherd in* The Faerie Queene (New Haven: Yale University Press, 1966), 65. For a perceptive discussion of Satyrane in the context of Reformed theology see Darryl J. Gless, *Interpretation and Theology in Spenser* (Cambridge: Cambridge University Press, 1994), 109–15. Gless views Satyrane's regular visits to his father (I.vi.30.1–4) as a "symbol of everyman's inescapably bestial origins and impulses" (110) but also sees in him "the cheering possibility that grace may at any moment effect a miraculous transcendence of natural limits" (115).

35. In purely pedagogical terms I am reluctant to say that Satyrane's bestial genealogy actually prevents him from learning. His bestial father is, after all, able to craft a sophisticated lesson that his half-human son cannot digest. Gless, 114, nicely sketches a series of theological perspectives on Satyrane's career: "Tridentine Catholicism could agree with Protestantism's insistence that human nature needs grace if it is to combat evil—though some versions of Catholic theology could then proceed to interpret Satyrane's behavior before his alliance with Una as preparation for grace, his subsequent works as actual contributions to his salvation. Protestant readings would be more likely to perceive that, by calling attention at its end to Satyrane's continuing need for special grace, *The Faerie Queene* I.vi concludes with an image that presents holy action as it must always appear in this life. Having received the call that enabled him to accept Una's 'discipline of faith and veritie,' Satyrane will nonetheless always achieve sin, even while pursuing his most charitable actions."

36. Artegall's attainments are also measured by the degree to which beasts fear him (V.i.8.4).

37. Richard Mulcaster, *Positions Concerning the Training Up of Children*, ed. William Barker (1581; Toronto: University of Toronto Press, 1994), 105.

38. Spenser's account of Satyrane's training is (no less than Mulcaster's praise for the hunt) may be the product of an extremely inventive engagement with Xenophon's *Cyropaedia*. Hunting is a pervasive feature of the *Cyropaedia*, but at the end of Book I Cambises (Cyrus' father) explains at length that the hunt has provided Cyrus with (to borrow Mulcaster's phrase) "a proper elementarie to warlike uses." Mulcaster does not make an issue of the scene, but Xenophon devotes several pages to Cambises' attempt to unpack the similarity between these spheres of action. Cambises insists that Cyrus must deviously maintain the upper hand on his enemies. Having been educated (at least in part) on a strict diet of Persian justice Cyrus is understandably surprised. I quote this remarkable exchange at length in William Barker's translation of *The VIII. Bookes of Xenophon, Containinge the Institution, schole, and education of Cyrus* (London, 1567): "Why than, said he [Cyrus], whan we were chyldren & yong men, dyd ye teache us the contrary? So truly do we now, said he [Cambises], toward our frends & cuntry men. But do ye not know that ye have lerned many subtilties how ye may do hurt to your enmies? No truly father. For what purpose, said he [Cambises] then, dyd ye lerne to shoote? For what purpose to dart? For what purpose to catche wyld bores with nettes & pittes? Wherfore hartes, with snares & traps? Why lyons, beares, & lybardes? Ye did not match with them of even hand, but alwais labored to encounter with them, you having thadvantage. Do ye not know, that al these things, be evill partes, deceits, craftes and getting of advantage? Yes truly, father, quod Cyrus, concerning wild beastes. But if I were but suspect, to go about to deceive any man, I remember full wel, that I had many a stripe. In dede, sonne, said he, we did not, as I think, trade you, to pick a dart at a man, but we taught you to drive it to the pricke. And nowe, ye may not hurt your frendes in no wise. But if warre did chance that ye might bee able to hytte, to deceive, and gette the advantage of men, we taught not you these feates in men, but in beastes, because you shoulde not hurte your fryndes" (Fii[r]–Fii[v]). Cyrus is troubled by this gap in his education and Cambises is at pains to justify Persian pedagogy to his son: "There is a sayeng, Sone, among our auncestours, that there was sometime a Scholemaister, that taught children justice, even as you nowe woulde have yt. Not to lye, and to lye. Not to deceyve, and to deceyve. Nat to slaunder, and to slaunder. Not to oppresse, and to oppresse. And did devide, whiche shoulde be done to frindes, whiche, to enemies. And wente so farre, that he taught to be lawfull, to deceive frindes, for a good purpose, to steale frindes goodes, for a good purpose. Children, beyng thus taught, muste nedes practise to do the same one agaynst an other, as yet the Grekes, men saye, teache theyr children in the common Schole, to deceive, and exercise them to be able to do it, one against an other. Therfore, some beyng verey towarde to deceyve conningly, and to get advauntage cunningly, and peradventure not untoward in coveting riches, did not spare their fryndes. But attempted to be enriched by them. By which occasion a lawe was made, which we use at this daye, that children shoulde one waye be taught, as we do now teache our servauntes, To doo trewly, not to deceyve, not to steale, not to be afore hand,

whiche thynges, yf they transgresse, we punishe them. That thus beyng accustomed to this trade, they myght be made the mylder men. But beyng at that age whiche you nowe be, yt was thought, they myght safely be taught, what was lawfull against enemies" (Fii[v]–Fiii[r]).

39.   Amoret grows "to perfect ripenes" (III.vi.52.1) with Pleasure as her "companion" (III.vi.51.8), and is "lessoned/In all the lore of love, and goodly womanhead" (III.vi.51.8–9) by Cupid and Psyche. For a persuasive account of Amoret's relation to Cupid, Psyche, and Pleasure in the Garden see Thomas P. Roche, Jr., *"The Kindly Flame": A Study of the Third and Fourth Books of Spenser's* Faerie Queene (Princeton: Princeton University Press, 1964) 126–27. Roche argues that "Amoret's presence in the garden completes Spenser's hierarchy of generation and presents a view of marriage that integrates the joys of human sexuality into the cosmic scheme of generation" (127). Roche sees the hermaphroditic reunion of Amoret and Scudamour at the end of the 1590 volume (a reunion that extends into Spenser's terminal plowman stanza) as "the most simple, the most satisfactory conclusion for the allegorical education of Amoret" (134). Georgic tropes thus bookend Amoret's education, which begins with her ripening in the Garden of Adonis and concludes with the 1590 *Faerie Queene*'s account of her union with Scudamour in the first lines of Spenser's georgic stanza: "Thus doe those lovers with sweet countervayle,/Each other of loves bitter fruit despoile" (III.xii.47.1–2).

40.   Sessions views Spenser's interest in labor as the earmark of a Protestant English *Georgics*.

41.   Loewenstein, 190.

42.   See Bruce Thornton, "Rural Dialectic: Pastoral, Georgic, and *The Shepheardes Calender*," *Spenser Studies* 9 (1991): 1–20. Thornton argues for a georgic strain in most pastoral literature, and suggests that competing attitudes to the natural world are held in tension in rural scenes in literature.

TODD BUTLER

That "Saluage Nation": Contextualizing the Multitudes in Edmund Spenser's *The Faerie Queene*

While early modern theology has long been used as a stable source for interpreting *The Faerie Queene*, this essay argues that both Spenser's poem and that theology must be placed within their immediate historical and political context—the struggle to reinvigorate the Church of England after the Marian persecution. Reading Una's encounters with Corceca and the satyrs (Book I) and Artegall's conflict with the Gyant (Book V) alongside contemporary religious tracts demonstrates how Spenser's poem reflects the difficulties England faced in attempting to reconstruct a Protestant religious polity. Images of the multitudes became politicized by both reformers and more conservative church officials, creating the potential for multiple interpretations of seemingly clear Biblical texts. The allegories of Spenser's *Fairie Queene* thus must be read in light of these conflicts, revealing that meanings once deemed transparently clear actually depend in large part upon the reader's own confessional allegiances.

*I*N BOOK I, canto 1 of Edmund Spenser's *The Faerie Queene*, Redcrosse Knight encounters the monster Error, a foul, misshapen beast whose womanly torso blends into a snake-like tail. The knight soon finds himself in desperate struggle with the beast and begins to strangle her, prompting a vicious counter-attack:

> Therewith she spewed out of her filthy maw
> A floud of poyson horrible and blacke,

93

Full of great lumpes of flesh and gobbets raw,

. . . .

Her vomit full of bookes and papers was,

With loathly frogs and toades, which eyes did lacke.

(I.i.20.1–3, 6–7)[1]

Although critics have traditionally interpreted Error's books and frogs as symbols of either heresy in general or specifically Roman Catholic propaganda, the poem's rhetoric suggests that a variety of interpretations may actually have been available to Spenser's contemporaries.[2] More conservative members of the Church of England could have found in Error the blowing forth of reformist polemics such as the Marprelate tracts, while reform-minded members may have interpreted the spew of books as an indictment of ministers who simply read homilies rather than composed their own sermons. In terms strikingly reminiscent of Spenser's Error, the Puritan *Cornish Supplication to Parliament* decries just such non-preaching ministers as destructive to England's nascent Protestant revival: "So that, though the excellent dignity of the Word and Sacraments do not depend on the worthiness of the men, yet their infectious breath, which savoreth of carrion, maketh God's children to abhor them."[3] The *Supplication*'s claims echo another similarly reformist appeal to Parliament declaring that if ignorant ministers remain in England's pulpits sedition surely will follow, just as "stinking puddles breedes plenty of Frogges and Toades."[4]

Such an interpretative conundrum exemplifies what historians increasingly recognize as the confused and ill-differentiated nature of Elizabethan religion, for by itself Elizabeth's ascension guaranteed little more than an opening for the return of Protestantism.[5] The task of defining this new (or renewed) Protestant church occupied not only the initial years of the queen's reign but also the decades that followed.[6] Instead of simply declaring what it was not—Catholic—the Church of England now needed to reach some consensus, however broad, as to what it was. To do so inevitably meant selecting among myriad theological, doctrinal, and practical positions that, while all generally Protestant, could also differ substantially. Further complicating matters was the presence within the population of a substantial number of subjects who, regardless of their current confessional allegiances, had experienced firsthand the uncertainty and instability that accompanied religious belief in sixteenth-century England.[7]

Given such a fluid environment, it should come as no surprise that modern scholars have thoroughly disagreed over the specifics of Edmund Spenser's own doctrinal allegiances, particularly when considering him as a writer who sought both poetic fame and the practical benefits of court preferment. As early as 1950 Virgil Whitaker exasperatedly concluded that "obviously Spenser could not be at once Calvinist and Catholic, a Puritan and a 'churchman.' "[8] The years since have failed to produce a consensus, with Spenser alternately labeled a militant Puritan or a restrained member of the national church.[9] Readers encountering such critical controversy might well echo the frustrated conclusions of the Edwardian preacher Hugh Latimer, whose "Homily Against Contention," reprinted in 1562, warns against such obsessions with confessional categorization: "he is a Pharisee, he is a Gospeler, he is of the new sort, he is of the old faith, he is a new-broached brother, he is a good catholic father, he is a papist, he is an heretic! O how the church is divided! O how the cities be cut and mangled!"[10]

Only recently have scholars begun to offer a solution to this critical impasse, suggesting that instead of ossifying Spenser between competing constructs of religious doctrine, we should begin to read Spenser's poetry as deeply invested in the complicated and varied constructions of English Protestantism, creating a site upon which multiple religious voices converge but do not dominate.[11] This essay pursues just such an approach, examining portions of *The Faerie Queene* alongside contemporary sermons and treatises not to establish Spenser's doctrinal allegiances but to illuminate the challenges faced by Elizabethans in pursuing the delicate task of constituting a new religious polity. Although these selections vary in their political and doctrinal positions, each evidences an intense concern for the particular subject of this study, namely the intensive struggle waged by all manner of devoted Protestants to extend the Reformation beyond the godly few to the often lukewarm multitudes.

Reading *The Faerie Queene* alongside these texts demonstrates how Spenser's epic poem both reflects and participates in this struggle. In three successive portraits of the common people—Una's encounter with Corceca and Abessa, the rescue by the satyrs (both Book I), and Book V's mighty Gyant—Spenser's poem reveals how, in grasping to build a stable religious polity, churchmen of all types saw in the tepidly Protestant multitudes a potentially distressing challenge to the Elizabethan religious settlement, one perhaps to be expected but nonetheless to be discouraged. It is in the disputes over extending church reform that the great religious debates of the 1580s and 1590s—particularly the demand for a preaching ministry and Presbyterian-influenced church organization—become intertwined with politicized representations of the weary and often reticent multitudes. As a poem deeply reliant upon representation for its method of argument, *The Faerie Queene* is inevitably invested in these controversies, resulting in allegories that—like Error's frogs and toads—depend primarily upon the reader's own confessional allegiances for their meaning. Bringing disparate representations of the common people together also helps chart the course of England's Reformation, for as *The Faerie Queene* moves to more explicitly contemporary events the multitudes are transformed from simple lost sheep into a dangerous symbol of disorder and religious schism, a shift that heralds the failure of communal religion to bridge the gap between the English gentry and the country's poor. Ultimately, by recognizing the poem's political and theological context rather than arguing over its explicit doctrinal allegiances, we gain not only a more nuanced interpretation of the text but also a vivid portrait of a nation haltingly attempting to recreate its political and religious identity.

★   ★   ★

Modern historiography of the English Reformation traditionally divides into two camps, with A. G. Dickens's seminal *The English Reformation*, which casts the Reformation as primarily an elite-driven movement readily accepted by the English masses, juxtaposed against the work of scholars such as J. J. Scarisbrick and Eamon Duffy, who present the Reformation as a fiercely contested struggle pitting a flourishing, traditional Catholicism against a more intellectual and elitist Protestantism.[12] More recent historians, however, increasingly have emphasized that the reality lies somewhere between these positions, in the gradual if at times fitful movement from resistance to a growing popular accommodation to Protestantism as a new communal tradition. Patrick Collinson's work demonstrates that despite some ambivalence and passivity, the arrival of Protestantism did not destroy popular religion, and recent work by Muriel McClendon and Christopher Marsh (among others) details the intense interest many Elizabethans had in defusing religious tension and maintaining social harmony at the expense of doctrinal or theological coherence.[13] Only with the later growth of Puritanism did these efforts become particularly contentious and fragmented. Stephen Braclow has seen in the Puritan movement a growing tendency toward godly separatism, and Keith Wrightson and David Levine have produced sociological and anthropological evidence charting a similar shift in the English village of Terling, where Puritanism's growth yielded a growing separation between the local elite and the village community.[14] The end result is a Reformation whose progress is more cyclical than linear, one that examines and alternately or even simultaneously tears down and builds upon traditional practices for its own advancement.

Studies like these invite a new focus for explorations of the English Reformation: the often vexed nature of the Elizabethan religious community. For readers of *The Faerie Queene*, the poem's evident concern with the internal church encourages such a study—a central motif in Book I is the stability or instability of foundations. Those buildings that are somehow suspect, such as the House of Pride, are described as rotten or unstable. Although the House of Pride's gilded roofs dazzle its inhabitants, the palace's foundations lie "on a sandie hill, that still did flit/And fall away," leaving the structure to sway beneath each windy gust from heaven (I.iv.5.5–6).

The Biblical source for such symbolism is Matthew 7:24–27, the story of the foolish man who builds his house upon sand. While this story traditionally represents the importance of Christ's Gospel, the passage's symbolism can also be read as proclaiming the need to re-form the once and perhaps still Catholic multitudes.[15] With an eye toward the decorative and ritual elements of Catholicism, John Calvin's commentary on these verses links building to preaching, drawing out a moral that is at once general and politicized: "Christ therefore compareth the vaine and windie profession of the Gospell, to a beautifull, but no sound building, which thoughe it was sette vppe to the shewe, yet it was ready to fall at euery moment, because it lacked a foundation."[16] The conclusion of Calvin's commentary seems to encapsulate Spenser's plan for Book I, and in particular the continuing challenge to Redcrosse Knight and the poem's readers to learn to recognize Archimago and other representations of falsity for precisely what they are: "In summe, this is the purpose, true godlinesse cannot bee discerned from counterfaite holinesse, vntil an examination and trial do come: for temptations wherwith we are tried, are like to floudes and stormes, which do easily beate downe unstable minds, whose lightnesse is not perceiued in a calme and quiet time."[17]

Calvin's analysis of this text, and in particular his connection between architecture and preaching, echoes the agenda of English Protestants, many of whom were bent on the continuing reform of not only the multitudes but also the church that served them. In his 1590 tract *A Treatise Wherein is Manifestly Proved*, the Puritan John Penry exhorts preachers "not only to beget fayth in men or to engrafte them into Christ, but being engrafted to build and aedifie them forwarde as liuely stones of that holy temple, whereof Christ Jesus is both the head & the foundation."[18] Yet despite the apparently universal character of this appeal, Penry's life highlights the extent to which such presumably orthodox claims could support positions deemed radical rather than moderate. Penry's involvement in producing the satirical Marprelate tracts would lead him to flee to Scotland, where his presence caused repeated diplomatic problems, and then to return to the growing Separatist movement in London, where his continuing agitation for reform brought his imprisonment, trial for contempt and sedition, and finally his execution in May 1593.[19]

The hostility that Penry and others like him engendered from officials in the Church of England stemmed primarily, though not exclusively, from their continuing demands for a genuine preaching ministry, one that would do more than simply read the Scriptures or homilies provided by their superiors. Such demands were not necessarily new to English Protestantism, nor were they the sole province of radicals.[20] The desire for a continuing Protestant evangelization of the country, however, and the suggestion of a preaching ministry as the means to accomplish that goal, warrant examination precisely because arguments for such evangelization often rely heavily upon a politicized representation of the English multitudes as unlettered and ignorant of even the very basics of Christian truth. For example, in a 1583 sermon later published with a dedication to some of Elizabeth's Privy Council, Thomas Gibson beseeches both his congregation and his readership to consider "the great inconueniences which followe in these places where the word is not preached, the people are still in ignoraunce and blindenesse . . . they know not the use of the sacraments, or to what ende they serue."[21] Penry similarly argues in A Treatise that the holy ordinances of God "are so farre from aedifying these people, who haue not bene instructed in the right vse of them by the worde preached, that vnto such they are nothing els but a sealed booke."[22]

This rather glum assessment of a people who seem insensibly immune to God's word is often echoed by modern criticism of The Faerie Queene's first depiction of the common people: Una's encounter with Corceca. Corceca, who represents spiritual blindness, is traditionally grouped with her daughter Abessa and Abessa's church-robbing lover Kirkrapine, the three symbolizing the degeneracy of the Catholic church that has lingered into Elizabethan times.[23] Michael O'Connell goes so far as to describe them as a "typological prophecy of the Marian years," while Anthea Hume suggests that the trio represents the continual abuses of the church that reoccur throughout English history, both Catholic and Protestant.[24]

In their rush to assemble these characters into a cohesive historical allegory, critics tend to overlook the poem's subtle yet crucial demarcation between Corceca and her daughter, a distinction that complicates the mother's smooth inclusion into this clearly negative family portrait. For, while Abessa flees from Una and the lion after being terrified of Una's beauty—a moment that clearly earns Abessa little sympathy from the reader—Corceca learns of the approaching danger only through her daughter, who arrives home terrified by the encounter. Homebound, Corceca becomes the passive recipient of Abessa's infectious fear:

> And home she came, whereas her mother blynd
> Sate in eternall night: nought could she say,
> But suddaine catching hold, did her dismay
> With quaking hands, and other signes of feare:
> Who full of ghastly fright and cold affray,
> Gan shut the dore.
>
> (I.iii.12.3–8)

The emotional and psychological dynamic of this moment reinforces the implicit hierarchy within this family, as the aging and blind mother unthinkingly takes on the fears of her daughter precisely because she has no other evidence upon which to rely. Indeed, Corceca has no means to acquire such evidence, since Abessa, suggestive of both an abbess and an absentee preacher, is the sole medium for her mother to comprehend the world, much as the masses relied on their local parish priest.[25] Although the narrator's subsequent description of Corceca's fanatic devotion to monastic prayer and penance conveys disdain, it also imparts a begrudging sense of respect. Even the narrator acknowledges that Corceca prayed "deuoutly penitent."[26] While Corceca's vengeful appeal to the disguised Archimago may evidence her inveterate sinfulness, her plea to Archimago also mirrors the appeals to knights accepted elsewhere in the poem.[27] The problem lies in identifying the proper object of such an appeal; in essence it is the poem's recurrent problem of reading correctly. Yet this failure should not necessarily damn Corceca, for just two stanzas later even Una is deceived by Archimago's appearance as Redcrosse Knight. Arguably, in this comparison Corceca actually comes out ahead—unlike Una she does not even have sight to help her distinguish good from evil.

The image of a blind woman foolishly caught in dead rituals likely would have resonated with contemporary readers of Spenser's poem,

as blindness provided a common trope to describe the reluctance of
many English subjects to become zealous Protestants. As early as 1572
a Parliamentary bill recognizing the continuing challenge of reform
admitted that "by reason of the late backsliding of the people from
true religion to superstition, divers orders of rites, ceremonies and
observations were therein permitted in respect of the great weakness
of the people then blinded with superstition."[28] Later Puritan texts,
cast as printed petitions to Parliament but likely meant for a wider
audience, employed similar language, using the description of the
rural multitudes as blindly ignorant of true religion as an almost
formulaic opening for their public appeals.[29]

Yet despite this common rhetorical language, the particular meaning readers ascribed to Corceca's blindness no doubt varied widely.
Initially, a Biblical reading of blindness appears to limit any sense of
sympathy one might harbor for these backsliding Englishmen, as both
the Old and New Testaments clearly link blindness with sin.[30] Yet
in Elizabethan England such clear Scriptural judgments existed alongside a belief that spiritual blindness was to be expected and perhaps
even pitied in a people who had endured generations of Catholicism.
The more contentious issue—as it often is in matters of politics—became where to assign blame for the continuing failure to extend the
Reformation throughout the populace.

The most commonly cited biblical verse in this debate, that of the
"blind leading the blind" (Mat. 15.14), appears to spread its concern
equally, yet in exegesis individuals could be much more selective in
their emphasis.[31] More zealous reformers tend to focus their attention
on the verse's blind guides. The anonymous *A Briefe and Plaine Declaration*, printed by the Puritan Robert Walgrave, exclaims, "How long
therfore shall we suffer the blinde to lead the blind, to the destruction
of both? Let vs therfore now at the legth, remoue these blind guides,
and place in their steeds faithfull ouerseers, that may lead the flock
of Christ into the way of saluation."[32] John Penry similarly lays the
blame for the masses' reprobation at the feet of England's ecclesiastical
hierarchy, citing Jesus' admonition that "the miserie of that people
is vnspeakably pitiful, where the blinde leadeth the blinde."[33] Comparing Penry's and Walgrave's arguments to those of other reformers
demonstrates the extent to which their readings are invested in immediate political circumstances. For example, the exposition of Matthew's gospel by Augustine Marlorate, a radical French Protestant
executed by Charles IX, applies Christ's rebuke to Pharisee and disci-
ple alike. Marlorate's text has little patience for those who would use
this Scripture solely against the ecclesiastical hierarchy, claiming it to

be "inexcuable" for those subjects who "beyng in errour and blyndn-
esse, say that they were so taughte by their teachers, and pastors,
under whom they ought to be gouerned, and say also that their errour
shall be imputed to the Byshoppes." The clear meaning of the verse,
according to Marlorate, is more universal: "But Christ here plainely
affirmeth that those blinde also shall fall into destruction on which
followed their blinde guides."[34] However unequivocal Scriptural
truth might be, the religious and cultural environment of an England
newly returned to Protestantism makes even the literary use of a
Biblical verse an issue of circumstance and political viewpoint as
much as theological doctrine. Indeed, in this case the two are
largely inseparable.

Darryl Gless has posited that Una's ongoing quest to rejoin Redcrosse Knight may echo the Israelites' own wanderings in the wilderness, a suggestion that offers yet another avenue to understand
Spenser's somewhat disdainful, somewhat pitying portrait of Corceca.[35] For many Elizabethans, Israel's forty-year sojourn in the wilderness could symbolize two historical occurrences: the retreat of the
English church into Wales after the Saxon invasion, or the church's
more recent suffering under the bonds of Roman Catholicism.[36] Puri-
tan-inclined readers of Spenser's text, however, might well have made
more contemporary connections, as the wilderness of Book I could
also represent the continuing absence of true preaching throughout
the land. Appeals by Puritans often portray their authors as residing
in a wilderness of ignorance. Walgrave claims "we thinke our selues
in a wilderness, or a fish out of the water," and *A humble petition*
bemoans that "if your Maiestie sawe that waste wildernes, wherein
the most parte of vs doe abide and dwell . . . we thinke your grace
coulde not forbeare."[37] It is important to note that these readings—and other additional interpretations offered here—do not necessarily supplant those of other critics. Indeed, in the case of the
wilderness these Puritan interpretations depend heavily upon the associations other critics have identified, for these more radical readings
exist within a system of signifiers in which a contemporary interpretation of the text is predicated upon associations that are historical or
even typological. For Elizabethan reformers viewing themselves as
inheritors of the Israelites' struggle in the Sinai, that wilderness must
exist in the text in order for their own spiritual wasteland to take
shape.

Whatever temporal links a reader might make with this episode,
it is clear that Corceca's life in the wilderness has left her bereft of
the true faith, which returns only with Una's sudden appearance.
While Corceca's outward rituals reveal her familiarity with the

Christian faith, her ignorance of true inward Grace renders her Pater Nosters and Ave Marias little more than hollow, mindless incantations. Yet Corceca's ignorance has not necessarily annulled her potential for membership within a true reformed church, as Protestant preachers initially were willing to make allowances for the multitude's inability to abandon the trappings of the Catholic faith. Augustine Marlorate, whose text reads so strongly against all the blind of Matthew 15.14, is willing to grant a distinction between "the weake (which are offended through ignorance, and are by and by conformable) and the proude and obstinate, whiche take offence to themselues."[38] In a similar appeal for toleration, Richard Hooker's 1585 sermon at Temple Church argues that "thousands of our fathers in former times, living and dying within her [the Catholic Church's] walls, have found mercy at the hands of God" and that because of the difficulty in judging "[w]e must therefore be contented both to pardon others and to crave that others may pardon us for such things."[39]

Given the Elizabethan government's implicit program of slow rather than vigorous reformation, it is perhaps no surprise that the language of Hooker and other moderates could allow a more gentle reading of Corceca's failure. More surprising is that Puritan texts provide a similar set of arguments. In his polemic tract *A defense of that which hath bin written* (1588), John Penry explicates Joshua 5.5–the Israelites' neglect of ritual circumcision in the Sinai—in order to reaffirm the faith of those born under Catholicism:

> But what shall we say vnto those that were vncircumcised in the wildernesse fortie yeres almost . . . . Did they never eate the passeouer all that time? . . . It is plaine that the passeouer was celebrated in the wildernes once at the least. Nom. 9.1. If euery yeare, why should the godly of the family be excluded from the action, the cause why they were uncircumcised not being in them.[40]

Recalling a wilderness suggestive of Corceca's own existence, Penry is strikingly willing to open the church's rituals to a particularly wide audience, and in doing so accommodate the at least nominal Catholicism practiced by many English subjects under Mary I. Even those Israelites without circumcision (a visible sign of election) are welcomed at Passover, understood in Penry's text as the Lord's Supper.

Penry's reading of this wilderness religion likely draws heavily on Calvin's own analysis of the same verse, one in which Calvin carefully explains that a lack of circumcision did not completely exclude the Israelites from their enduring covenant with God. Noting that while the problem is similar to admitting unbaptized or improperly baptized Christians into the Lord's Supper (an issue that will be significant to my discussion of Book V), Calvin explains that God could "chaunge the ordinarie use for a time, to make those men partakers of other holie things, from whom he had taken circumcision away for a season. So in one part the people were excommunicated : and yet releeued with sufficient helpes."[41] While not diminishing the differences within religious communities, both Penry and Calvin are thus unwilling to transform these differences into eternal judgments. The multitudes instead carry a reduced responsibility and are welcomed into the fold. Penry's argument suggests that even those Elizabethans who supported thorough religious reform may not have viewed a Catholic Corceca as negatively as modern critics have assumed.

Where moderate and zealous readers of Spenser's poem could have differed, however, is in making sense of Spenser's distinction between Corceca's blind ignorance and the active immorality of Abessa and Kirkrapine. While moderate readers might well have remained content with a reading that addressed Catholic rapaciousness or even Henry VIII's dissolution of the monasteries, the period's Puritan rhetoric could provide a more aggressive interpretation, one that reveals the increasing tension within the Church of England and the extent to which images of the multitude could become weapons of political rhetoric. For example, Penry begins A Treatise with a now familiar acceptance of popular ignorance: "with all their wickednes, [they] may seeme to deserue some excuse because they never as yet had anye meanes to know God aright . . . They are poore, they are foolish, for they haue not knowen the way of the Lord." A marginal note refers readers to Jeremiah 5.3–4, a text which provides a clear Biblical source for Una's and her lion's encounter with Corceca's family:

> Therefore I said, Surely thei are poore, thei are foolish, for thei knowe not the way of the Lord, nor the iudgement of their God. I will get me vnto the great men, and wil speake vnto them: for thei haue knowen the way of the Lord, and the iudgement of their God: but these haue altogether broken the yoke, and burst the bondes. Wherefore a lion out of the forest shal slay them . . .

This text probably would have been familiar to nearly all of Spenser's readers, as it was part of the Scripture commonly read at morning prayer on the fourteenth Sunday after Trinity Sunday. In moderate hands, these verses were often interpreted as a more general warning against the fruits of wickedness. Bishop Thomas Cooper, for example, glosses the text as an universal injunction against the contemptuous denial of God's word.[42] Interestingly, however, the Geneva Bible's gloss to this passage intensifies the text's focus on religious leaders, as "[h]e speaketh this to the reproche of them, which should gouerne and teache others, & yet are farther out of the way than the simply people." Following this lead, Penry directs the passage's prophetic anger onto the church establishment. Immediately after he grants the common people allowance for their ignorance, Penry attacks "our supposed ministry" as "nothing els, but a troup of bloody foule murtherers, sacriligious church robbers." Such explosive language is found in other Puritan publications as well. Regarding the Church of England's "idol ministers," Robert Walgrave proclaims that "we think it to be playn ynough, that these men entred not in at the doore into the sheepe-folde, but climed vp another way, and therefore, by the verdict of our sauiour Christ, they are theeues and robbers, whose coming tendeth only to steale, to kil, and to destroy."[43] When placed together Penry's treatise and Walgrave's petition provide us with all three members of Spenser's wilderness family—the ignorant Corceca, whose sin may be forgiven, and the more despised pair of Abessa and Kirkrapine, whose theft of church property signals both England's Catholic heritage and the continuing abuse of the English populace by the Church of England.

★   ★   ★

At this point in *The Faerie Queene* the church and the multitude have traveled two separate paths. While in his portrait of Corceca Spenser mixes judgment with pitying indulgence, he has offered little in the way of suggesting how to integrate such subjects into the new church. Corceca's house exists only as a waystation for the wearied Una, a brief respite before her lonely journey must continue. The encounter with Corceca becomes only a static snapshot of the English religious community rather than an exposition of its construction. This exposition comes with Una's rescue by the satyrs, in which the wider populace is figured as a multitude whose impulses fitfully drive them toward a newly established church.

The encounter with the satyrs begins as Una's captor Sansloy leads her through a wild forest. As his anger transforms into lust, Sansloy first follows the strictures of courtly love, wooing Una with "fawning wordes" and love-struck sighs. Una's steadfast refusal of his advances only further spurs his lust, and Sansloy resolves to take by force what he could not by guile. Una's helpless cries prompt the narrator to beg justice from the heavens, and "eternal providence" responds in the form of fauns and satyrs, who leave their dancing merriment to investigate the commotion:

> Vnto that place they came incontinent:
> Whom when the raging Sarazin espide,
> A rude, mishapen, monstrous rablement,
> Whose like he neuer saw, he durst not bide,
> But got his ready steed, and fast away gan ride.
>
> (I.vi.8.5–9)

In introducing the satyrs, Spenser creates a rather muddled portrait of the masses, for while he echoes stereotypes of the rabble, he crafts this portrait through the eyes of the pagan Sansloy, subtly suggesting that a Christian reader might see these unwitting instruments of Providence quite differently. Like Corceca, Una sits in a rumpled heap, provoking the satyrs to "pittie her vnhappie state" (vi.9.7). Although pictured as a "saluage nation," the satyrs possess an instinctual sympathy that allows them to "read her sorrow in her count'-nance sad" and offer Una their humble submission as evidence of their goodwill.

Finally calmed by the satyrs' fawning obedience, Una returns with her rescuers and meets their leader Sylvanus. Una's subsequent residence in the wood inspires a variety of different responses: a nostalgic love from Sylvanus, jealousy from the nymphs, and surprisingly chaste adoration from the satyrs.[44] Una soon seizes upon this adoration as an occasion to displace their devotion from her and onto the true religion:

> Glad of such lucke, the luckelesse lucky maid,
>   Did her content to please their feeble eyes,
>   And long time with that saluage people staid,
>   To gather breath in many miseries.
>   During which time her gentle wit she plyes,
>   To teach them truth, which worship her in vaine,
>   And made her th'Image of Idolatryes;
>   But when their bootlesse zeale she did restraine

From her own worship, they her Asse would worship fayn.
(vi.19.1–9)

For the first time in *The Faerie Queene*, the "truth" (left conveniently vague) is preached not to a single hero but to the multitude.[45] The results, of course, are uneven. While their hearts are in the right place, the satyrs cannot seem to discard their propensity for idolatry—they apparently understand Una's lesson, but they apply it in a manner that is at once both amusingly comical and deeply disappointing.

Critics of Spenser have usually glossed this encounter with a general explanation that the satyrs represent both natural human impulses toward God and humanity's inability to grasp God's truth without grace.[46] However, an interpretation that rests primarily on Protestant doctrine should not necessarily eliminate a historicized or particularized understanding of this encounter. Given Spenser's own writings on "savagery," critics examining this episode might fruitfully (and perhaps reflexively) refer to *A View of the Present State of Ireland* as an interpretative aid for the rhetoric at this portion of the poem.[47] Yet doing so offers us less insight on how Spenser's epic might have been read, particularly by those Elizabethans who never had Spenser's remarkably unfortunate experience with Ireland and its native populace. John Calvin's commentary on a seemingly unrelated biblical moment—Christ feeding the multitude with five loaves and two fishes—instead provides sufficient echoes to suggest a more broad-based interpretation of the satyrs' interaction with Una. According to the Biblical account, Christ retires from the crowds after having learned of John the Baptist's execution, only to be followed by a great mass of people. After healing their sick, Christ feeds the multitudes.[48] Much like Spenser's presentation of the satyrs, Calvin's interpretation of this miracle appears ambivalent. The fact that the masses followed Jesus, Calvin explains, signals that the Jews knew well Christ's power, and thus cannot complain if their "owne slothfulnes" would later deprive them of salvation. Yet only a few lines later Calvin seems to moderate his reading, deploying turns of phrase strikingly similar to Spenser's poem:

The other two [Mark and Luke] doe expresse more plainely, and especaly Mark, why Christe tooke this compassion : to witte, because he saw hungry souls caried by their hot and zealous desire from their owne dwelling places into the desert. And that wante of doctrine was a token of a miserable dissipation: therefore Marke saieth, that Christ had compassion on them, because they were as sheepe wanting shepheards . . . For this was no small token of piety, to leaue their owne houses, and to come in flockes to the Prophet of God.

Both Calvin's and Spenser's texts maintain parallel descriptions of the masses, people whose zealous lust for spiritual sustenance simultaneously disguises an inability to recognize the proper route to salvation and earns them at least begrudging admiration from their readers.

For many English reformers Calvin's masses and Spenser's depiction of a "saluage nation" would have conformed quite nicely to their understanding of their fellow subjects. As suggested earlier, the religious rhetoric of the time provided ample opportunity for divines to see unlettered, traditional multitudes inhabiting England's own untamed wilderness. As early as 1559 John Jewel wrote to friends in Zurich regarding his recent trip to the West country, where "the wilderness of superstition . . . had sprung up in the darkness of the Marian times."[49] Later Elizabethan rhetoric offers evidence that readers of *The Faerie Queene* may also have looked for such savages in their own backyard. In *A Covnter-poyson* (1584), the reformist Dudley Fenner worries that without an increase in preaching ministers the English nation will "become more sauage then Painims and wilde Irish."[50] Yet again at this point in the reestablishment of Protestantism in England such portrayals of the common people, while disparaging, were not uniformly negative. Echoing his discussion of the Israelites' sojourn in the wilderness, John Penry presents savagery as part of an almost evolutionary process toward Protestantism:

for there be many regions nowe professing popery, where not so much as the name of Christ was heard, vntill they were become grossely popishe. So that their first step was out of paganisme vnto poperye. And this is the estate of all those poor oppressed vassals the west Indians, who now in great nombers profes Romish Idolatrie. (*Defense* 18)

At issue then in Spenser's depiction of the satyrs is not their initial savagery—the period's religious rhetoric could make sufficient exceptions for such a state. Instead, it is the inability of the satyrs to assimilate the lessons of faith—rather than merely recognize them—that ultimately drives Una to abandon this "colony." Not to be disregarded, however, are the steps the satyrs make toward a new understanding of religion: they hastily forsake their traditional merriment to rescue Una and then at least manage to fixate their veneration and devotion on a paragon of human virtue.

The satyrs' developmental process appears to illustrate what Keith Wrightson and David Levine have identified as a particularly vexing problem in the 1580s: while most English subjects became increasingly willing to direct their beliefs to a tepid Protestantism based on anti-Catholic nationalism, few preachers could spur their flocks toward "enthusiastic Protestant devotion."[51] Una's abortive attempt at developing a truly Protestant community illustrates an ambivalent view of popular religion, for while the satyrs' impulses are proper, the beasts seem strangely unable to make the full transition away from the traditional rituals that have marked their merry lives.[52] Together Una's brief sojourns with both Corceca's family and the satyrs offered Spenser's readers an opportunity to recognize their own acceptance or exasperation with the slow pace of reform, tempered by the recognition that the remnants of Catholicism would not easily be cleansed from England's shores.

* * *

Attempting to link these episodes of Book I with those in Book V might initially appear a difficult task, as, along with the other books published as part of the expanded 1596 version of *The Faerie Queene*, Book V is separated from the earlier portion of Spenser's epic by both time and place. In the intervening years Spenser had secured a pension from Queen Elizabeth and a governmental post in Ireland, where he composed the second portion of his poem. Yet despite these changes in Spenser's life, modern critics have regularly remarked upon the apparent topical and thematic links between Book V and Book I, particularly with regard to the apocalyptic elements that structure the legend of Justice.[53] Such criticism has generally concentrated on the second half of Book V, which contains a thinly-veiled allegory on the Spanish domination of the Low Countries and the attendant religious and political anxieties it provoked.

Yet another set of thematic similarities exists between Book I and Book V, specifically the poem's continuing interest in the portrayal of the multitude, figured here in the early encounter between the "mighty Gyant" and Artegall. Unlike Spenser's previous characters, the masses in this episode are obtuse, undifferentiated figures without any identifying characteristics—even the giant who leads them appears to be nameless. While the rhetorical and physical aggressiveness of this episode has drawn interest from critics searching for hints of subversion within Spenser's poem, the faceless uncertainty of the masses appears to have complicated attempts to situate the Gyant and his mob within any specific historical or theological context, reducing readings of this allegory to a more general economic and moral message.[54]

As has been demonstrated, however, the common people offered Puritans a powerful rhetorical weapon to secure an independent preaching ministry. Yet Penry and the other reformers were not the only voices in this debate, as more conservative members of the Church of England were often willing to respond in kind. Prominent among these ministers was Richard Bancroft, who had ferreted out a group of libelous Brownists at Cambridge University and had led the somewhat successful search for the writers of the Marprelate tracts. Such endeavors helped Bancroft become both the bishop of London (1597) and archbishop of Canterbury (1604), but most immediately they garnered him an invitation to preach at St. Paul's Cross in 1588 on the first Sunday of the new session of Parliament.[55] In his *Sermon at Paules Crosse* (1588)—a document that was to become a major salvo against the English reformists—Bancroft answered Penry's attacks by portraying English Puritans as inextricably linked with the Presbyterians of Scotland, whose dissent had endangered the life of the king and the safety of the state. Reading *The Faerie Queene*'s clash between Artegall and the Gyant alongside both Bancroft's depiction of the Scottish rebellion and Puritan demands for a preaching ministry reveals how charges of Anabaptism and economic radicalism provided divines with a language for pursuing more parochial goals, ultimately signaling the increasing politicization of the multitudes by the Elizabethan religious elites.

Initially a comparison between the Gyant's rabble and England's radical reformers might appear incongruous, as Spenser's rude portrayal of Gyant and his desire for radical reform often seems driven more by economics than theology. As the Gyant in Book V has no formal name, critics have variously named the character "the communist giant, the egalitarian giant, [and] the demagogic giant," descriptions that signal the apparently obvious nexus between class and political justice operating in Spenser's text.[56] Yet the presence of an apparently obvious reading of Spenser's allegory again need not foreclose the existence of more particularized interpretations. Indeed, there is much in late sixteenth-century religious and political rhetoric to suggest that charges of economic radicalism were often deployed to undermine Puritan-led campaigns for greater church reformation. To some extent the vulnerability to such charges lay with the Puritans themselves, and in particular with their continuing desire to expand Protestantism's reach via a preaching ministry. Such a ministry, all involved conceded, would cost the Church of England money that was in short supply during an era in which pastoral livings were routinely and often dramatically underfunded. Deploying language similar to that of Book I, for example, the Puritan appeal *A Humble Motion with Submission* declared that "If our forefathers in blindness, thought nothing to much for the Churches advancement, neither almost had any ende in giuing their lands and goods that way, shall wee thinke that God cannot another way blesse vs as much, if we parted from alitle, for the competent and decent erecting of his ministery?"[57]

Despite the motion's appearance of unity, appeals for the funding of a preaching ministry regularly devolved into bitter debates about the source of such funding, and by extension who would lose financially in this redistribution. Given their rhetorical stance as defenders of those multitudes abused by the ecclesiastical hierarchy, Puritans directed their ire and demands toward what was seen as a well-funded nobility and ecclesiastical hierarchy that had grown rich off previously Catholic church lands. In a sermon later published for members of the Privy Council, Thomas Gibson would trenchantly suggest to his congregation that if the nobility might remember the importance of preaching there might be better funded livings. Gibson cites for emphasis Genesis 47.22, Pharoah's funding of his priests during Egypt's famine, and darkly notes that the example of an idolater providing for an idolatrous ministry would condemn many Christians who "rather dayly by deceit or violence, they take that from the Minister, which long agoe was giuen by others."[58] Even for a listener who had not encountered Spenser's Kirkrapine, the allusion to Catholicism and its remnants in the Elizabethan church is difficult to miss.

Both sides in the debate understood the potential explosiveness of such claims. Taking a more conservative line in his 1591 sermon *The Poore Mans Teares*, Henry Smith bemoans "Oh howe liberall were people in times past to maintaine superstition : and nowe howe harde hearted are they growen to keepe the poore from famine."[59] While acknowledging the potential wealth of England's Catholic past, Smith subtly alters the contemporary frame of reference, placing a matter of religious evangelization into a general moral framework. The liberality shown to the monks of times past, Smith contends, should now be shown to the poor directly, implicitly bypassing those Puritans who would presume to speak to and for them. There is some evidence that the Puritans themselves were similarly ambivalent about the implications of their demands. The reformist *A petition made to the Conuocation house*, which employs the now-familiar language of church robbery, insists that "We in this our request, doe openly and from our heartes testifie, that wee doe nothing desire the spoyle of your possessions, by any of the Court whatsoeuer, nor yet in speache complaine of your aboundance."[60] Clearly, making their rhetoric reality was delicate business for the Puritans of Spenser's time.

Further complicating matters was the ease with which such redistributive impulses could be elided into charges of Anabaptism. To some extent the issues were simply economic—Henry Smith would proclaim to his congregation that those beggars not satisfied with Lazarus's crumbs "are of the opinion of the Anabaptists, that eurie mans goods must be common to them . . . [and they] ought to haue almes at Tiburne."[61] Yet Anabaptism's program for redistribution extended into the religious and political realm as well, as its emphasis on adult baptism and the inward calling reoriented spiritual authority from the church hierarchy toward the laity. It was at this point that English Separatists such as Penry and his co-defendants Henry Barrow and John Greenwood were most vulnerable. Barrow recorded his interrogation by Elizabethan authorities in some detail, and a reader of the text (published posthumously in 1596) will recognize the repeated attempts made by his questioners to align Barrow with Anabaptism.[62] Barrow, who had not baptized his own son because of his inability to find a suitably reformed congregation, tries to walk a delicate balance between denying that he was an Anabaptist and acknowledging that he believed previous baptisms in the Church of England had been improper. In a parenthetical aside Barrow darkly notes that "I doubt least the Arch B. hearing my answer of rebaptising/caused it to be left out of the question and my answer/ taking that which might best serue their owne turne/ to bring us into suspition of error and hatred." In his own interrogation Penry would also note resignedly that "We and our cause/are neuer brought before her/but in the odious weeds of *Sedition/rebellion/schisme, heresie* ect. and therfore it is no mervaile too see the edge of her sword turned against us."[63]

Sedition and rebellion certainly mark both Spenser's Gyant and the greedy and vulgar multitude that congregates around him. Yet one need not rely solely upon the interrogations of Penry and his followers for evidence that readers might have applied this allegory of justice to Puritan reformers rather than to the Irish or a vague mass of poverty-stricken subversives. Instead Bancroft's sermon reveals the ease with which these characteristics—and the accompanying label of Anabaptism—could serve as a rhetorical stand-in for the ecclesiastical hierarchy's more immediate opponents. According to Bancroft, King

James viewed the Scottish presbyteries—the same militants who had
sheltered Penry from Elizabeth's wrath—as "an introduction to An-
abaptisme and popularitie: that it tended to the overthrow of his
state and Realme, and to the decaie of his crown."[64] For Bancroft,
Presbyterianism and its associated reform movements were Penry's
religious evolution in reverse, stepping stones to a return to religious
and political chaos. Failure to recognize the rhetorical fluidity inherent in the term "Anabaptist" may lead critics of Spenser to neglect
a significant division of power between the Gyant and the rabble.
Spenser casts the Gyant as a powerful and prideful being whose promises to reduce all things "vnto equality" captivate the easily-swayed
masses:

> Therefore the vulgar did about him flocke,
>   And cluster thicke vnto his leasings vaine,
> Like foolish flies about an hony crocke,
>   In hope by him great benefite to obtaine.
> All which when *Artegall* did see, and heare,
>   How he mis-led the simple peoples traine,
> In sdeignfull wize he drew vnto him neare,
> And thus unto him spake, without regard or feare.
>
>   (V.ii.33.1–9)

While the vulgar common folk elicit little sympathy from Spenser's
hero, their foolishness does seem to absolve them of some blame for
their rebellion—the common folk have been misled by their own
cupidity and the impressive-sounding proclamations of the Gyant,
whose only impulse for this rebellion seems to be pride: "he boasted
in his surquedrie,/That all the world he would weigh equallie"
(V.ii.30.3–5).

Such an anatomization of rebellion matches the beginning of the
Paul's Cross sermon, which argues that pride is the original cause of
heresy.[65] Avarice and covetousness, the sins of Spenser's rabble, come
only fourth in Bancroft's list. Addressing what many reformists saw
as their greatest strength—Scripture proclaimed individually and in-
dependently—Bancroft echoes Spenser's depiction of the multitudes
as foolishly immoderate: "but you through your rashness in following
of euerie spirit, are growen to a woonderfull newfangleness: and are
indeed become meere changelings."[66] Although certainly interested
in matters of doctrine and ecclesiastical organization, Bancroft's public sermon also emphasizes the concern of its author (and by extension
the church hierarchy) for the rhetorical dynamism of the reformist

cause, a concern that suggests that readers of this episode in *The Faerie Queene* should consider not only the theological substance of the Gyant's arguments but also the method by which the Gyant pursues the debate. The preaching ministry of the Puritans, an occasion for the presumably proper redistribution of Catholic wealth in the service of Protestant evangelism, has itself now become a threat not only to ecclesiastical but also political stability. For both Bancroft and Spenser, the main fault of the multitude lies in its pervasive inability to recognize truth from falsehood, and its increasing tendency to believe in preachers whose rhetorical skill and fire disguise a dangerous threat to the established social order.

Rhetoric becomes the core of the confrontation between Artegall and the giant, as much of the entire encounter is consumed by a running debate whose terms offer a variety of interpretative possibilities. Artegall's case rests firmly on God's providential determination of the social order, a position common enough in Elizabethan England to make it impossible to tie it to one single source. By contrast, the narrator's description of the Gyant's futilely inquisitive attempts to understand the world through his balance beam more closely echoes the charges leveled by Bancroft against the burgeoning numbers of Puritan polemicists: "they sticke at all things which are injoined, they require the reason of everything."[67] When the Gyant rages at his inability to weigh right and wrong, Artegall guides him to realize that "right sate in the middest of the beame alone," an artful description of the delicate doctrinal balance the Elizabethan church sought to maintain. Worried over attacks on the *Book of Common Prayer*, Bancroft offers a similar argument for right's position in the middle of extremes: "I haue read that if anything . . . may in reasonable construction admit two interpretations, the best and the mildest is ever to be received."[68]

Spenser's poem offers the giant only two stanzas to argue his case (Artegall gets more than eight), yet in this brief space are further hints that Spenser may have drawn on the contemporary conflicts within the Church of England to help structure this episode. Warming to his egalitarian claim, the Gyant declares:

> Were it not good that wrong were then sucreast,
> And from the most, that some were giuen to the least?

> Therefore I will throw downe these mountaines hie,
> And make them leuell with the lowly plaine:
> . . . .

> Tyrants that make men subject to their law,
> I will suppresse, that they no more may raine;
> And Lordlings curbe, that commons ouer-aw;
> And all the wealth of rich men to the poore will draw.
>
> (V.ii.37.8–9, 38.1–2, 6–9)

The giant opens his defense with a seemingly egalitarian focus, namely that the world has become corrupt and uneven, in need of a massive redistribution of wealth. Yet despite this interest in community and the presence of his assembled followers, the giant's methods seem conspicuously singular—the repetitive use of "I" suggests that the responsibility for such changes rests solely with the giant, leaving the multitudes beholden to him. Bancroft warned his listeners against believing such promises:

> They [Puritans] will furthermore (the better to creep into your harts) pretend great humilitie and bitterly exclaime against the pride of Bb. as though they affected nothing else by their desired equalitie, but some great lowlines . . . whereas in deed they shoote at greater superioritie and preeminence, then euer your Bishops did use.[69]

Bancroft's depiction of his opponents emphasizes their selfish manipulation of the masses, for while the reformists proclaim their desire for equality they actually seek the destruction of the ecclesiastical hierarchy precisely for their own advancement. More than just partisan posturing, Bancroft's charge does seem to carry some evidentiary weight, at least in terms of Puritan rhetoric. The Puritan authors of the anonymous *A Humble motion* would declare soon after Bancroft's sermon that "As touching the L. Bb. and great clergy men, which haue soe laden themselues with thicke claye, that they haue much adoe to get vp in the pulpit of God . . . is it a smal matter for them to leaue their thousands, and bee content with their hundrethes."[70]In Spenser's poem the Gyant, who has already advanced himself to the head of the multitude, signals a similar disdain for religious hierarchy by paraphrasing Isaiah 40.4, a standard passage employed by Tudor reformists to satirize clerical failures: "Eurie vallie shalbe exalted, and eurie mountaine and hill shalbe made lowe."[71] Clearly this Gyant knows Scripture, but he wields it as a challenge to the established order—much as Bancroft accused the Puritans of doing.

From this beginning assault the Gyant moves to a more explicitly secular concern with the interconnected nature of economic and political tyranny. While concluding with a promise of distributive justice, the bulk of the Gyant's speech in stanza 38 centers on an incipient political revolution, a radical rearrangement of law-making within the kingdom. In decrying political tyranny, Spenser's Gyant displays the sort of subversive nature found in conservatives' descriptions of their reformist opponents. After smarting under the Puritans' relentless insistence on Scripture as a foundation for argument, the ecclesiastical hierarchy had finally found in the association of Puritans and rebellion an opportunity to rearrange the terms of the quarrel. For Richard Bancroft, the ideal symbol in this regard was not the Anabaptists but John Knox, whose insistence upon the power of the people and magistrates to regulate and depose their monarchs promised a dangerous shift in political power. Conservatives in the Church of England feared John Knox perhaps even more than the Anabaptists. Indeed, Bancroft structured much of his continuing assault on English Puritans around Knox's work. Bancroft's *Dangerovs Positions and Proceedings*—published at approximately the same time as Book V—reprints and cites large portions of Knox's writings as an example of the inherently lawless impulses that existed with Puritanism.[72]

Modern scholars have generally employed this Elizabethan fear to explain the violence that concludes the debate between Artegall and the giant. As the Gyant is engrossed in the inevitably impossible task of attempting to balance truth and falsehood on his beam, Artegall's squire Talus suddenly throws him over a cliff, simultaneously killing the monster and inciting the disappointed multitude into open revolt. Talus then swings his flail into action against this "swarme of flyes," transforming the misled mass into so much early modern cannon fodder (53.6).[73] This abrupt movement from rhetoric to violence has been explained by Michael O'Connell as an unavoidable necessity: "Spenser knew that his readers would recognize the radical threat of this vision in the egalitarian giant and would generally acquiesce in the necessity of its destruction. The threat to society was felt to be too real and pressing to require full consideration of all the philosophic or juridical questions."[74] O'Connell's certainty aside, even a brief glance at current criticism on Elizabethan literature and religion should convince one of the difficulty of categorizing the Elizabethan population—let alone resurrecting for it any uniformly stable ideology.[75] In addition to interpretations attributing Book V's violence to Spenser's personal frustration with the Irish peasantry, I would like to suggest another possible reading of the episode, one that emphasizes not Spenser's individual motivations but the possible reception of the poem among its English readership and what, together with Book I, this Gyant's story might reveal about the anxieties and course of the Elizabethan Reformation.[76]

While in Book I the multitude of satyrs possess at least an impulse (however improperly applied) toward godliness, in Book V the multitude—portrayed much as Sansloy viewed the satyrs—possesses instincts that tend only to dissolution and outright violence. Such a shift in characterization may mirror what modern scholars have seen as a growing disillusionment among English elites with the slow pace of reconverting the multitudes. According to Wrightson and Levine: "By the turn of the century, however, the tone of clerical comment on the common people was souring. Where they had been prone to see fields ripe for the harvest, hungry sheep left unfed, they tended increasingly to see 'silly ignorants' or an 'earthly minded' multitude."[77] Wrightson's and Levine's argument precisely characterizes the distinction found between Books I and V, for while the Gyant's multitude still retains some vestiges of unthinking innocence, the tone of Spenser's presentation has become much more stark and aggressive.[78] The contrast between these two episodes also reveals another significant element: the growing gulf between representatives of the aristocracy (Una, Artegall) and the wider mass of the realm's inhabitants, identified specifically in the later episode as the poor. Unlike Una, Artegall makes no attempt to reeducate the masses. Instead, after his brilliant display of rhetoric against the giant, Artegall lapses into a confused silence when confronted by the multitude, who stand arrayed for battle yet motionless as if awaiting Artegall's response. By not speaking Artegall neglects a statutory duty required of the queen's officers, who were obliged to address unlawful assemblies and offer them time to disperse before unleashing force against them.[79]

Rather than continuing his argument, the knight selects for his emissary the unspeaking Talus, who is sent to inquire after the multitude's reasons for arming themselves and to pursue a truce. According to the poem the choice is made primarily due to the wide social gulf that exists between the mob and Artegall, who as a noble hero can neither shed the blood of such base subjects nor retire from them for fear of shame. Yet by any reasonable standard Talus remains a poor choice for a diplomat, having just summarily executed the mob's leader and dashed their hopes for gain. Additionally, as early as the beginning of Book V Spenser has described Talus as less of a negotiator and more of an automaton:

His name was *Talus*, made of yron mould,

Immoueable, resistlesse, without end.
Who in his hand an yron flale did hould,
With which he thresht out falshood, and did truth vnfould.

(V.i.12.6–9)

Talus's description echoes John the Baptist's prophecy of Jesus' coming, a passage which has unavoidably apocalyptic overtones: "Which
hathe his fanne in his hand & wil make cleane his floore, and gather
his wheat into his garner, but wil burne vp the chaffe with unquen-
cheable fire" (Mat. 3.12). The Geneva Bible's marginal notes to Matthew 3.12 refer the reader to Mark 1.9 and Luke 3.22, both stories of
Jesus' baptism and the subsequent revelation of his divine parentage.
Together these verses emphasize the association of threshing with
election, with the separation of truth and falsehood leading to a
polarization between the godly and ungodly. Gone are the impulses
toward accommodation found in Book I—election here appears re-
served for those blessed with social and political power. In Book V
theological justification appears possible only for those Elizabethans
who found their social positions unassailable.[80]

Taken together, Talus's flail, Artegall's confusion, and the new
characterization of the multitude illustrate the Elizabethan elite's increasing tendency to associate the masses with not only poverty but
also ungodliness and disorder.[81] In contrast to earlier episodes in *The
Faerie Queene*, Book V makes little allowance for the multitude's
ignorance—disregard for order and right religion no longer stems
from sojourns in the Catholic wilderness but instead springs from a
lawlessness dramatically opposed to social and religious hierarchy. As
the similarities between the Gyant's rebellion and Bancroft's sermon
suggest, such antagonism to the poor does not necessarily require a
specifically conservative or reformist subtext. Demonizing an opponent through the commons instead became a common tactic deployed by both Penry and Bancroft. Together Spenser's depiction of
Corceca's family, the satyrs's rescue, and Artegall's encounter with
the Gyant provide a diverse portrait of an English church and its
members struggling to make a transition to established Protestantism,
a struggle that when viewed through the lens of contemporary rhetoric on the subject seems to have been challenging at best. In this
sense Spenser's epic figuratively illuminates the period, transforming
theological doctrines into recognizable characters that illustrate the
growing Elizabethan preoccupation with their internal religious
community. To some extent *The Faerie Queene*, as an item of cultural
capital, may have even helped to shape these discourses. In turn,

the further development of *The Faerie Queene* was likely shaped by contemporary religious disputes, suggesting an instance of intellectual hybridization whose effects are tantalizingly evident but whose course becomes increasingly difficult to unravel.

Washington State University

Notes

1. *The Faerie Queene*. Ed. Thomas P. Roche, Jr. (New York: Penguin, 1987). All references to Spenser are from this edition and noted in the text.

2. Reading Spenser alongside John Bale leads Hume to see this passage as representing the continual eruption of heresy within Christian history, while Waters and Gless both identify the frogs specifically with Catholicism. See Anthea Hume, *Edmund Spenser: Protestant Poet* (Cambridge: Cambridge University Press, 1984), 77–80; D. Douglas Waters, *Duessa as Theological Satire* (Columbia: University of Missouri Press, 1970), 21–25; and Darryl Gless, *Interpretation and Theology in Spenser* (Cambridge: Cambridge University Press, 1994), 67–68. King posits the books as representative of religious polemicism in general. John King, *Spenser's Poetry and the Reformation Tradition* (Princeton: Princeton University Press, 1990), 87.

3. H. C. Porter, *Puritanism in Tudor England* (Columbia: University of South Carolina Press, 1970), 218.

4. Also *The lamentable complaint of the communalitie, by way of Supplication to the high court of Parliament, for a learned ministerie, renued and augmented.* (1588, new edition of Walgrave, 1585), sig. I4.

5. See Patrick Collinson, *The Religion of Protestants: The Church in English Society, 1559–1625* (Oxford: Oxford University Press, 1982) and Christopher Haigh, *English Reformations: Religion, Politics, Society under the Tudors* (Oxford: Oxford UP, 1983). In addition to Gless (9–16), Richard Mallette's book offers a useful summary of these changes in historiography. Richard Mallette, *Spenser and the Discourses of Reformation England* (Lincoln: University of Nebraska Press, 1997), 7–11.

6. Patrick Collinson's recent observation on the impact of the Elizabeth's 1559 ascension puts the matter succinctly: "Was anything 'settled' by the so-called religious 'settlement' of 1559? Not much, and not yet." "Comment on Eamon Duffy's Neale Lecture and the Colloquium." *England's Long Reformation, 1500–1800*. Ed. Nicholas Tyacke. (London: University College London, 1998), 72.

7. That religious beliefs and allegiances could range widely within not only communities and institutions but also individual families is one of the major points of emphasis in Norman Jones's recent study *The English Reformation: Religion and Cultural Adaptation* (Oxford: Blackwell, 2002).

8. Virgil Whitaker, *The Religious Basis of Spenser's Thought* (Stanford: Stanford University Press, 1950), 7.

9. Criticism of this sort generally revolves around works by Hume, who argues for the more militant Spenser, and King, who takes the more moderate position (also argued for by Whitaker).

10. Quoted in Jones, 105.

11. For example, see Mallette, who contends that critics of Spenser should work towards "determining how religious discourses have been rooted subterraneously in the text and of identifying subtle negotiations . . . between literary and religious discourses." Mallette, *Spenser*, 208. Daryl Gless emphasizes the potential variability of messages contemporary readers could have found in *The Faerie Queene*. Gless, *Interpretation*, esp. 16–18. Carol Kaske takes a somewhat similar approach, though she also does not shy away from making firm readings of the religious meaning behind Spenser's allegories. *Spenser and Biblical Poetics* (Ithaca: Cornell University Press, 1999).

12. J. J. Scarisbrick, *The Reformation and the English People* (Oxford: Blackwell, 1984); Eamon Duffy, *The Stripping of the Altars* (New Haven: Yale University Press, 1992).

13. For Collinson, in addition to the works cited earlier, see also *The Birthpangs of Protestant England* (Basingstoke: Macmillan, 1988) and "Elizabethan and Jacobean Puritanism as Forms of Popular Religious Culture." *The Culture of English Puritanism, 1560–1700* Ed. Christopher Durston and Jacqueline Eales (New York: St. Martin's Press, 1996), 32–57. For work in the same vein, see Muriel McClendon, "Religious toleration and the Reformation: Norwich magistrates in the sixteenth century." *England's Long Reformation, 1500–1800*. Ed. Nicholas Tyacke. (London: University College London, 1998), 87–115; and Christopher Marsh, *Popular Religion in Sixteenth-Century England: Holding Their Peace* (New York: St. Martin's Press, 1998).

14. See Stephen Brachlow, *The Communion of Saints: Radical Puritan and Separatist Ecclesiology 1570–1625* (Oxford: Oxford University Press, 1988), and Keith Wrightson and David Levine, *Poverty and Piety in an English Village, Terling 1525–1700* (Oxford: Clarendon Press, 1995).

15. King reproduces an interesting visual illustration of this symbolism—a woodcut in Stephen Bateman's *Christall Glasse of Christian Reformation* that portrays a Catholic monastery collapsing as a flood sweeps it along. The gloss to the woodcut reads: "The house which standeth on the rocke, signifieth the stedfast beliefe of the faythfull: The other which standeth in the valy and on sandy ground, is the church of Antichrist and all popishe preaching." King, *Spenser's Poetry*, 88–90.

16. John Calvin. *A harmonie vpon the three euangelists, Matthew, Mark and Luke, w. comm. of J. Caluine*. Trans. E. P[aget]. (1584), 224.

17. Calvin, *A harmonie*, 225.

18. Penry's choice of words is interesting—"aedifie" sounds much like "edifice." The awkward title of Penry's work stems from the occasional difficulty of separating titles and subtitles in early modern publications. The running title in the book is a manageable "Reformation No Enemie to Hir Majestie and the State," but I have provided the full title for reference purposes. John Penry, *A Treatise Wherein is Manifestlie Proved, That Reformation and Those that sincerely fauor the same, are unjustly charged to be enemies vnto hir Majestie and the state* (London, 1590).

19. The diplomatic maneuvering to secure Penry's banishment from Scotland extended to even the most important state occasions, a fact that suggests the seriousness with which the Elizabethan government viewed this combative reformer. The day before James was to crown his new bride, Anne of Denmark, the Elizabethan ambassador Robert Bowes paid the king an official visit, ostensibly to congratulate the

king on his wedding. During the visit, however, Bowes also took the occasion to press further Elizabeth's displeasure with the continued freedom of Penry and Robert Walgrave, who had printed the Marprelate tracts. William Pierce, *John Penry: His Life, Times and Writings* (London: Hodder and Soughton, 1923), 278.

20.   For example, Elizabeth had already clashed with Edmund Grindal, bishop of London, over his interest in enforcing obedience through such independent sermonizing. See Patrick Collinson, *Archbishop Grindal 1519–1583: The Struggle for a Reformed Church* (Berkeley: University of California Press, 1979), esp. 231–52.

21.   Gibson's sermon is dedicated to the earl of Bedford and Sir Walter Mildmay, who was also the chancellor of the queen's Court of Exchequer. *A Frvitful Sermon, Preached at Occham, in the Countie of Rutland, the Second of Nouember. 1583.* (London, 1584), sig. D2v.

22.   Similar language is found in Penry's first work, the *Aequity of an Humble Supplication* (1587), which appealed to Parliament to remedy the shortage of trained ministers in Wales, without whom the common citizens remained backward and idolatrous. Robert Walgrave's *A Lamentable Complaint of the Commonalty, By Way of Supplication to the High Court of Parliament, for a Learned Ministry* (1585), likewise calculates that "not aboue 2. or 3. of 100. (we suppose) of vs country people throwout the land where these blind guides be, can make any better answer to the purpose, whereby you may probably coniecture that the seed of eternal life is sowen in our hearts," sig. B4r.

23.   Douglas Brooks-Davies, *Spenser's Faerie Queene* (Manchester: Manchester University Press, 1977), 38; Humphrey Tonkin, *The Faerie Queene* (London: Unwin Hyman, 1989), 69.

24.   Michael O'Connell, *Mirror and Veil: The Historical Dimension of Spenser's* Faerie Queene (Chapel Hill: University of North Carolina Press, 1977), 50; Hume, *Edmund Spenser*, 86–87. More recently, Carol Kaske has reiterated the Catholic elements of these characters, and in particular the "ignorant, ineffectual, unhospitable, and grotesquely Romanist Corceca." Kaske, *Spenser*, 30.

25.   Elizabeth Heale, The Faerie Queene*: A Reader's Guide* (Cambridge: Cambridge University Press, 1987), 86–87.

26.   The narrator becomes even more accommodating in canto X, the visit of Una and Redcrosse to the House of Holiness. Here the lady of the house "was busie at her beades," but unlike Corceca has the good sense to put them aside when Una arrives (I.x.8.3). It seems as if the issue in these two stories is the proper place and limits on ritual, rather than the mere existence of ritual itself. Whitaker, *Religious Basis*, 25–27.

27.   See for example Una's encounter with Prince Arthur (I.vii.29–42). Additionally, throughout the verbal assault on Una that occurs prior to Archimago's appearance, Spenser avoids specifying just who is speaking. Although Archimago's conversation with Corceca may provide evidence that the old woman does much of the railing, stanza 24's reference to a seeing individual (Abessa) complicates this assumption: "But when she saw her prayers nought preuaile,/She backe returned with some labour lost" (1–2). Of course "saw" might also mean simply "realized," but it remains an interesting choice of words.

28.   Porter, *Puritanism*, 148.

29. Cf. *An humble petition of the Communaltie to their most renowned and gracious Sovereigne, the Lady Elizabeth* (London, 1588), sig. A3r; and Walgrave, *The lamentable complaint of the communalitie*, sig. B4r.

30. Psalm 115 recounts the idolaters who have eyes but cannot see, and both Ephesians (4.18–19) and Romans (1.21) present blindness as a physical sign of a spiritual ignorance and obstinacy. The Geneva Bible's gloss on the verses from Ephesians seems particularly apt for Spenser's wandering Una: "He sheweth what great vanitie it is to aske helpe of them, which not only have no helpe in them, but lacke sense and reason."

31. The Geneva Bible's gloss on Matthew 15.14 offered additional grounds for this conflict. According to the commentator, "this [verse] declareth that there is an horrible disorder among that people, where the true preaching of Gods worde wanteth." "True preaching," as my argument will suggest, became a major sticking point between conservative and more radical reformers.

32. *A Briefe and plaine declaration, concerning the desires of all those faithfull Ministers, that haue and do seeke for the Discipline and reformation of the Church of Englande* (1584), 50.

33. The marginal note to Penry's sermon refers readers not only to Matthew 15.14 (the source of Penry's allusion) but also to Mark 6.34: "Then Iesus went out, and sawe a great multitude, and had compassion on them, because they were like shepe which had no shepherde." All Biblical passages in this essay are taken from the Geneva Bible (1560). *The Geneva Bible, a Facsimile of the 1560 Edition* (Madison: University of Wisconsin Press, 1969).

34. Augustine Marlorate, *A Catholike and Ecclesiasticall exposition of the holy Gospell after S. Mathewe, gathered out of all the singuler and approued Devines.* Trans. Thomas Lymme. (London, 1570), 55, 56. In France Marlorate was a well known member of the first wave of Genevan Protestantism. In 1562 he helped lead the Protestants of Rouen to seize their city in order to ensure their freedom of worship. After a series of sieges the royal army stormed the city, capturing Marlorate and delivering him for trial and execution. See Marlorate's entry in *The New Schaff-Herzog Encyclopedia of Religious Knowledge* vol. 7 (New York: Funk and Wagnalls, 1910), 186.

35. Gless, *Interpretation*, 83.

36. Humphrey Tonkin, *The Faerie Queene* (London: Unwin Hyman, 1989), 60; King, *Spenser's Poetry*, 204–05.

37. Walgrave, *The lamentable complaint*, sig. B4r; and *An Humble Petition*, sig. A3r.

38. Marlorate, *A Catholicke*, 55.

39. Quoted in Jones, *The English Reformation*, 33.

40. John Penry, *A defense of that which hath bin written in the questions of the ignorant ministrie, and the communicating with them* (London. 1588), 47.

41. Jean Calvin, *A Commentarie of M. Iohn Caluine, vpon the booke of Iosue, finished a little before his death.* Trans. William Fulke. (London, 1578), 23r.

42. Thomas Cooper, *A briefe exposition of suche Chapters of the olde Testament as vsually are saide in the Church at common praier on the Sundayes* (London, 1573), 279–86. Interestingly, Cooper does at least glance at the possibility of a more contemporary interpretation of the Biblical text; he acknowledges that "the manner of the Prophets is oftentimes, by a time Past to note the time to Come, as well in the threatenings of punishments, as in the Promises of Gods good blessings." 282r.

43.　Waldegrave, *The lamentable complaint*, sig. B4iv.

44.　While the satyrs do gaze at Una longingly, there is little of the unbridled lasciviousness the Elizabethans commonly ascribed to satyrs.

45.　On the importance of preaching to understanding *The Faerie Queene*, see Mallette's *Spenser and the Discourses* and his "The Protestant Art of Preaching in Book One of *The Faerie Queene." Spenser Studies* 7 (1986): 3–25.

46.　Gless, *Interpretation*, 108. Reading the episode alongside John Calvin's accounts on natural religion, Anthea Hume similarly argues that "we are faced with an episode which depicts a characteristic experience of the true church rather than a particular historical moment." Hume, *Edmund Spenser*, 89.

47.　While he concentrates primarily on the savages of Book V, Andrew Hadfield takes just this approach regarding Ireland's formative influence on Spenser. Andrew Hadfield, "The 'sacred hunger of ambitious minds': Spenser's Savage Religion." *Religion, Literature, and Politics in Post-Reformation England, 1540–1688*, ed. Donna Hamilton and Richard Strier (Cambridge: Cambridge University Press, 1996), 27–45.

48.　The account of this story is the only miracle found in all four gospels: Matthew 14.13–21, Mark 6.30–44, Luke 9.10–17, and John 6.1–13. Calvin's commentary can be found in *A harmonie*, 425.

49.　Claire Cross, *Church and People 1450–1660: The Triumph of the Laity in the English Church* (Atlantic Highlands, NJ: Humanities Press, 1976), 135.

50.　[Dudley Fenner], *A Covnter-Poyson, modestly written for the time* (London, 1584), 69.

51.　Wrightson and Levine, *Poverty*, 26. The mention of nationalism seems particularly apt at this point, as the poem here appears to make the link between Una and Queen Elizabeth relatively explicit. The satyrs "wonder of her [Una's] beautie soueraine" and "[d]o worship her, as Queene" (I.vi.12.6; 13.9).

52.　The difficulties in enflaming the commons to a fervent Protestantism are perhaps best described by Richard Greenham, who by all accounts was a particularly devoted pastor who sought to heal both his parishioners' spiritual and social ills. After toiling in the small parish of Dry Drayton for over twenty years, Greenham left for London, remarking to his successor that "I perceive no good wrought by my ministry but one family." Everett Emerson, *English Puritanism from John Hooper to John Milton* (Durham: Duke University Press, 1968), 145.

53.　See, for example, Hadfield "The 'sacred hunger' " and Mallette, *Spenser*, 155–57.

54.　On subversion and the Gyant, see Susanne Wofford, who explores how the Tudor iconography of giants could both represent and undermine the monarch's claim to legitimacy. Susanne Wofford, "Spenser's Giants." *Critical Essays on Edmund Spenser*, ed. Mihoko Suzuki (New York: G.K. Hall, 1996), 199–220. See also Stephen Greenblatt, "Murdering Peasants: Status, Genre, and the Representation of Rebellion." *Representing the English Renaissance* (Berkeley: University of California Press, 1988), 1–29.

55.　See Stuart Babbage, *Puritanism and Richard Bancroft* (London: Published for the Church Historical Society, 1962), esp. 8–42.

56. Jane Aptekar, *Icons of Justice: Iconography and Thematic Imagery in Book V of* The Faerie Queene (New York: Columbia University Press, 1969), 35. Since such naming is itself an interpretative act, one that closes off interpretative options as much as opens them up, I will distinguish this character only through Spenser's spelling.

57. *A Humble*, 74.

58. Gibson, *A Frvitful sermon*, sig. E4iiv

59. Henry Smith, *The Poore Mans Teares*. (London, 1591), 27.

60. *A petition made to the Conuocation house, 1586* (London, 1588), sig. Pv. Similarly, Waldegrave's *A Briefe and Plaine Declaration*, while using the poor as a means to reemphasize the need to pattern the English church after the non-hierarchical organization of the early church, takes a rather traditional line against the potentially subversive inclinations of the wandering poor. Waldegrave, *A Briefe*, 101–06.

61. Smith, *The Poore Mans Teares*, 12.

62. Interestingly, charges of Anabaptism were leveled by both sides during the interrogations. While debating whether commissions of ministers initially ordained under Queen Mary were still valid, John Greenwood manages to get his questioner, a minister, to respond that he knew inwardly that his commission was valid. Greenwood then responds, "Do you hold that by an inward calling a man may exercise as Office in the Church of GOD without an outward calling thervnto? If I should hold it, I should quicklye be drawne forth for an *Anabaptist*." One can imagine that at that moment at least the briefest of smiles must have flickered across Greenwood's face. Henry Barrow, *A collection of certain letters and conferences lately passed betvvixt certaine preachers and tvvo prisoners in the Fleet*, 52.

63. Henry Barrow et al., *The examinations*, sigs. Biiv, Diir.

64. Richard Bancroft, *A Sermon Preached at Paules Crosse the 9. of Februarie*. (London, 1588), 75.

65. Bancroft, *A Sermon*, 15. Pride, of course, is also the original cause of sin, going as far back as Satan's rebellion against God. Greenblatt proposes that this rebellion may be circulating within the story of the Gyant. Greenblatt, "Murdering," 20.

66. Bancroft, *A Sermon*, 90.

67. Bancroft, *A Sermon*, 96.

68. Bancroft, *A Sermon*, 59.

69. Bancroft, *A Sermon*, 93.

70. *A Humbe Motion with Submission unto the Right Honorable LL. of Hir Majesties Privie Covnsell*. (Edinburgh?, 1590), 108.

71. King, *Spenser's Poetry*, 42.

72. Richard Bancroft, *Dangerovs Positions and Proceedings* (London, 1593). Penry's personalized response to Bancroft's sermon reveals the increasing uneasiness the Puritans felt with this new state of affairs: "But let it bee graunted, that the true Church gouernours in Scotland, behaued themselues rebelliously towards their Prince . . . Do you thinke it a good reason to say, that the Archbishop is a Traitour, therefore the Archbishopricke is gilty of Treason? You cannot deny, but Thomas Becket was a traitor, so were diuers others that haue beene Archbishops of Canterbury, but I trust you will not therefore attaint the Archibishopricke of treason" John Penry, *A Briefe Discovery Of the Vntrvthes and Slanders Against the Trve Gouernement of the Church of Christ* (London, 1588), 43.

73. The extent of Talus's violence can be judged by the propensity of modern critics to use twentieth-century military comparisons such as this one. Discussing this scene of violence, Greenblatt describes Talus as one "who can no more receive dishonor than can a Cruise missile." Greenblatt, "Murdering," 23.

74. O'Connell, *Mirror and Veil*, 138–39.

75. As Darryl Gless has noted, "awareness that Elizabethan orthodoxy was unevenly received should somewhat inhibit whatever impulse literary interpreters might still feel to assert confidently what 'the English reader' thought about religious issues raised in *The Faerie Queene*" (11).

76. See, for example, Peter Bayley, *Edmund Spenser: Prince of Poets* (London: Hutchinson University Library, 1971), 138–40; and O'Connell, *Mirror and Veil*, 139, 158. The *View* was entered for publication in 1598, but it did not actually appear in print until 1633, making its use as a key to the reception of Spenser's epic somewhat limited. Greenblatt offers a similar caveat to biographical interpretations of Sidney's *Arcadia* and its understanding of the common people. Greenblatt, "Murdering," 16.

77. Wrightson and Levine, *Poverty*, 13. Christopher Marsh has identified evidence of this disillusion coming from Puritans as early as the late 1570's. See Marsh, "Piety and Persuasion," 150.

78. Although length does not permit a full reading of the cannibalistic multitudes of Book VI, they too display a similarly aggressive and disputatious character.

79. T. K. Dunhseath, *Spenser's Allegory of Justice in Book Five of* The Faerie Queene (Princeton: Princeton University Press, 1968), 110–11. Elizabethan statues could even offer the tongue-tied Artegall a set text to proclaim. The standard response to unlawful assemblies was to proclaim "The Queene our Soveraigne Ladie chargeth and commandeth all persons beeing assembled, immediately to disperse themselves, and peaceablie to depart to their habitations, or to their lawfull business, upon the paines contained in the Acte lately made against unlawfull and rebellious assemblies. And God save the Queene." Dunsheath, 111. While Dunsheath suggests that Artegall's disregard for this requirement "is no great matter," both literature and English history offers critics repeated examples of nobles such as Sir Thomas More defusing the mob through speech. Aptekar, *Icons*, 36. Some might argue that in the debate with the Gyant Artegall has already spoken. I would suggest, however, that the primary reason for Artegall's silence is that the period's standard rhetoric against mobs explicitly foregrounds the possibility of violence. As Greenblatt notes, Spenser accommodated the notion of state force against the commons by relying "upon the allegorical separation of rhetoric and violence" in Artegall and Talus. Greenblatt, "Murdering," 23. Artegall' s use of the Elizabethan proclamation against mobs would undermine such a careful balancing act.

80. Gless, *Interpretation*, 200.

81. Wrightson and Levine, *Poverty*, 180.

PAUL SUTTIE

Moral Ambivalence in the Legend of Temperance

This essay considers the long-running debate as to whether, in the person of Guyon, Spenser means to champion or reject a particular conception of temperance, arguing instead that the moral ambivalence of all Guyon's achievements is itself the point. Guyon's world does not make available to him an ideal middle course between "forward" and "froward" extremes; rather he has *two* chief paradigms of virtue on which he can draw, themselves respectively "forward" and "froward" in character, and hence themselves open to the charge of being forms of the very intemperance they are meant to remedy. Whereas Book I establishes a Protestant as against a Catholic basis for morally interpreting the poem's action, Book II looks to build on that ground by testing against one another two leading Protestant notions of the virtuous life in such a way as to grapple seriously with the difficulties posed by each.

*I*N MISSION TERMS, Sir Guyon's quest is as successful as the Redcross knight's before him; and the authority that morally endorses the mission is in either case the same. Nonetheless, the modern critical traditions surrounding the completion of the two undertakings could hardly be more different. Whatever failings Redcross may display in the course of his quest, it has always seemed clear that its object, slaying the dragon, is offered to us as a good and glorious deed. Not so the destruction of the Bower of Bliss, the poem's moral endorsement of which has been a matter of persistent debate, both pre- and post-Greenblatt.[1]

My purpose here is not to take a side in that debate, but rather to look into the problem in Book II of moral ambivalence as such, of which Guyon's actions in completing his quest are the

crowning but by no means the only significant example. For it seems
to me that Spenser actively cultivates moral ambivalence throughout
this book, and in this book especially. Not, however, in an unstruc-
tured way, as though it were simply the poet's skeptical habit of
mind to cast doubt equally everywhere. Rather the ambivalence itself
has a structure—a particular form and cause—which I shall try to describe.

Uncertainty about what constitutes the good features in Book I,
as well: the straying Redcross pursues evil precisely under the guise
of virtue, and even the good often looks unsettlingly like an evil
already rejected. However, the dragon quest, assigned by the legitimate and godly monarch Gloriana, becomes, amidst the ambiguity,
a much-needed beacon of moral clarity, the very sign of the hero's
having been "chosen" for salvation. Guyon's quest, in contrast, is
itself caught up in moral ambivalence from start to finish. That is
partly a function of the mission's nature: where Redcross was to
rescue Eden from a monster—clear enough—for Guyon the two are
conflated, such that the Eden *is* the monster. It has also to do, though,
with how the quest figures in the story at large, from how it is
initiated to how its hero is received after completing it; and it is to
that context that I now turn.

To take the reception after the fact first: Redcross reappears at the
beginning of Book II as a figure of exemplary moral self-control, to
whom shame will not stick, and receives rapturous praise for his "late
most hard atchieu'ment" (II.i.32); whereas Guyon, in the analogous
scene in Book III, encounters at his successor's hand not praise but
tremendous "shame," and his response, till restrained by his friends,
is "wrath" and a "fierce" impulse "to reuenge," which looks like
anything but the attained virtue of temperance (III.i.9). So that,
where the Redcross knight's accomplishment is underscored, by both
explicit praise and his own example, Guyon's is made to look suspect,
raising a big retrospective question about the ethical value of his
whole prior quest. However, it would be simplistic just to label
Guyon a failure on those grounds. For such vengeful wrath, while
undoubtedly problematic from the point of view of any classical
definition of temperance (and greeted with alarm even here by the
stoic Palmer), far from simply having been the enemy of Guyon's
quest, has been intrinsic to its motivation from the very start. There
is a contradiction at the heart of his project, which we do not touch
merely by saying that Guyon never successfully becomes in practice
the classically temperate man.

For in fact, there are two very different models of heroism in play
in Book II, of which the self-restraint that defines temperance is only

one. The other is an outgoing, militaristic ethos of valor, (broadly speaking, a chivalric ethos), which marks as noble not one's capacity to restrain the passionate nature but its native strength: where temperance would rein in and subdue irascibility and concupiscence, this valor ethos makes it the sign of nobility "to be borne by natiue influence/ . . . feates of armes, and loue to entertaine" (II.iv.1).[2] Of course, the book at points satirizes such a conception of virtue, most notably in the proudly passionate characters of Pyrochles and Cymochles. By no means does it simply disown it, though, any more than it unambiguously champions the opposite, stoic ideal—which is, for example, made to look as ludicrous as Pyrochles and Cymochles ever do, when in the Palmer's advice to Phedon it is reduced to the supremely trite as well as (to use Harry Berger's term) "gynophobic" notion that the kind of love that aims at marriage is the "monster" at the root of Phedon's woes.[3] The simultaneous presence of these two value systems, not only in the story but in Guyon's own thinking, makes the moral significance of all his actions radically ambivalent, because each one's ideal of virtue is from the other's perspective a type of vice. Moreover, while it is tempting to imagine that the book's deeper moral project would be to mark out a middle way between the respective extremes of these stoic and aristocratic paradigms, in fact the Legend of Temperance consistently rejects that pat solution.

We can see that already in the first two cantos, where the hero gets his quest underway; for he gives it, as it were, a double launch, first by Amavia's grave, then again at Medina's court, and in each case he cuts such a different heroic figure as to come away looking like a walking self-contradiction. At the graveside, "temperance" may be on the Palmer's lips (II.i.58), but could not be more alien to Guyon's actual deed, which is deliberately to work himself up into a sufficient passion resolutely to assume the tragic revenger's role:

> Sir *Guyon* more affection to increace,
> Bynempt a sacred vow, which none should aye releace.
>
> . . . Such and such euill God on *Guyon* reare,
> And worse and worse young Orphane be thy paine,
> If I or thou dew vengeance doe forbeare . . .
>
> (II.i.60–61).

At Medina's table, in contrast, it is not towering, vengeful passion but humble duty that Guyon makes the motive of his quest. "My Soueraine," he explains,

> Whose glory is in gracious deeds, and ioyes
> Throughout the world her mercy to maintaine,
> Eftsoones deuisd redresse for such annoyes;
> Me all vnfit for so great purpose she employes.
>
> (II.ii.43).

His own painful experience is appealed to now only in a forensic vein: of Acrasia's crimes, he declares, "I witnesse am" (II.ii.44). Indeed, it would have sounded very strangely to have had recourse to his former motive here. For his hostess has already spoken out categorically against "wrath" and "mortall vengeaunce," even where there is "rightfull cause of difference" or a "crime abhord" has been committed (II.ii.30). One might try to salvage logic from Guyon's change of tack by arguing that in visiting Medina's house the hero corrects his own motives, bringing them into line with reason. But the poem does not depict any such process of correction, in the way it depicted Redcross as having to be chastened into subordinating his own motives for chivalric endeavour to his duty to the godly queen who knighted him. Rather Guyon's two motives for his quest are merely juxtaposed. When he departs from Medina's house "mindfull of his vow yplight," this might *include* his recently reported vow to Gloriana, never to "rest in house nor hold,/Till I that false *Acrasia* haue wonne" (II.iii.44), but any sense that that dutiful oath may have subsumed his other, impassioned vow of vengeance vanishes when he hands the bloody-handed baby to Medina, enjoining her of all people to teach him, "so soone as ryper yeares he raught . . -. T'auenge his Parents death on them, that had it wrought" (II.-iii.1–2). Ruddymane, after all, has not been given his sovereign's orders to do any such thing: we are back, here, to the passionate vendetta that animated Guyon at the graveside. Nor can we even say, in view of this parting act, simply that Guyon has failed to learn Medina's lesson, as though that lesson itself were patently right. Rather her philosophy is itself suspiciously over-simple, in the same sort of way as is the Palmer's later advice to Phedon. As Lauren Silberman observes, Medina "makes accord itself a value, at the expense of any substantive meaning the dispute may have. The difference between two [parties] is granted no significance except insofar as that difference allows a mean to be struck."[4] Such indiscriminate peacemaking hardly looks like an adequate ethical basis for Guyon's task. So not only does the passionate vengeance ethos remain a part of the hero's moral makeup, but the question whether that ethos can appropriately play a part in motivating his quest remains unresolved.

All that is clear is that the different models of morality in play cast doubt on one another's legitimacy.

The parallel and in either case precarious standing in the book of each of these ethics is seen with particular clarity in canto nine, where Guyon and Arthur come face to face with Shamefastnesse and Prays-Desire. Here the two potential models of virtue, the self-restraining on the one hand and the high-aspiring on the other, are themselves linked to two strong, contrasting passions dwelling in the human heart. The encounter radically challenges the notion that virtue might consist simply in steering a rational course between the extremes of excess and defect, "forward" and "froward" passions: rather the potential motives for virtue are themselves seen as powerful "forward" and "froward" passions respectively.[5] Hence, too, both are laid open to a charge of being themselves forms of the very intemperance that the one ethos, at least, had promised to remedy—a charge made against each, ironically, by the very knight in whose moral life it is especially active. Nor does the episode offer to resolve the confusion: it quickly rebuffs the knights' simplistic attempts to disown their animating passions, but leaves resolutely unclear whether their error is to reprove in others excesses they ought to reprove in themselves, or rather, to reprove qualities necessary to their own heroism and hence in practice good; it leaves tellingly unresolved, that is, whether either of these passions is properly understood as a morally enabling or disabling energy.

These two points—that there is no neutral moral stance between the extremes of passion, and that the "forward" and "froward" motives for virtue are both ambivalent in their real moral value—can be seen demonstrated throughout Guyon's adventures. Though in one encounter after another, our hero attempts to assume the part of the temperate judge, who reproves passionate excesses from the authoritative stance of the golden mean, with telltale regularity the possibility of taking such a place above the fray is called seriously into doubt. Even in Medina's house, which seems of all the book's settings most clearly and schematically to offer him such solid middle ground to stand on, the action he takes, interposing himself between the champions of Excess and Defect, does not in practice display but put into question his capacity for assuming the arbitrator's role: for it is the ironic levelling of the aspiring mediator with the two other combatants, rather than Guyon's high intention, that proceeds to dominate the episode's development. But it is in the hero's later encounters, especially his notoriously ambivalent adventures at the Cave of Mammon and the Bower of Bliss, that these problems receive their deepest exploration. For it is there that the "forward" and "froward" motives for virtue are themselves put on trial.

Those two great scenes have in common the nature of a Catch-22. The Mammon episode begins as a critique of the "forward," acquisitive model of virtue, the ethos of Prays-Desire. For Guyon relies on that ethos to summon up disdain for the offered treasure—as he puts it, "Regard of worldly mucke doth fowly blend,/And low abase the high heroicke spright,/That ioyes for crownes and kingdomes to contend" (II.vii.10)—but only to find that his own announced goals themselves fall within his adversary's worldly purview: if he rejects gold for pursuit of kingdoms, he will be offered kingdoms (II.vii.10–11); if he rejects political climbing by ignoble, mercenary means, he will be offered advancement "for workes and merites iust" (II.vii.49); if he disdains the court at which the advancement is offered (II.vii.50), he will be offered an object of heroic aspiration abstracted from political considerations (II.vii.54*ff*). The exchange has the effect of inducing Guyon progressively to retreat from the very motives for heroism he himself begins by declaring. But here comes the trick: that finally the episode will be a critique not only of the "forward" but of the "froward" ethos, on which Guyon falls back in systematically shunning the moral ambivalence of heroic aspiration. He may not give in to Mammon's temptations, but the process of never giving in is itself pursued to a reductio ad absurdum. For Mammon, in reply, so refines the nature of the "gold" he offers as to expose Guyon's underlying premise: that all desire whatever is morally suspect, and every object suspect insofar as it is an object of desire. Trying to set himself apart from all morally dubious ends, Guyon cuts the ground from beneath his own feet, till left with nowhere to stand: presented at last with the objects of the inalienable human aspirations towards food and rest (II.vii.63), he is obliged by his own premises to push from beneath himself those two "pillours" of "food, and sleepe" which "vpbeare . . . this fraile life of man" (II.vii.65), and promptly falls into a faint (II.vii.66).

As for the Bower of Bliss, it constitutes a similar, but in some respects opposite trap for the hero. Here it is the adequacy of the "froward" ethos of self-restraint that is most obviously on trial, as Guyon's self-control falters before "sights, that courage cold could reare" (II.xii.68). But with the Palmer always at his shoulder here to keep him in check (as the fiend is in Mammon's cave) ultimately the Bower's more dangerous incitement to Guyon is, not to let go of his quest in Verdant-like sensual self-abandon, but rather to carry it through: carry it through, that is, in terms that will reveal in his very success something potentially as culpable as his failure would have been. That deeper incitement structures the whole scene, making what stands between Guyon and the goal of his quest a concentric series of the very kind of false barrier that the Bower everywhere interposes between desire and its object: flimsy and weakly guarded gates, transparent veils, and permitted crimes, whose real function is not to dissuade but to solicit the force that will breach them. With its elaborate and insistent pretence of denying entry, the whole island is one grand exercise in inciting the kind of impassioned violence with which the hero does in fact respond to it at every stage. If, by the time he chains Acrasia and unleashes on her Bower "the tempest of his wrathfulnesse" (II.xii.83), his level of violence seems linked to his susceptibility to the place's charms, and even suggests a kind of erotic possession by other means,[6] then that, I think, is the trap into which the Bower has been concertedly luring him. Mortdant himself was drawn here not initially by lust, but "As wont ye knights . . . / . . . his puissant force to proue" (II.i.50); and Guyon, even in pursuing his quest, becomes Mortdant's successor as much as his avenger. Whereas the Cave of Mammon corners Guyon into disowning his own enabling heroic passions, the Bower provokes him into expressing them in a form that implicates them in the disabling vice that his violence was meant to remedy. In sum, he looks damned if he doesn't, and also damned if he does.

So, if Book II presents all Guyon's actions as morally ambivalent, still it does not construct that situation as a matter of personal failing, as though in similar circumstances another hero with a firmer grip on virtuous motives could have succeeded more convincingly. Rather it suggests that Guyon really is between a rock and a hard place, in that the very motives for virtue from which he has to choose may be indistinguishable from the vices they are meant to conquer. In those circumstances, "God guide thee, *Guyon*" (II.i.32).

Now, in criticising not so much an individual's failure to live up to a given ethos, as the shortcomings of the ethical systems themselves according to which he models his actions, Book II does resemble Book I. In fact, it is Book I that sets up the problem Guyon inherits, by marking out as its ideal a course between the extremes of the arrogant moral self-assertion that takes Redcross to the House of Pride, and the despairing quietism from which (ironically) Contemplation finally rouses him. The first book associates those pernicious extremes with Catholic worldliness and Catholic unworldliness respectively, marking as moral a Protestant middle way according to which one shoulders the responsibility of the active life even while humbling one's personal sense of right and wrong before the tasks set out for one by God. Its touchstone for that humble active life is loyalty to a divinely authorized monarch. But such unqualified turn-ing to divine and concomitantly to human authority leaves the actual content of the faithful subject's moral life all but unexplored. Indeed, for Redcross the problem hardly exists, because in his case the task of acting morally in the world is straightforwardly represented by a single symbolic act, spelled out by a direct order from above; it is Guyon, whose quest comes next, to whom are devolved the diffi-culties of negotiating practical moral problems, and the moral uncer-tainties inherent even in loyal action. As Book II kicks off, and Guyon and Redcross pay homage to one another's nominal virtues, it looks briefly as though the first book's lesson in faithfulness will be fur-thered straightforwardly by one in self-restraint—as though there will simply be two complementary guides, piety and moderation, to keep in check the potentially loose cannon of heroic aspiration.[7] What I am arguing, though, is that it is precisely the weaknesses of that facile solution that the rest of the book explores. If Book I extols a Protes-tant as against a Catholic basis for moral action, then Book II looks to build on that ground by seeking in the Protestant camp an adequate practical definition of the faithful active life. It tests what might summarily be described as a "Cecilian" Protestant Stoicism against a "Dudleian" Protestant Militarism;[8] and while, prudently, not trum-peting the inadequacy of either—in the way that the first book ex-plicitly demonizes Catholicism—it does grapple seriously with the difficulties of each, finding in them a Scylla and Charybdis between which it will be no mean task to steer.

University of Cambridge—Robinson College

NOTES

1. Pre-Greenblatt: see A. C. Hamilton, ed., *The Faerie Queene*, (Longman, 1977), 168. Stephen Greenblatt, *Renaissance Self-Fashioning: From More to Shakespeare*, (Uni-versity of Chicago Press, 1980), chapter 4. Post-Greenblatt: e.g., Lauren Silberman, "*The Faerie Queene*, Book II, and the Limitations of Temperance," *MLS* 4 (1987), 9–22, esp. 20; Harry Berger, Jr., "Narrative as Rhetoric in *The Faerie Queene*", *ELR* 21 (1991): 2–48, esp. 43–44; and Jay Farness, "Disenchanted Elves: Biography in the Text of *Faerie Queene* V", in Judith Anderson et al., eds., *Spenser's Life and the Subject of Biography* (University of Massachusetts Press, 1996), 18–30, esp. 21–24.

2. It will be seen that I think the book is less interested in discriminating among the different definitions of temperance offered by the various classical schools of thought than in pitting a syncretic amalgam of those against a radically different

conception of virtue, one that is predominantly chivalric in its terms but itself widely enough conceived to include classical strains, notably the tragic and the Homeric.

3.　*The Faerie Queene*, II.iv.35; Berger, 30 ff.

4.　Silberman, 11.

5.　Cf. William Nelson, *The Poetry of Edmund Spenser: A Study*, (Columbia University Press, 1963), 182.

6.　Greenblatt, 173; Madelon S. Gohlke, "Embattled Allegory: Book II of *The Faerie Queene*", *ELR* 8 (1978): 123–40, esp. 137.

7.　Cf. e.g. F. M. Padelford, "The Virtue of Temperance in *The Faerie Queene*," *SP* 18 (1921): 334–46, esp. 336.

8.　Recent work on the political and cultural context alluded to here includes Richard Helgerson, *Self-Crowned Laureates: Spenser, Jonson, Milton, and the Literary System* (University of California Press, 1983) and *Forms of Nationhood: The Elizabethan Writing of England* (University of Chicago Press, 1992); Mervyn James, *Society, Politics and Culture: Studies in Early Modern England* (Cambridge University Press, 1986), esp. chapters 7–9; and Richard McCoy, *The Rites of Knighthood: The Literature and Politics of Elizabethan Chivalry*, (University of California Press, 1989).

JAMES W. BROADDUS

Renaissance Psychology and the Defense of Alma's Castle

A Renaissance Aristotelian-Galenic look at Guyon's faint and
at the frailties exhibited earlier by Guyon and the Palmer calls
attention to the physiological as well as the psychic in the episode at Alma's Castle. Approached physiologically, Maleger
represents the curse of mortality understood either within or
without the Christian faith, the curse as found in the Garden
of Adonis: that because of which "All things decay in time, and
to their end doe draw." Through his agents Maleger effects
occasions of decay by exploiting psychic weaknesses; Maleger
himself destroys through the "course of kinde." Guyon, even
if aided by the Palmer, could not contend with Maleger because
Maleger preys on frailties apparent in both Guyon and the
Palmer. That Arthur successfully defends the Castle further differentiates the relationship of Guyon and the Palmer to Maleger's agents from the relationship of the two to Maleger himself.

*T*HE QUESTION HERE IS FAMILIAR: Why should Guyon, the
patron of temperance, continue on to the Bower of Bliss and leave
Arthur to defend the house of temperance against Maleger, the most
formidable villain in Book II and arguably the fundamental threat to
the virtue of temperance? The answer is also familiar because, as in
theological interpretation, in psychological analysis as practiced here,
natural powers can contend with Maleger's agents but not with Maleger himself. However, rather than original sin, Maleger will represent the curse of mortality whether that curse is understood within
or without the Christian faith, the curse as it appears in the Garden
of Adonis: that because of which "All things decay in time, and to
their end doe draw." In the Garden, mortality is both blessing and
curse, and both appear in that lovely part of, or aspect of, the Garden

135

occupied by mature and sexually active lovers. The curse is that the bond that enables matter to live deteriorates slowly "By course of kinde" or is severed "by occasion" (III.vi.38–42). Maleger's agents, those like his troops who assist him directly and those like Acrasia who are his agents only conceptually, effect occasions for destruction by exploiting psychic weaknesses. Maleger himself destroys through the "course of kinde."[1]

I will begin with Guyon's faint, which is central to my argument (but not from symbolic significance) and then move to the frailties, physical and psychic, that Guyon exhibits in his initial encounters. Had the term psychology been available to Spenser, it would have constituted a literal description of the science of the corporeal soul and would have included the physical as well as the psychic actualizations of that soul. The aged, frail Palmer can compensate for Guyon's psychic but not his physical frailty. The assault on the Castle will be approached through the characterization of Maleger's troops rather than determined by the introductory stanzas to cantos ix and xi. And all of the foregoing prepares for an understanding of Maleger as the "course of kinde." My argument will unfold not unlike a periodic sentence.

Having spent the three day limit in Mammon's underworld, Guyon must be taken back to the surface,

> But all so soone as his enfeebled spright
> Gan sucke this vitall ayre into his brest,
> As ouercome with too exceeding might,
> The life did flit away out of her nest,
> And all his senses were with deadly fit opprest.
>
> (II.vii.66)

The physical cause of Guyon's faint is usually identified as exhaustion: "want of food, and sleepe, which two vpbeare,/Like mightie pillours, this frayle life of man . . . ." Clearly these two contribute; but however "weake and wan" Guyon's "vitall powres gan wexe" toward the end of his three day trial (65), he faints "all so soone" as he "Gan sucke this vitall ayre into his brest . . . ." Paul Alpers reads this as paradox, but James Nohrnberg correctly identifies air as the precipitating cause. Nohrnberg mixes the physiological and allegorical: Guyon is sanguine in temperament and so air is his proper element. But his "too sudden exposure to *fresh* air" (emphasis added) after having been in the earth for three days results in "an adverse reaction to a too violent application of a contrary."[2] Nohrnberg's appeal to balance and proportion, the core of Galenic theory, is appropriate. However, Renaissance respiration theory, in which air is drawn from the lungs into the heart to nourish and regulate the vital spirits created in the heart, provides a clearer and more direct explanation of the faint than does humor theory. The "too exceeding might" of *cooling* air, sucked in rather than merely breathed in, precipitates the faint by suppressing Guyon's vital spirits. "[A]ll life [in the sense of vivification]," declares the Renaissance anatomist Helkiah Crooke, "is from the heart and the vital spirit."[3] And the physiology specific to the faint takes place in the two upper cavities of the heart:

> The use of these eares [the auricles, or atria] is that whereas the bloud and ayre rush violently toward the heart [blood into the right and air into the left ventricle] these should take them vp . . . and let them into the heart by degrees, otherwise the creature should bee in danger of suffocation . . . [by] their sudden affluence.
>
> (Crooke, 374)

Guyon so overcools his heart that his "life did flit away out of her nest . . . ." Weak from hunger and a lack of sleep, Guyon faints from Galenic hyperventilation.[4]

This explanation does not separate Guyon's faint from his visit to Mammon's underworld, but it does introduce a factor not originating there. No psychic stresses are evident; and the immediate, physiological cause is respiratory. Thus a physical frailty inherent to humankind but separate from the need for food and sleep is included, a frailty that also locates the action of the poem within Guyon's heart. That physical temperance, like emotional temperance, requires a balance of forces in the heart enlarges the concept of temperance beyond what Spenser has been understood to derive from "Aristotle and the rest" and consequently calls for an adjustment of the vocabulary of temperance. Within the Aristotelian-Galenic body-soul relationship, temperament, temperance, temperature, and temper are closely related concepts of mixture and balance with both psychic and physiological application. And since the difference between continence and temperance, Aristotelean or otherwise, is not germane to my purposes, I will use "temperance" as an inclusive term for the management of the passions. As I will also be concerned with the temperament or temper of the body, I will use Spenser's sometime spelling, "temperaunce," to indicate the state of the entire corporeal soul as embodied.[5] My use of historical materials and my concern with inwardness resemble that found in Michael Schoenfeldt's examination of the stomach-kitchen in Alma's Castle as an expression of the physiology and consequently the psychology of temperance. My focus, however, is on the heart, initially on the vital spirits created in the heart but later also on the passions which are seated in the heart and are, as E. Ruth Harvey explains, constituted by movement of the vital spirits.[6]

The oppression of Guyon's vital spirits also accounts for the details of his subsequent unconsciousness. His overall corpse-like state is the direct result of severely diminished vital spirits, Guyon's loss of his senses being caused by a lack of animal spirits, which are produced by further concoction of vital spirits in the brain. The term "deadly fitt," used by the angel (viii.7) as well as the narrator (vii.66), associates Guyon's extended unconsciousness with serious conditions such as the suffocation of the uterus, more popularly known as "fits of the Mother" (Crooke, 421). To a modern reader the two "fits" may appear to be completely dissimilar, one originating in the uterus and the other in the lungs; but a fit of the mother can also involve an oppression or suffocation of the vital spirits. There can be "a cessation of breathing" and even the

> intermission of the pulse at least to the feeling, the vse of them both being taken away by a venemous breath, which dissolueth the naturall heate of the heart; and such women liue onely by transpiration, that is by such aer as is drawn through the pores of the skin into the Arteries & so reacheth vnto the heart: so that it is impossible almost to perceiue whether such women do yet liue or no.
>
> (Crooke, 253)[7]

Guyon is described as "he that breathlesse seems" (viii.7), which could mean that he appears to breathe only through the pores of his skin or that his breath is so light as to escape detection or both. Crooke says if women in a fit of the mother are able to breathe, they breathe so lightly as not to move even a "downy feather." The fits "will last sometimes 24. houres or more, and the bodies grow colde and rigid like dead carcasses" (253). Guyon's swoon does not last so long, but he is so corpse-like he is continually taken for and described as dead. The theological implications of Guyon's "death" have occupied the scholarship, but my interest is in the dependence of his physical constitution upon forces precariously balanced. And that Guyon's vulnerability is comparable to a specifically female vulnerability would impress that fact upon Spenser's patriarchal contemporaries. Hugh MacLachlan's reading of the faint "not as a physical collapse, but as a metaphor for his spiritual state after (and before) his stay in the Cave of Mammon" provides a useful contrast. MacLachlan examines, in a particular episode, how Guyon symbolizes theological concepts. I examine, in a sequence of episodes, how Guyon embodies and consequently dramatizes human qualities, those qualities prompting allegorical interpretation when related to Maleger's attack on Alma's body-castle. My interest is in allegory that emerges rather directly from character and story.[8]

Physical frailty, which had evoked divine protection for Guyon, remains the focus after the angel leaves. The Palmer,

> At last him turning to his charge behight,
> With trembling hand his troubled pulse gan try,
> Where finding life not yet dislodged quight,
> He much reioyst, and courd it tenderly,
> As chicken newly hatcht, from dreaded destiny.
>
> (viii.9)

Hamilton's annotation of "it" to refer to "his charge," to Guyon, captures the Palmer's protectiveness but does not explain one of Spenser's looser pronoun references.[9] "[L]ife" is the closest possible referent but does not provide an object to be "courd" (covered). "[P]ulse," however, points to the implied referent if we visualize the Palmer trying Guyon's pulse where it resides, in his heart. In Galenic theory, the pulse is not the mechanical effect of a pump on fluid; it is, in and of itself, the faculty that propels the life force. As Crooke explains, the "motion of the heart and the Arteries" arises "from a naturall pulsatiue faculty of the Soule residing in the heart . . . and thence deduced by influence or irradiation into all the arteries at one instant" (410). The pulse is the faculty by which the heart "hurleth forth (as lightning passeth through the whole Heauen) his spirits into the whole body" (401). Viewed in this way, both "life" and "pulse" direct us to the implied referent for "it."

I believe we are to visualize the Palmer feeling Guyon's chest and "finding life not yet dislodged quight" from the heart, that is, finding a faint heartbeat, or pulse. The Palmer then covers Guyon's heart with his hand: "He much reioyst, and courd it tenderly, / As chicken newly hatcht, from dreaded destiny." The Palmer, in an act unreflective of any notion of right reason, does what he can to preserve the vital heat in the hearth of Guyon's body. The fictional situation created by Guyon's faint is resolved after Arthur dispatches Pyrochles and Cymochles and, "Life hauing maystered her sencelesse foe," Guyon's pulse regains strength. The pulse brings vital heat and consequently color to his extremities: the Palmer is glad "With so fresh hew vprysing him to see" (viii.53–54).

Understood as part of a religious experience, the faint prepares Guyon for his visit to Alma's Castle. Understood physiologically, besides preparing the reader for a psychological (in the extended sense) reading of the subsequent episode, the faint directs the reader's attention to frailties Guyon and the Palmer exhibit in previous episodes. Guyon's faint is only the most obvious and severest manifestation of an inherent frailty evidenced in the initial episodes where his "temperaunce" (the condition of his entire corporeal soul as embodied) is more, but not exclusively, psychic. According to Thomas Wright, the passions or affections are "certaine internall acts or operations of the soule, bordering vpon reason and sense, prosecuting some good thing, or flying some ill thing, causing therewithall some alteration in the body."[10]

First then, to our imagination commeth by sense or memorie, some obiect to be knowne, conuenient or disconuenient to Nature . . . [and when the imagination is engaged] . . . presently the purer spirits, flocke from the brayne, by certain secret channels to the heart, where they pitch at the dore, signifying what an obiect was presented, conuenient or disconuenient for it. The heart immediately bendeth, either to prosecute it, or to eschew it : and the better to effect that affection, draweth other humours to help him.

(45)

Without affection, until the heart "bendeth," there is no activity. In the faint, the heart connects the corporeal soul to the body; in Wright's observation, the heart connects the mind to the body. In modern physiology, the heart responds to forces coming from all parts of the body; in the old physiology, vital spirits and passions originate in the heart and their influence spreads out through all parts of the body.

The physiological results of passion have been important to Book II scholarship as indications of the passions' strength and the consequent difficulty of exercising rational control. However, Guyon's first three encounters should make clear that the moderation of, or control of, the passions is an important aspect of his "temperaunce," but not its equivalent. Guyon's encounter with Archimago and Duessa is a textbook illustration of the internal process by which aroused affections exercise control over bodies. The manipulation of Guyon by that pair of shrewd rhetoricians illustrates, however corruptly, Bacon's pronouncement that the function of rhetoric is to apply reason to imagination for the better moving of the will.[11] Archimago's vivid account of the rape of an innocent maid, enhanced by his acting out the appropriate emotions, and the consequent affecting image of Duessa as wronged maid so capture Guyon's imagination as to produce a psychic, then physical response: an unknightly attack on Redcrosse. Although Guyon learns the identity of the alleged rapist, his imagination of Redcrosse, drawn from memory—"he surely is/A right good knight, and trew of word ywis . . . [who] hath great glorie wonne, as I heare tell" (i.19)—lacks vividness and force and is powerless to counteract the rhetoric.[12] Only Guyon's passionate and consequently physical reaction to the cross on Redcrosse's shield breaks off the attack.

In the next episode, the sight of the dead Mordant, the dying Amavia, and Ruddymane dabbling his hands in his mother's blood initiates a reaction that retraces the previous physiological sequence. But rather than moving Guyon immediately to action, the object presented to his imagination so powerfully "oppresses" his vital spirits that he suffers a momentary loss of his senses that anticipates his deeper and more prolonged faint:

> Whom when the good Sir *Guyon* did behold,
> His hart gan wexe as starke, as marble stone,
> And his fresh blood did frieze with fearefull cold,
> That all his senses seemd berefte attone:
>
> (i.42)

This is not poetic embroidery. Neither Spenser specifically nor Crooke generally explains the mechanism by which Guyon's heart "wexe[d] as starke, as marble stone," that is, became rigid, stopped beating and lost its vital heat. However, a medieval rabbi comments most helpfully on the physiology of a comparable event, Jacob's hearing that Joseph was alive and well and ruler of Egypt:

> His heart became paralyzed, and his breathing stopped, since the movement of his heart had ceased. He was just like a dead

person. This is known to occur when joy comes upon suddenly, and it is noted in the books on medicine. The old and the weak cannot bear it, and many of them faint when joy comes upon them suddenly. The heart expands and opens suddenly; the natural heat leaves and spreads out to the exterior parts of the body; and the heart is numbed due to the cold.[13]

And Thomas Wright describes the larger system that accounts for the effect both of Guyon's sorrow and Jacob's joy: "Al passions may be distinguished by the dilation, enlargement, or diffusion of the heart: and the contraction, collection, or compression of the same . . . in all Passions the hart is dilated or coarcted more or less" (24). That contraction precedes paralysis of Guyon's heart is not specified, but impairment of the heart and a consequent oppression of the vital spirits is apparent.[14]

When Guyon recovers, he demonstrates in his tenderhearted care of Amavia and especially of Ruddymane the emotional vulnerability that precipitated the astonishment. Taking the "litle babe vp in his armes" (ii.1), he is moved to a tearful lament by the babe's innocence; and, in Spenser's carefully constructed, visual, and dramatic image, Guyon

> Then soft him selfe inclyning on his knee
>   Downe to that well, did in the water weene
>   (So loue does loath disdainefull nicitee.)
>   His guiltie handes from bloody gore to cleene . . . .
>
>   (3)

(The ambiguity in "guiltie" lies outside my present scope; nevertheless, the discussion here should enhance efforts of those interested in relating Guyon to Adam's sin.) Guyon's emotions are evident to the end of the episode. Prior to the last rites for Mordant and Amavia, Guyon, "more affection to increace," vows vengeance. And then he and the Palmer, "shedding many teares, . . . closd the earth agayne" (60, 61).

Guyon emerges from his first encounters as youthful, vigorous, and virtuous and also as physiologically and psychologically vulnerable. He characterizes the corpses of Amavia and Mordant as the "ymage of mortalitie"; but he is a much more important image of "feeble nature [the corporeal soul], cloth'd with fleshly tyre" (i.57)—a phrase that serves as the Book II counterpart to "images of

God in earthly clay" (I.x.39). But such characterizing does not establish his allegorical role. Unlike the emergence of Redcrosse's allegorical significance from the totality of his initial encounters, Guyon as patron of temperance emerges neither from his actions nor from his words—I read his characterization of Amavia and Mordant as unintentional irony. We know him to be the patron of temperance from statement, as in the prologue where he is proclaimed to be one "In whom great rule of Temp'raunce goodly doth appeare" (Prol.5) and in his initial description as "comely," "vpright," "demure," and "temperate" (i.6). This assessment is echoed in Redcrosse's comment on his previous acquaintance with Guyon: "For sith I know your goodly gouernaunce" (29). Harry Berger, Jr.'s, understanding of Guyon as an "Aristotelian sophrosyne" is based almost solely on such statements.[15]

The two vignettes bracketing the encounter with Archimago and Duessa complete Guyon's introduction by including his relationship with the Palmer. The second vignette is merely expository: the Palmer is said to have guided Guyon's "race with reason, and with words his will" and "From fowle intemperaunce he ofte did stay . . . " (34). Both vignettes image an ideal state in which the passions are under rational control, but the first has a larger purpose. Guyon possesses qualities generally necessary for heroic achievement: nobility, youth, energy, physical prowess, and adventurousness. And the Palmer provides the knowledge, experience, and restraint necessary for heroic achievement in a legend of temperance. But this does not explain the Palmer's age and physical decay. A representation of reason and reason only would more appropriately resemble the "man of ripe and perfect age" in the middle room of the turret in Alma's Castle (ix.54). The Palmer's advanced age and "feeble steps" (i.7) will, however, figure importantly in the relationship of the pair to Maleger and "the course of kinde."

To approach Alma's Castle with the "temperaunce" of both Guyon and the Palmer in mind is to escape reading the assault merely as an attempt by "misrule" (Maleger) to subvert the "forte of reason" (the Castle) by means of an attack by "passions bace" (Maleger's troops) but remain within the temporal. Misrule is only one of Maleger's weapons; and the subversion of rationality that produces misrule appears *in the action* in Acrasia's domain but not, I contend, *in the action* at the Castle. Maleger's siege of the Castle is a direct attack on the body and consequently on the corporeal soul, but pursuit of this theme requires a fresh look at the introductory stanza to canto ix:

Of all Gods workes, which doe this world adorne,

> There is no one more faire and excellent,
> Then is mans body both for powre and forme,
> Whiles it is kept in sober gouerment;
> But none then it, more fowle and indecent,
> Distempred through misrule and passions bace:
> It growes a Monster, and incontinent
> Doth loose his dignity and natiue grace.
> Behold, who list, both one and other in this place.

Although the stanza has served as a template to shape the siege into an attack by the passions on the "forte of reason" (xi.1), it looks back on the previous encounter with Pyrochles and Cymochles more clearly than it anticipates the siege. Alma or Arthur (Arthur in either episode) equally could be the "one" whose body is "kept in sober gouerment," but Pyrochles and Cymochles are better referents for the "other" than is Maleger. Both brothers are "Distempred through misrule and passions bace" and grown into monsters, and both have qualities that can be imagined as having been so "[d]istempred." But one cannot imagine a previous state of "dignity and natiue grace" for Maleger. Nor does "in this place" refer more clearly to the Castle than it does to the locale of the previous canto. Immediately after the introductory stanza, the story continues from the point at which Guyon and Arthur have reached knightly accord at the end of canto viii. The pair proceeds together engaged in a lengthy conversation about the Faery Queen: "So talked they, the whiles/They wasted had much way, and measured many miles"(9). Much has taken place before they reach the Castle in stanza 10.

More importantly, the customary use of the stanza misrepresents Maleger's troops, who resemble vices resulting from habitual exercise of passions rather than the passions themselves. The attack is from the outside, but passions are inward forces. Wright calls them "internall acts or operations of the soule" (28). Passions can be aroused internally by an interaction of memory, imagination, and appetite; but an attack from the outside designed to arouse concupiscent passions would come from enticement. One can imagine a siege of a "virgin bright" like Alma in which enticement poses a threat because the virtuous also have appetites and emotions. But the enticements and the passions aroused would logically proceed, especially in the virtuous, by subterfuge. As Wright says, "For these rebellious Passions are like craftie Pyoners [miners], who, while Souldiers liue carelessly within their Castle . . . [,] vndermine the vnderstandings of men . . . [and creep] vp into their hearts" (69–70). In such a siege the senses would serve as entrances to the higher faculties, as weak places in or under the walls rather than as "Bulwarke[s]" or "fort[s]" (xi.10).

Maleger's siege proceeds through an open bombardment of the castle walls; and the troops as well as their weapons are, in the main, too repulsive to represent enticements—only beauty and money would serve as such. The other "wicked engins" used in the attack on sight, "lawlesse lustes, corrupt enuyes,/And couetous aspects," are more like the practices of those who have habitually yielded to enticement, an impression solidified by the attack on the sense of taste. Not only are the latter troops repulsive, their repulsiveness is the product of the practices represented by their weapons. They are "a grysie rablement . . . Like loathly Toades, some fashioned in the waste/Like swine" and armed with "luxury,/Surfeat, misdiet, and vnthriftie waste,/Vaine feasts, and ydle superfluity" (xi.8–12). As Kellogg and Steele observe, to understand the attack as the threat posed by the passions to the reason (as they do) is to stipulate allegorical meanings for the troops rather than to infer those meanings from appearances.[16]

Nevertheless, the subversion of the deliberative faculties is the initial stage of the assault on humankind that Maleger effects through his agents. In this episode that stage is supplied through statement in the introductory stanzas: each describes a sequence beginning with the subversion of the higher faculties and ending with the creation of monsters corrupted in mind and flesh. The result of bodies turned into monsters is explicit in the introduction to canto ix and implicit in that to canto xi through its focus on the "captiuitie," "bondage," and "vellenage" resulting from passions cultivated into vices, a process facilitated by the 'infirmitie/Of the fraile flesh":

> What warre so cruel, or what siege so sore,
>   As that, which strong affections doe apply
>   Against the forte of reason euermore
>   To bring the sowle into captiuity:
>   Their force is fiercer through infirmity
>   Of the fraile flesh, relenting to their rage,
>   And exercise most bitter tyranny
>   Vpon the partes, brought into their bondage:
> No wretchednesse is like to sinful vellenage.

Understanding the attack of Maleger's troops as only part of Maleger's assault on humankind focuses attention on Acrasia's subversion of the hierarchy of faculties. And the consequent understanding of the complex of Maleger's agents focuses attention on the role of Maleger himself.

More physiology will clarify the nature of our physical being and Maleger's appropriateness as the agent who attacks that being through the "course of kinde." In his initial introductory chapter, Crooke describes four excellencies of the human body, all of which recall commonplaces in Alma's Castle. Three excellencies are absolute. The first is "an vpright frame and proportion, that . . . [we] might behold & meditate on heauenly things" (5). The third is "due proportion, composition or correspondencie of the parts of Mans body," illustrated by Crooke's description of the Vitruvian man with arms and legs outstretched and forming a perfect circle with an enclosed quadrate. This, Crooke says in words applicable to Spenser's most obviously numerological stanza (ix.22), is the "true quadrature of the circle, not those imaginarie lines whereof Archimedes wrot, and which haue troubled the heads of all our Mathematitions for many ages, when as euery one might haue found it in himselfe" (6). The fourth and last excellence is that the human body constitutes "a Little world, and the paterne and epitome of the whole vniuerse" (6). The second excellence, the body's temper, however, is not absolute. Its excellence is that, unlike the other creatures that are "either too Earthy, or too Watry," "Man hath . . . a moderate Temper, and is indeed the most temperate of all Bodies . . . ." The temper of human flesh is necessary to human complexity and adaptability: "[T]he Matter of Man's body . . . is soft, plyable and temperate, ready to follow the Workeman [the corporeal soul], in euerie thing and to euerie purpose" (4–5). The complexion of a body must be adequate to the complexity of its corporeal soul. The simple complexion of plants, for example, allows only for a vegetable soul capable of nutrition, augmentation, and reproduction. But the temper of flesh necessary to actualize the complex human soul is a prime source of human frailty. Our moderate temper makes us vulnerable to imbalances of various kinds, including those moderns call diseases, because we are "equally distant from both extreames" (5). (This passage is pertinent also to the physiology of Guyon's faint and to his earlier astonishment.)

In a later introductory chapter, Crooke presents a starker view of our physical temper. The postlapsarian body, he says, is "but the Sepulchre of that which God at first created . . . infirme and weakely defended":

To death and diseases [imbalances] we lye open on euery side.
The World is a Sea, the accidents and diuers occurrents in it

are Waues, wherin this small Barke is vexed, tossed, and beaten
vp and downe, and there is betwixt vs and our dissolution, not
an inch boord, but a tender skinne, which the slenderest violence euen the cold aire is able to slice through.

(61)

The resemblance of Crooke's observation to Alma's Castle is not
merely a product of their shared commonplaces. Apparently our com-
parative longevity, despite the fragility of our flesh, moved Crooke
to quote the numerological description of Alma's Castle ("The frame
thereof seemd partly circulare, / And part triangulare, O worke diu-
ine," and so forth [ix.22]) in its entirety. Then, together with the
remark on the quadrate cited earlier, he provides the very first commentary on that much-discussed stanza: "So that trueth to say, it is
not the matter, whose commencements are dust, and consummation
clay, but the excellent proportion and structure that maketh this
Paper-sconce high perill-proofe" (61).

Crooke's comment accurately reflects Spenser's ambivalent view
of the castle-body. Sometimes the focus is on the stability provided
by its form (of which Alma's "sober gouernment" is an aspect) even
though the Castle is under constant attack. At other times the emphasis is on the brevity of life inherent in that made of "*AEgyptian* slime"
(fertile Nile mud as in III.vi.8, also the slime from which the Vulgate
says Adam was formed): "But O great pitty, that no lenger time / So
goodly workemanship should not endure: / Soone it must turne to
earth; no earthly thing is sure" (ix.21). In addition to reminding
readers of their ephemerality, the transitory castle-body reinforces
the significance of the Palmer's advanced age. In the earlier episodes
his age enables a control of the emotions denied to the youthful
Guyon. Now the Palmer's age reminds us that, in "the course of
kinde," Guyon's youth is temporary.

Maleger conducts the siege by marshaling his troops, but he exercises his own power in his combat with Arthur. Maleger's attributes
and capacities represent a complex of forces—disease, decay, cold,
the desiccation of age, and death itself—against which the postlapsarian body is inherently vulnerable no matter how we conduct our-
selves. Maleger wears a skull as a helmet (xi.22). He is of "such subtile
substance and vnsound, / That like a ghost he seem'd, whose graue-
clothes were vnbound" (20). He is withered: "pale and wan as ashes"
and "lean and meagre as a rake" (22). These reflections of weakness,
as has often been noted, are the sources of Maleger's power, he being
"most strong in most infirmitee" (40). Maleger's arrows can inflict

wounds beyond the curative power of any medicine, "so inly they did tine" (21); and Arthur's apparently imminent death at the hands of Maleger evokes a lament on mortality. That Maleger "lives" but without blood, heart, or vital spirits ("Flesh without blood, a person without spright" [40]) makes him immune to normal injury and also reflects his power over the normal life processes in human beings. Arthur defeats Maleger by separating him from the earth, that to which all mortal creatures return and, consequently, the source of Maleger's "life."

And so, finally, to address the question of the essay directly, Maleger's power exercised through his functionaries is profitably distinguished from that exercised through his own capacities. Guyon, aided by the Palmer, captures Acrasia; and the pair could have defeated Maleger's troops because vices result from the subversion of the hierarchy of faculties, the correction of which is the Palmer's specialty. Why, if the temperance team is capable of defeating Maleger's troops, do we not see them do so in the poem? Perhaps in an earlier stage of the poem's composition, Guyon and the Palmer were given that task. That Guyon and Arthur are traveling together at the beginning of Book III having been cured of their wounds by Alma (III.i.1) cannot be explained by the fiction of Book II.[17] In any event, the choice of Guyon, with or without the Palmer, to defend the Castle against Maleger would have obscured an important theme in Book II because both Guyon and the Palmer embody the physical weaknesses on which Maleger preys. In addition to Guyon's other frailties, the energy and strength of youth proves through the "course of kinde" to have been a delusion. Guyon and the Palmer leave the Castle and proceed to the Bower of Bliss and to a task for which the two, as a team, is well suited.

Two phrases describing Maleger, "cold and dreary as a Snake" and "withered like a dryed rooke" (22), relate Maleger to the "course of kinde" with special clarity. A predominance of heat and moisture is necessary to life; cold and dry militate against life when they do more than temper warmth and moisture. The danger that cold poses to life "by occasion" has been featured in the essay; the cold and desiccation wielded by Maleger progresses inevitably. Crooke tells us that

This forme we call Life . . . continueth so long therein, as it is supplied with nourishment, which nourishment is the radical moysture of the spermaticall parts [the white, structural parts of the body generated from the combined male and female seeds]. Nature therefore being not able to generate anie part of seede whose moysture should not in time bee exhausted, could not produce any particular creature eternall or immutable."

(198)

Crooke does not explain how radical moisture nourishes life and why the moisture "must in time bee exhausted," but André du Laurens does. He says vital or radical heat is nourished by moisture in the same way as the flame of a lamp is nourished by the oil. The radical moisture is in time exhausted because although it is continually replenished by arterial blood, that blood's moisture is not as rarefied, as highly concocted, as that in the seed which originally formed the spermatical parts of the body. Seed is the product of a further concoction in the testicles. Consequently, du Lauren says, "the radicall heate and moisture waxe weaker and weaker euery houre, by the coupling of them with new nourishment, which is alwaies infected with some aduersarie and vnlike qualitie."[18]

The theological implications of the weaknesses and limitations found in Guyon and the Palmer resonate in the choice of Arthur to contend with Maleger and in the demise of Maleger in "a standing lake" (46). Even though Arthur's characterization in Book II lacks the evidences of grace—his shield, for example, is mentioned only once, in canto viii, and is covered—his appearance in Book II evokes irresistible theological implication. This does not mean, however, that Guyon necessarily either takes on or is limited to such significance. Understanding the move from Mammon's underworld to Alma's Castle to the Bower of Bliss to reflect a development or progression within Guyon depends upon borrowing a sense of progression from Book I; and to make the transfer, critics have understood Guyon's stay in Alma's Castle to compare to Redcrosse's stay in the House of Holinesse (see especially Hamilton, *Structure of Allegory*, 101–02). But rather than having been educated or reformed by any of his experiences in the latter episodes, Guyon is at least as dependent on the Palmer in the final episode as he was at the beginning of Book II.

Whatever significance we may see in Arthur's disposal of Maleger, Guyon's quest as an expression of temperance, a secular or even pagan virtue, has a major role in the grand theme of *The Faerie Queene*, indeed the grand theme of Spenser's poetry: the search for, the striving after, stability in a world of change. Physical temperance, the temperance of hot and cold and of wet and dry, is essential to the maintenance of life; and psychic temperance is essential to the sustained exercise of purposeful activity necessary to civil life. The expression of temperance, both physical and psychic, however, is confined to the actualizations of the individual corporeal soul and consequently, unlike holiness (through the immortal soul) and chaste love (through offspring), temperance offers no remedy for the "course of kinde."

Indiana State University, emeritus

NOTES

1. All citations to the poem are from *The Faerie Queene*, edited by A. C. Hamilton (London: Longman, 2001). The text is edited by Hiroshi Yamashita and Toshiyuki Suzuki.

Beginning with A. S. P. Woodhouse ("Nature and Grace in *The Faerie Queene*," *ELH* 16 [1949]: 194–228) and continuing through efforts to bridge Woodhouse's separation of nature from grace (importantly in A. C. Hamilton's *The Structure of Allegory in* The Faerie Queene [Oxford University Press, 1961]), Maleger has, in the main, been understood as a threat to the immortal soul and consequently a force beyond the capacities of temperance, a threat that could be met only by Arthur as an agent of grace or a Christ figure. Philip Rollinson ("Arthur, Maleger, and the Interpretation of *The Faerie Queene*," *Spenser Studies* 7 [1986]: 103–21) has worked to revive the secular view of Maleger as misrule and Arthur as magnificence. Rollinson also thoroughly and fairly documents opposed views of Maleger as misrule and as original sin.

The theological implications of Arthur's defeat of Maleger are both inescapable and perplexing. Arthur's disposal of Maleger in a "standing lake" has been read as baptism although the water is static, even, perhaps, stagnant rather than flowing and although Maleger is already dead and even if alive would not be baptizable. Hamilton reads the act analogically as Ruddymane's baptism (*Structure of Allegory*, 115). For Darryl Gless, the event is only semi-baptismal: "Arthur's action symbolizes, that is, the destructive first half of any experience of spiritual renewal, which always includes both a death and a rebirth, as in baptisms" (*Interpretation and Theology in Spenser* [Cambridge: Cambridge University Press, 1994], 191). Despite the difficulties, if one reads Book II theologically, there is no plausible alternative, as Harold Weatherby observes, to an identification of the lake as the font (*Mirrors of Celestial Grace: Patristic Theology in Spenser's Allegory* [Toronto: University of Toronto Press, 1994], 186).

Brief references to Maleger as mortality appear in the *Variorum* commentary; James Carscallen's "The Goodly Frame of Temperance: The Metaphor of Cosmos in *The Faerie Queene*," *UTQ* 37 (1968), reprinted in *Essential Articles for the Study of Edmund Spenser*, edited by A. C. Hamilton (Hamden: Archon Books, 1972), 361; and James Nohrnberg's *The Analogy of* The Faerie Queene (Princeton: Princeton University Press, 1976), 321–22. Maurice Evans (*Spenser's Anatomy of Heroism: A Commentary on* The Faerie Queene [Cambridge: Cambridge University Press, 1970], 134–35, understands Maleger as the mortality consequent upon sin. Weatherby's extensive treatment of Maleger as mortality as viewed by the eastern fathers (*Mirrors of Celestial Grace*, 179–87) has been most helpful to me. I do not follow Weatherby in the specifics of his argument, either in his theological reading of Book II or, in particular, his use of the patristic view of the passions "not as natural impulses to be governed by reason but as diseases of the soul and legacies of the Fall to be extirpated by an ascetical mortification . . . ." (114). My debt to *Mirrors of Celestial Grace* is that it rescued me from equating Maleger with original sin.

David Quint anatomizes Book II as epic and uses Platonic rather than Aristotelian-Galenic psychology; nevertheless, his conclusion about Arthur's defeat of Maleger is similar to that advanced in the present essay:

> In this case allegorical internalization boils down the heroic impulse, perhaps the impulse of all human endeavor, to a struggle against biological necessi-ty . . . . It is a victory of sorts, a partial victory over the bodily decay that Maleger represents. But Spenser's fiction also draws a darker conclusion: the fight with Maleger is one that no mere epic hero can win (The Hugh Maclean Memorial Lecture 2002, "The Anatomy of Epic in Book 2 of *The Faerie Queene*," *The Spenser Review*, 34.1 [2003]: 40).

Maleger appears as something completely different from the above in what Harry Berger, Jr. ("Narrative as Rhetoric in *The Faerie Queene*," *ELR* 21 [1991]: 1–48) calls the "suspicious" readings of Madelon Gohlke and Lauren Silberman, readings in which temperance rather than intemperance is the object of critique (18). Berger does not discuss Maleger in his own "suspicious" reading of Book II; but for Gohlke ("Embattled Allegory: Book II of *The Faerie Queene*," *ELR* 8 [1978]: 123–40), "[t]he temperate body appears as a fortress built specifically to exclude the pleasures of the senses, which appear as violent, monstrous, and grotesque" (130). For Silberman (*The Faerie Queene*, Book II and the Limitations of Temperance," *MLS* 17 [1987]: 9–22), the Castle's defenses against the attack reflect the inability of temperance to cope with "sensual experience" (17, 18) or "sensuality" (18), Maleger's troops being understood to represent passions as perceived through the distortion of temperance.

2.   Paul Alpers, *The Poetry of* The Faerie Queene, (Princeton: Princeton University Press, 1967), 265; James Nohrnberg, *Analogy*, 297–99. Richard D. Jordan (*The Quiet Hero: Figures of Temperance in Spenser, Donne, Milton, and Joyce* [Washington: Catholic University of America Press, 1989], 31) explains the faint as "the natural result of too quick an exposure to fresh air after three days in underground fumes." Peter Stambler ("The Development of Guyon's Christian Faith," *ELR* 7 [1977]: 51–89) reads the "vitall aire" as baptismal: "With that breath he is 'ouercome as with too exceeding might.' Guyon seems to have undergone the kind of baptism—not the symbolic immersion, but the thing itself . . . ." (73). The scholarship on the faint has been summarized recently by Richard Mallette, *Spenser and the Discourses of Reformation England* (Lincoln: University of Nebraska Press, 1997), 238–39, notes 43 and 44, and by Weatherby, *Mirrors of Celestial Grace*, 132–39. Weatherby's use of the pre-Augustine and Greek fathers on the passions and on our inheritance from Adam provides a critical perspective on interpretations of the faint deriving from the west-ern, or Augustinian, view.

3. Helkiah Crooke, ΜΙΚΡΟΚΟΣΜΟΓΡΑΦΙΑ. *A Description of the Body of Man. Together With The Controversies Thereto Belonging. Collected and Translated out of all the Best Authors of Anatomy, Especially out of Gasper Bauhinus and Andreas Laurentius* (1615; 1631 ed., 373).

Renaissance psychology posited a soul as the source of life and then proceeded to explain how the soul manifested itself in activity. Spirits enabled the faculties of the soul to actualize their powers until well after Spenser, when chemical reaction and electricity began to provide alternatives. From Crooke:

> the distance is not so great betweene the highest Heauen and the lowest Earth, as is the difference betwixt the Soule and the Bodye. It was therefore verie necessary that a spirite should be created, by whose intermediate Nature, (as it were by a strong though not indissoluble bonde) the Diuine soule might be tyed to the bodie of Earth . . . Our definition of a spirit . . . *A subtile and thinne body always moouable, engendred of blood and vapour, and the vehicle or carriage of the Faculties of the soul.* (373–74)

Crooke's 1012 folio pages provide details not found in the popular compendia of medicine and anatomy and also a thorough account of what he called in his preface to the Barber-Chyrurgeons "the Principles and Theory or Contemplatiue part of your profession," both of which have been essential to my comprehension of the physiology in *The Legend of Temperaunce.*

C. D. O'Malley ("Helkiah Crooke, M. D., F. R. C. P., 1576–1648," *Bulletin of the History of Medicine* 42 [1968]: 1–18) notes that Crooke "gave allegiance to the conservative opinion, sometimes first presenting the new, correct description of some anatomical structure, but then closing his eyes upon what he had just written and subscribing to the older, incorrect, and often Galenic doctrine" (12). What for O'Malley is unfortunate retrogression has been essential to my purposes.

Recent interest in the Renaissance body has made Crooke fashionable. My *Spenser's Allegory of Love: Social Vision in Books III, IV, and V of* The Faerie Queene (Madison: Fairleigh Dickinson University Press, 1995) leans heavily on Crooke. Jonathan Sawday (*The Body Emblazoned: Dissection and the Human Body in Renaissance Culture,* [London: Routledge, 1995], 167–70) argues that in Crooke's anatomy "can be glimpsed Spenser's vision of self-reflection, culled from Crooke's reading of *The Faerie Queene* (167). And references to Crooke appear throughout a collection of essays, *The Body in Parts: Fantasies of Corporeality in Early Modern Europe,* edited by David Hillman and Carla Mazzio (New York: Routledge, 1997). Gail Kern Paster's contribution, "Nervous Tension: Networks of Blood and Spirit in the Early Modern Body," is especially dependent on Crooke.

Unlike the physiological, the more psychic actualizations of Guyon's and the Palmer's corporeal souls are for the most part adequately understood and are readily accessible by reference to Thomas Wright's much used, comprehensive, and more than usually analytical treatise, *The Passions of the Minde in Generall,* 1601.

4. Galen accounts for the creation in the heart of vital heat (essential to, if not quite the same as, life in the sense of vivification) through an analogy to the generation of observable flames. Every flame "requires the surrounding air to be cold in

due proportion, for the excessively hot, by making . . . [the flame's] outward motion out of proportion, and the excessively cold its inward motion [out of proportion], both quench it . . . ." Working securely within his core principles, Galen understood that a properly functioning flame requires a balance of opposing forces, a temperance of hot and cold. Summing up the physiological implications, he followed his mentors, Aristotle and Hippocrates, and declared that the principal use of breathing is "for regulation of heat" (*Galen on respiration and the arteries*, translated and edited by David J. Furley and J. S. Wilkie (Princeton: Princeton University Press, 1984), 133). Consequently, for the next fifteen hundred years the respiratory system was believed to achieve that purpose in the way stipulated by Galen.

The centrality of the heart in Galenic physiology is apparent when its role in generating "vital heat" is contrasted to that of its essential but different role in modern physiology to move blood so that metabolic processes can generate "vital heat" in individual cells.

5.   Weatherby ("Spenser's Legend of Temperance," *SP*   93 [1996]: 207–17) makes a convincing argument that Spenser followed the sixteenth century translators of the Bible rather than Aristotle and followers (Cicero, Aquinas, Castiglione, translators of the *Ethics*, et al.) and used "temperance" to denote control of all passions, thereby limiting "continence" to the control of sexual desire. Weatherby's essay most helpfully obviates unrewarding attempts to accommodate the vocabulary of temperance in Book II to Aristotle's. More important for my purposes, Weatherby's demonstration that capacity could differentiate "temperance" from "continence" indicates that the further capacity of "temperance" to include the physiological could be important to *The Legend of Temperaunce*.

6.   Michael Schoenfeldt, "Spenser's Castle of Moral Health," chapter 2 in his *Bodies and Selves in Early Modern England: Physiology and Inwardness in Spenser, Shakespeare, Herbert, and Milton*, Cambridge Studies in Renaissance and Culture 34 (Cambridge: Cambridge University Press, 1999). E. Ruth Harvey, *The Inward Wits: Psychological Theory in the Middle Ages and the Renaissance* (London: The Warburg Institute, 1975), 17.

7.   Edward Jorden describes a comparable effect of a fit of the mother on the respiratory system (*A Briefe Discourse of a Disease Called the Suffocation of the Mother*, 1603, 6–7).

8.   Hugh MacLachlan, "The Death of Guyon and *The Elizabethan Book of Homilies*," *Spenser Studies* 4 (1983): 97. Treatment of Spenser's creations as fictional personages has been unfashionable for some time. C. S. Lewis cautioned us not to concentrate on passages such as the conversation between the lovesick Britomart and her nurse: "The novel calls for characters with insides; but there are other kinds of narrative that do not" (*Spenser's Images of Life*, edited by Alastair Fowler (Cambridge: Cambridge University Press, 1967], 113. Lewis does not deny "insides" to Britomart; he insists that they are unimportant to the allegory. Thomas Roche explicitly denies to Spenser's creations the kind of insides novelists trick us into accepting for their creations. For Roche, "character" is a misnomer because "no figure in Spenser has an interior life that lets us ascribe our judgments to that figure's actions in the poem" ("Britomart's at Busyrane's Again, or, Brideshead Revisited," *Spenser at Kalamazoo 1983*, edited by Francis G. Greco, [Clarion: Clarion University

Press, 1983], 140). In part and in effect, Lewis and Roche object to the use of modern psychology as a framework within which to understand Spenser's characters.

Those who avoid story in *The Faerie Queene* are more unlikely to treat Spenser's creations as characters. Weatherby says "Or perhaps, since neither is a character in a fiction, we can say that Alma is simply Ruddymane in another allegorical context—Ruddymane, let us say, after he has been taught by Medina" (*Mirrors of Celestial Grace*, 185). Alpers says Spenser's creations are not "coherent dramatic individuals" but "congeries of characteristics that [Spenser] can exploit to reveal fundamental realities of all human personality" ("Review Article: How to Read *The Faerie Queene,*" *Essays in Criticism* 18 [1968]: 434). I think Maleger fits Alpers's description of Spenserian characterization better than does Guyon.

On the other hand, in less argumentative *Spenser Encyclopedia* articles, Spenser's creations appear as characters or fictional personages as a matter of course. R. Rawdon Wilson ("Character") specifies for Spenser's major characters "attributes and conflicts that do not belong altogether to allegory but rather to romances and the heroic poem" and "typify the human possibilities of their virtues." For Maurice Evans ("Guyon"), Guyon is "not simply an abstract virtue but a character whose temptations and adventures demonstrate the nature and practice of his virtue." And Darryl Gless ("Nature and Grace") declares that Guyon is "above all a representative man seeking to live by the virtue of which he is the patron." (*The Spenser Encyclopedia*, edited by A. C. Hamilton [Toronto: Toronto University Press, 1990]).

9. Subsequent annotations in Hamilton's Longman editions will be identified as such in the text. Those in the body of the essay are from the 1977 edition.

10. Thomas Wright, *The Passions of the Minde in Generall*, 1601, ed. 1621, p. 8.

11. Bacon, *The Advancement of Learning*, quoted by Herschell Baker in *The Dignity of Man*, (Cambridge: Harvard University Press, 1947), reprinted as *The Image of Man* (New York: Harper and Row, 1961), 285.

12. For Guyon's attack on Redcrosse as sin, see Gless, *Interpretation and Theology*, 178–79.

13. This translation from the original Hebrew was posted to Medsci-L on December 24, 1996 by Tzvi Langermann, National Library, Jerusalem. In the published English translation edited by C. B. Chavel, *Commentary on the Torah by Moshe ben Nachem (Nochmanides)* (Jerusalem, 1962), the passage appears in Vol. 1, 244.

14. Una's collapses, each caused by her fears for Redcrosse, are similar to the collapse suffered Guyon at the sight of Mordant and family. When Archimago reports that Redcrosse is dead, sorrow disables Una's heart and its vital spirits causing an oppression of her senses:

> That cruell word [i.e., "death"] her tender hart so thrild,
>   That suddein cold did ronne through euerie vaine,
> And stony horrour all her sences fild
>   With dying fitt, that downe she fell for paine.
>
> (I.vi.37)

Her collapse upon seeing the dwarf with Redcrosse's armor is even more serious:

> She fell to ground for sorrowfull regret,

> And liuely breath her sad brest did forsake,
> Yet might her pitteous hart be seene to pant and quake.

> (I.vii.20)

She suffers three relapses before her "life" finally "recouer'd had the raine,/ And ouer-wrestled his strong enimy" (24). Una's life and her love for Redcrosse, both of which are centered in her heart, are indivisible. When she recovers from seeing Redcrosse's armor, she asks why she should continue to live, why her eyes should "feed on loathed light"

> Sith cruell fates the carefull threds vnfould
> The which my life and loue together tyde.

> (I.vii.22)

15.   Harry Berger, Jr., *The Allegorical Temper: Vision and Reality in Book II of Spenser's* Faerie Queene (New Haven: Yale University Press, 1957) esp. 10–11.

16.   Edmund Spenser, *Books I and II of* The Faerie Queene, *The Mutability Cantos, and Selections from the Minor Poetry*, edited by Robert Kellogg and Oliver Steele (Indianapolis: Bobbs-Merrill, 1965), 72. Not only is the siege unlike an assault of passions, the interior of the Castle is not organized as a fort of reason. Indeed, the interior of the Castle is not organized to defend against a threat of any kind. The activities there seem unrelated to the siege until the walls are about to collapse and Arthur is called upon to save Alma and her Castle.

I do not think the interior of the Castle relates significantly to the siege—I dwell on this as a way of responding to a problem in the fictional situation from my point of view: why would a host of vices be attacking the body of a young and virtuous lady? Within the Castle we observe Alma, the corporeal soul, functioning through her vegetable, sensible, and intellectual faculties as those faculties engage in daily activities. Lewis H. Miller ascribes the quietude of the interior to the presence of Guyon, which quells the passions, and so the siege resumes upon his departure ("Arthur, Maleger, and History in the Allegorical Context," *UTQ* 35 [1966]: 177). However, although Guyon and the Palmer are able by various means to quiet passions, nowhere else has Guyon been thought to do so simply by his presence.

For Gohlke and Silberman (see: note 1), the siege reflects an internal, a psychological dislocation of some kind, but no emotions concerning the siege are expressed in the parlor-heart. The visit to the turret most clearly separates the interior of the Castle from the attack of Maleger's troops because the faculties there, which one would expect to be instrumental in resisting such a siege, do not combine to form a defensive complex. Nor do they reflect an achieved indifference to passion or a resistance or immunity to vice. Each of the three sages is busily looking after those affairs most suitable to his stage of life: the youthful Phantastes "could things to come foresee"; the mature, unnamed but clearly cogitative, reflective figure in the middle room "could of thinges present best aduize"; and old Eumnestes "things past could keepe in memoree" (ix.49). The stability reflected in this complex of figures does not derive from control of passions. If the middle sage is to advise of things present, he must be able properly to meditate on the images of "lawes, of iudgements, and of decretals;/All artes, all science, all Philosophy" (53). And to do so, he must have access to the past as well as to projections about the future. The stability reflected in the turret is that generally achieved by imaginative insight, careful thought, and knowledge and is consequently unrelated to any particular circumstance such as a siege by vices or passions. (Of course, if the siege were proceeding by subterfuge rather than through a bombardment of the walls, it would be appropriate for the personified faculties to go carelessly about their daily activities).

Lynette C. Black says that the three sages constitute Wise Counsel and argues that Guyon's visit to the turret results in an acquisition of prudence that enables his victory over Acrasia ("Prudence in Book II of *The Faerie Queene*," *Spenser Studies* 13 [1999]: 65–88, esp. 70, 77–78). But neither the siege nor Arthur's combat with Maleger figures in Black's argument. Nor do they figure in David Lee Miller's Lacanian analysis of the Castle (*The Poem's Two Bodies: The Poetics of the 1590 Faerie Queene* [Princeton: Princeton University Press, 1988], 164–214). Miller refers briefly to Maleger's troops as they appear in canto ix (185), but he does not discuss canto xi and he does not mention Maleger. In a "footnote to Miller's account of cantos ix and x," Berger connects interior and exterior for Miller's "suspicious" reading, but the connection depends upon accepting Maleger's troops as affections:

> The strong affections that do not evade the repressive defenses of castrative sublimation are expelled outside "the fort of reason" (xi.i) which, under Maleger's leadership, they have besieged for seven years, forcing the well-tempered body to keep its "gates fast barred . . . /And every loup fast lockt, as fearing foes despight" (ix.10) ("Narrative as Rhetoric," 34).

17.   In the 2001 Longman edition, Hamilton's annotation of III.i.1 follows Upton's inference that Guyon had returned to Alma's Castle where Arthur is recuperating from his wounds:

> The famous Briton Prince and Faery knight,
>   After long wayes and perilous paines endur'd,
>   Hauing their weary limbes to perfect plight
>   Restord, and sory wounds right well recur'd,
>   Of the faire *Alma* greatly were procur'd,
>   To make there lenger soiourne and abode;
>   But when thereto they might not be allur'd,
>   From seeking praise, and deeds of armes abrode,
> They courteous conge tooke, and forth together yode.
>
> (III.i.1)

Thus, according to Upton and Hamilton, only Guyon has endured the "long wayes and perilous paines" and has had his "weary limbes" restored; and only Arthur has suffered "sory wounds" that have been "right well recur'd." The stanza can be so read (with some effort), but even so it is nothing more than a patch on a bad connection in the narrative. The stanza can also be read as a remnant of an earlier version of the poem in which Guyon (and the Palmer?) defeat Maleger's troops and Arthur defeats Maleger.

18.   André du Laurens, *A Discourse of the Preservation of Sight; of Rheumes, and of Old Age*, translated by Richard Surphlet, 1599.

RAPHAEL LYNE

Grille's Moral Dialogue: Spenser and Plutarch

Guyon and the Palmer do not have much time for the opinions of Grille, the recalcitrant pig who complains at being released from Acrasia's enchantment. But Grille has literary antecedents (in Plutarch, Montaigne, Erasmus, Gelli and others) who add to his impact on the reader's experience. Spenser does not give an explicit role to the tradition in which Grille's predecessors' views – ironically or otherwise—have some validity. Nevertheless it has a role, partly because Spenser's character resonates with tradition, and partly because the silencing of Grille might actually heighten interest in what he has to say. The story is a microcosm of *The Faerie Queene* in more than one way. It shows the rich and complex interaction between the poem and its contexts. It also shows the tense interaction between the central threads of meaning in the allegory and the other possibilities that the poem evokes.

T HE FINAL TWO STANZAS of Book II of *The Faerie Queene* briefly introduce the figure of Grille to the ruins of the Bower of Bliss. The recalcitrant pig who refuses to be freed from Acrasia's enchantment provides a curious discordant note despite the confident condemnation of Guyon and the Palmer. His brief appearance invokes the story of the classical Gryllus, one of Odysseus' companions who prefers to stay under Circe's spell, a story most memorably found in Plutarch's *Moralia*. Grille also calls up the myriad intervening versions of his story, versions that form a complex web of related threads from which significant contradictory dynamics emerge. Modern readers of Spenser have straightforward access to this intertextual web, through such resources as the *Spenser Encyclopedia*, the notes to A. C. Hamilton's edition, and critical works, with James Nohrnberg's *The Analogy of "The Faerie Queene"* to the fore.[1] Which of its dynamics

159

governs the mood of the end of Book II is a complex but significant question.

Literary reference resources provide the raw material for establishing connections, but they tend not to explore the implications of
the emerging contradictions between authorities. In establishing the
purpose of the story of Grille they usually associate Spenser's meaning
with those sources that align best with the main thread of Book II,
namely those who condemn Grille's example. As will be seen, not
all writers before Spenser present an opinionated pig who attracts
pure condemnation. Furthermore, the attempts in modern reference
resources to reconstruct the characteristic literary associations of a
contemporary reader (perhaps an ideal contemporary reader) do not
always register the nuances of these associations when they contrast
with one another. This is not just a question of space or decorous
practicality; it is also testimony to a real problem in reading Spenser's
poem. In this tiny example the strange richness of *The Faerie Queene*
comes through: so adept at making connections, it then confronts
the reader with the problem of unscrambling mixed messages. The
solution does not simply lie in a moral ambiguity that has often been
identified in the end of Book II. It also encompasses the tone of
Spenser's epic, and the attitudes and moods that it struggles to embrace. Grille/Gryllus proves a curious, indirect, short-lived, yet pene-
trating commentator on Spenser's project.

The two stanzas that tell Grille's story are succinct. Their brevity
might be read as forestalling the character's complex connections.
Indeed, there is nothing explicit in these lines that invites the reader
to attempt a reading against the stated significance of the grumbling
hog. However, such a counter-interpretation might still exist in the
reader's response, especially because the terse conclusion to Book II
reads as if it is introducing, inhibiting, and silencing the character
quickly before moving on:

> Streight way he with his vertuous staffe them strooke,
>   And streight of beasts they comely men became;
>   Yet being men they did unmanly looke,
>   And stared ghastly, some for inward shame,
>   And some for wrath, to see their captive Dame:
>   But one above the rest in speciall,
>   That had an hog beene late, hight *Grille* by name,

Repined greatly, and did him miscall,
That had from hoggish forme him brought to naturall.

(*FQ* II.xii.86)[2]

The end of Book II is often compared with the end of Book V, where Envy, Detraction, and the Blatant Beast darken the success of the knight of Justice. They are both incursions of an unregenerate sinful humanity that will not yield to virtue. The end of Book V, however, is more grim and shocking, and it reverberates more strongly through the following book. Grille, despite or because of the complex literary tradition surrounding his antecedents, recedes quickly. Nevertheless he may leave an impression. Readers of *The Faerie Queene* are used to dealing with coded names, and to thinking laterally in response to images in the stories. This name leads in directions that, to the observers within the text, seem easily mapped:

Said *Guyon*, See the mind of beastly man,
   That hath so soone forgot the excellence
   Of his creation, when he life began,
   That now he chooseth, with vile difference,
   To be a beast, and lacke intelligence.
   To whom the Palmer thus, The donghill kind
   Delights in filth and foule incontinence:
   Let *Grill* be *Grill*, and have his hoggish mind,
But let us hence depart, whilest wether serves and wind.

(*FQ* II.xii.87)

There is something smug (or worse—even sinister) about this, as the conquering pair share a clear view of the incident. They agree on the basic moral interpretation of the story, one that aligns with the current of Book II while accepting that virtue is the individual's business at the last, and those like Grille are beyond salvation.[3] James Nohrnberg is right to emphasize the importance of the forgetfulness of the metamorphosed pig: it is clear that he has made a morally wrong choice.[4] However, he is basing this judgment on Guyon's interpretation of the scene. The short sharp story has caused many readers to sympathize with Grille in an affectionate way, and it also creates interest in the things he does not get to say in his defence—not least because he has such well-known literary predecessors. Grille has more to say for himself in other versions of the story, and in the experience of Spenser's readers, as a result, he may not meekly lie down despite the strong truncation of his appearance. This is an interesting instance of a clash between the poem's capacity (its vast range of reference and intersection) and its remarkable clarity of purpose (often if not always visible). Here understatement serves both causes, preserving clarity, but hinting as eloquently as any copious exploration that there is much more to this than can be included.[5]

In the emblem tradition, specifically in the *Pegma* of Pierre Coustau (Costalius), the explication of Gryllus aligns with that of Guyon and the Palmer. He is the embodiment of how essentially evil people choose vice and cannot be persuaded from it.[6] This work may be a source for the physical configuration of the Graces in *Faerie Queene* VI, so Spenser could well have seen the Gryllus emblem.[7] The influential *Mythologiae* of Natalis Comes (Natale Conti) gives a version of the Odysseus-Circe story, and the transformation of his companions, which brings it close to Spenser's interests. Like Guyon a figure of temperance, Odysseus stays strong while others give in to animal emotions:

Atque ut summatim dicam; per hanc fabulam significare voluerunt antiqui sapientem virum in utraque fortuna oportere se moderatè gubernare, et ad omnes difficultates invictum consistere, cum reliqua multitudo tanquam levissima navis huc illuc fluctibus deferatur, et quocumque ventorum inconstantia impulerit: quare mutati fuerunt in belluas Ulyssis socii, cum ipse invictus ob sapientiam, quae verè est Dei munus, perstiterit.[8]

I summarise it like this: through this fable the ancients wanted to indicate that the wise man should rule himself with moderation in every eventuality, and that he should remain uncorrupted in the face of all difficulties, since everyone else is carried hither and thither by the sea like the lightest ship. This is why the companions of Ulysses were changed into beasts, while he remained unbeaten thanks to his wisdom, which is certainly a gift from God.

Earlier Comes attributes the transformations to the particular lusts of the shipmates, and these are contrasted with the man who behaves "moderatè," temperately. Given his long voyage, there is a degree of irony in seeing Odysseus as the temperate man and others as the ones tossed about on the waves. Gryllus is not mentioned, but temperance is in fact a key issue in many of the versions of his story. In commentary that sees this episode as a coda working within the moral theme of the book, other passages are recruited to the cause. The Bible gives images of those who refuse to bend to morality: Revelation 22.11 says that the filthy man should remain filthy; 2 Peter 2.22 cites dogs returning to their vomit, and pigs wallowing in dirt, as examples of the same. Plotinus is a classical authority that pigs, specifically, are not good at controlling themselves.[9] Another voice to line up on this side is Calvin, in whose *Institutio Religionis Christianae* Gryllus makes a brief and incongruous appearance:

> Proinde sapientissime quoque ille apud Plutarchum Grylus ratiocinatur: Dum homines affirmat, si ab eorum vita semel absit religio, non modo brutis pecudibus nihil excellere: sed multis partibus esse longe miseriores. Ut qui tot malorum formis obnoxii, tumultuariam et irrequietam vitam perpetuo trahant. Unum ergo esse Dei cultum, qui superiores ipsos faciat: per quem solum ad immortalitatem aspiratur.[10]

> Plutarch's Gryllus reasons very wisely when he affirms that as soon as religion is absent from their lives men are in no way superior to brute beasts—indeed in many respects they are far more miserable. And so, subject to so many kinds of wickedness, they drag out their lives in endless disorder and anxiety. Therefore, it is worship of God alone that makes men superior to the animals, and through that alone they aspire to immortality.

Calvin is resourceful here, using a funny little vignette from a broad-minded Pagan author to illustrate a fundamental principle right at the beginning of his work. Calvin praises the skilful reason of the recalcitrant pig, but the proof extracted is that men are significantly like beasts only when they forget their true divine nature. So this Gryllus argues essentially against the dignity of himself and other animals.

Calvin's reading of Plutarch's version in the *Moralia* is shrewd. For Plutarch makes Gryllus a notable voice of dissent against the superiority of humans. The "Gryllus" dialogue, also known as "Bruta animalia ratione uti" (Beasts are rational), is slight and comic in comparison with most of the *Moralia*, and it is almost certainly fragmentary and truncated. It ends abruptly at the point where Gryllus has slurred Odysseus's name by referring to the atheism of his ancestor Sisyphus. Its premise is that not all of the people transformed into beasts by Circe want to be turned back: one is chosen as a spokesman, and he defends life as a beast on the grounds that animals show virtues more readily and more naturally than human beings. Early in their exchange Odysseus asks an incredulous question of Gryllus that echoes the confident assumption of the Palmer:

'Ἐμοὶ σύ, Γρύλλε, δοκεῖς οὐ τὴν μορφὴν μόνον ἀλλὰ καὶ τὴν

διάνοιαν ὑπὸ τοῦ πόματος ἐκείνου διεφθάρθαι καὶ γεγονέναι μεστὸς

ἀτόπων καὶ διαλελωβημένων παντάπασι δοξῶν· ἢ σέ τις αὖ συηνίας

ἡδονὴ πρὸς τόδε τὸ σῶμα καταγεγοήτευκεν;

To me, Gryllus, you seem to have lost not only your shape, but also your intelligence under the influence of that drug. You have become infected with strange and completely perverted notions. Or was it rather an inclination to swinishness that conjured you into this shape?[11]

More important than Gryllus' simple rejection of these theories is his promotion of animal virtues in an espousal of "theriophily" (respect for animals). First is courage, which (he argues) appears in beasts spontaneously and without self-interest. The most ingenious argument concerns epithets applied to humans ("wolf-minded", "lion-hearted"): like "wind-footed" and "godlike" these are hyperbolic, Gryllus argues, and represent an unattainable ideal.[12]

The Spenserian connotations of Plutarch's dialogue increase when (as in *The Faerie Queene*) temperance is the second virtue tackled. In sixteenth-century editions of Plutarch marginal notes sometimes reiterate this point, marking the passage in which Gryllus discusses animal "σωφροσύνη" as a "temperantiae descriptio."[13] Gryllus makes a series of comparisons which set animals over humans, of which the first is particularly pointed: widowed crows are said to stay chaste for nine generations of men, which is nine times better than Odysseus's wife Penelope. This is partly comic, though Plutarch is participating in a larger and long-lasting debate about the nature of animals and human beings.[14] So there is a serious edge when Gryllus argues that beasts do not live luxuriously, as he illustrates with his own example:

'Εμὲ γοῦν ποτε καὶ αὐτὸν οὐχ ἧττον ἢ σὲ νῦν ἐξέπληττε μὲν χρυσὸς ὡς

κτῆμα τῶν ἄλλων οὐδενὶ παραβλητόν, ᾖρει δ᾽ ἄργυρος καὶ ἐλέφας· ὁ δὲ

πλεῖστα τούτων κεκτημένος ἐδόκει μακάριός τις εἶναι καὶ θεοφιλὴς ἀνήρ,

εἴτε Φρὺξ ἦν εἴτε Κὰρ τοῦ Δόλωνος ἀγεννέστερος καί τοῦ Πριάμου

βαρυποτμότερος. ἐνταῦθα δ᾽ ἀνηρτημένος ἀεὶ ταῖς ἐπιθυμίας οὔτε χάριν

οὔθ᾽ ἡδονὴν ἀπὸ τῶν ἄλλων πραγμάτων ἀφθόνων ὄντων καὶ ἱκανῶν

ἐκαρπούμην.... ἀλλὰ νῦν ἀπηλλαγμένος ἐκείνων τῶν κενῶν δοξῶν καὶ

κεκαθαρμένος χρυσὸν μὲν καὶ ἄργυρον ὥσπερ τοὺς ἄλλους λίθους·

περιορῶν ὑπερβαίνω, ταῖς δὲ σαῖς χλανίσι καὶ τάπησιν οὐδὲν ἂν μὰ Δί᾽

ἥδιον ἢ βαθεῖ καὶ μαλθακῷ πηλῷ μεστὸς ὢν ἐγκατακλιθείην

ἀναπαυόμενος. τῶν δὲ τοιούτων τῶν ἐπεισάκτων ἐπιθυμιῶν οὐδεμία ταῖς

ἡμετέραις ἐνοικίζεται ψυχαῖς· ἀλλὰ τὰ μὲν πλεῖστα ταῖς ἀναγκαίαις ὁ βίος

ἡμῶν ἐπιθυμίαις καὶ ἡδοναῖς διοικεῖται, ταῖς δ᾽ οὐκ ἀναγκαίαις ἀλλὰ

φυσικαῖς μόνον οὔτ᾽ ἀτάκως οὔτ᾽ ἀπλήστως ὁμιλοῦμεν.

Certainly there was a time when I myself, no less than you now, was dazzled by gold and held it to be an incomparable possession; so likewise I was caught by the lure of silver and ivory and the man who had most property of this sort seemed to me to be a blissful favorite of the gods, whether he was a Phrygian or Carian, one more villainous than Dolon or more unfortunate than Priam. In that situation, constantly activated by these desires, I reaped no joy or pleasure from the other things of life, which I had sufficiently and to spare . . . But now I am rid and purified of all those empty illusions. I have no eyes for gold and silver and can pass them by just like any common stone; and as for your fine robes and tapestries, I swear there's nothing sweeter for me to rest in when I'm full than deep, soft mud. None, then, of such adventitious desires has a place in our souls; our life for the most part is controlled by the essential desires and pleasures. As for those that are non-essential, but merely essential, we resort to them without either irregularity or excess.[15]

Gryllus goes on to discuss humans' indulgence of sensuous pleasure and their lurid appetites for sex and elaborate food. In this passage (which also has a discussion of superfluous finery in clothing) Gryllus comes close to an inverted critique of the Bower of Bliss—inverted not because the essential point about the need to avoid meaningless luxury is any different, but because the tables are turned on the epic hero. Up to a point Spenser's epic can easily accommodate this, as Guyon finds his own temperance tested in the Bower, and passes the test. However, in Plutarch we hear Grille's voice (in a sense) speaking, and Grille is a figure who appears briefly in *The Faerie Queene* as a concluding shake of the head about the irredeemable nature of some of mankind. So, if the moral allegory is to sit comfortably, this ironically anticipatory retort from Grille is hard to square.

Calvin's moral reading of the Gryllus dialogue is, however, far from anomalous. The first English translation of the complete *Moralia*, by Philemon Holland in 1603, takes a similar tone in its "Summarie."[16] He makes a careful distinction between Plutarch's understanding of the comparisons of men with beasts, and a Christian's. However, he does point out that Plutarch did at least get the point that human "intelligence and cogitation" of God were crucial. Holland ends his "Summarie" by mentioning the truncation of the extant version, but asserts the value of the surviving part: "this which remaineth and is come unto our hands, may serve all men in good stead for their instruction and learning, not to glory and vaunt themselves, but in the mercy of him, who calleth them to a better life wherein brute beasts, (created onely for our use, and for the present life, with which they perish for ever) have no part or portion at all."[17] The translation of the text itself is close, though there are some apparent alterations that are consistent with Holland's interpretation. The first passage quoted above (Ulysses' question to Gryllus) is slightly expanded:

> It seemeth *Gryllus* that the potion which you dranke at *Circes* hands, hath not onely marred the forme and fashion of your bodie, but also spoiled your wit and understanding; having intoxicate your braine, and filled your head with corrupt, strange, and monstrous opinions for ever; or else some pleasure that you have taken by the acquaintance of this body so long, hath cleane bewitched you.[18]

This should be compared with the French version of Jacques Amyot, not least as a measure of its significant influence on Holland:

Il semble Gryllus que ce breuvage là que te donna Circé ne t'a
pas seulement corrompu la forme du corps, mais aussi le discours
de l'entendement, et qu'elle t'a remply la cervelle d'estranges et
totalement depravées opinions, ou il fault dire que le plaisir que
tu prens à ce corps pour le long temps qu'il y a desia que tu y
es, t'a enforcelé.[19]

The "pleasure" or "plaisir" of being a pig is present in both Holland
and Amyot, and takes a rather sharper line on the Greek "ηδονη"
than the Loeb translation's "inclination." Amyot is admirably concise
in matching single French words to single Greek words, while Holland here, as elsewhere, offers pairs of words ("forme and fashion,"
"wit and understanding") and perhaps a more telling expansion in
his tricolon "corrupt, strange, and monstrous opinions." Although
his translation clearly shows the burden of paraphrasing, it also adds
a further note of revulsion—"corrupt" helps to imply the sinfulness of
Gryllus' position. However, while the first English translator shared
Calvin's slant on Plutarch, this does not preclude a different potential
emerging when a slightly earlier inheritor, Spenser, ventures onto
this territory.

Another chapter in the *Moralia* is a source for Spenser's several uses
of the story of Isis and Osiris (especially in *Faerie Queene* V.vii). Again
Plutarch is not simply a source for stories: this section, like the *Gryllus*,
also talks back to Spenser, especially in its explicit and implicit analysis
of religious allegory. Plutarch attributes the use of symbols to a desire
to guide human intelligence toward the divine. The worst potential
pitfall is that this can lead to superstition, or (among those who reject
superstition too assiduously) toward atheism.[20] This makes Plutarch's
approach congenial to Protestants opposed to the practices of Catholicism. There are differences, though, in that Spenser approaches allegory as a literary technique, and also perhaps as an instructive tool,
whereas Plutarch treats it as an anthropological phenomenon. Plutarch's idea of allegory tends against Spenser's use also in that he sees it
as a process by which a single truth is translated into diverse culturally
appropriate forms. The same truths may be hidden beneath all the
different gods and symbols.[21] Clearly Spenser does not share this rela-
tivistic view of religious truth: for him the many false paths religion
can take may parallel the potential for confusion in allegory. However, his poem's many strands and opaque moments provide the
pitfalls and opportunities for individual interpretation that Plutarch
implies. The *Moralia* is a source that does not just quietly offer up its
material. In his treatment of allegory and his treatment of Gryllus,

Plutarch is tolerant, open-minded, and somewhat ironic, a quality D. A. Russell associates with the philosopher's opposition to the Stoics:

> Plutarch sees in Stoicism something fundamentally hostile to his ethical belief in the value of kindness and humanity, and to that sense of human frailty and comic imperfection in which he reminds us of the classic attitudes of early Greece, the modest confidence and tempered pessimism of a Herodotus or a Sophocles.[22]

The figure of Grille may well indicate to readers that it is worth thinking about the presence or absence of that "sense of human frailty and comic imperfection" in *The Faerie Queene*. Russell's acute observation captures the genial serio-comic tone that does not always fit easily within Spenser's epic. (Plutarch's Gryllus confesses to having been a Sophist philosopher in his human days, which adds further irony to his ability to argue—and requires a bit more scepticism from the reader.) The Grille episode may be a brief entrance of a serio-comic tone, quickly stifled. It is a microcosm of the way poetic resources are marshaled by Spenser: the possibilities evoked by things within the poem are sometimes so complex that they need to be inhibited—or rather, the text includes within itself the inhibition of its own rich, contradictory potential, and that inhibition need not be complete or successful. The reader's response to Gryllus depends partly on how clearly such a tone is evoked and how this affects the dynamics of the intertextuality: the Plutarchan source does not, perhaps, exert sufficient pressure on its own, but its tone is evident in some major works within the Gryllus tradition, and they add to the pressure.

One is Erasmus's *Praise of Folly*, in which Gryllus speaks up once, as the goddess develops her idea that Nature's rules show humanity to be ridiculous. Erasmus was the translator of several of Plutarch's *Moralia*, and was linked with a plan to publish a translation of "Gryllus" alongside *Praise of Folly*.[23] This suggests that there may have been a specific harmony of tone between Plutarch and his later imitator.[24] Folly emphasizes the harmony and happiness of bees, which live simply and according to a natural pattern. (Horses, conversely, have lapsed into bad human habits befitting their subjugation.) She then asserts the inferiority of human beings:

> Proinde numquam satis laudarim, gallum illum Pythagoram, qui cum unus omnia fuisset, philosophus, vir, mulier, rex, privatus,

piscis, equus, rana, opinor etiam spongia, tamen nullum animal
iudicavit calamitosius homine, propterea quod caetera omnia,
naturae finibus essent contenta, solus homo sortis suae limites
egredi conaretur. Rursum inter homines, idiotas multis partibus
anteponit doctis ac magnis, et Gryllus ille non paulo plus sapuit,
quam πολυμῆτις Ὀδυσσευς, qui maluerit in hara grunnire,
quam cum illo tot miseris obiici casibus. Ab his mihi non dis-
sentire videtur Homerus nugarum pater, qui cum mortales
omnes subinde δειλους και μοχθἠρους appellat, tum Ulyssem
illum suum sapientis exemplar, saepenumero δυστῆνον vocat,
Paridem nusquam, nec Aiacem, nec Achillem. Quamobrem id
tandem? Nisi quod ille vafer et artifex nihil non Palladis consilio
agebat, nimiumque sapiebat, a naturae ductu quam longissime
recedens?[25]

And so I could never have had enough praise for the famous
cock who was really Pythagoras. When he had been everything
in turn, philosopher, man, woman, king, commoner, fish,
horse, frog, even a sponge, I believe, he decided that man was
the most unfortunate of animals, simply because all the others
were content with their natural limitations while man alone
tries to step outside those allotted to him. Again, amongst men
in many ways he preferred the ignorant to the learned and
great. Gryllus was considerably wiser than the many-counseled
Odysseus when he chose to grunt in his sty rather than share
the risks of so many dangerous hazards. Homer, the father of
fables, seems to take the same view when he calls all mortals
wretched and long-suffering, and he often describes Ulysses, his
model of wisdom, as unfortunate, though he never does this to
Paris or Ajax or Achilles. The reason for this is clear: that cun-
ning master of craftiness never did a thing without Pallas to
advise him, and became far too wise as he moved further and
further away from Nature's guidance.[26]

In this work Erasmus can always deny that Folly is blasphemous or
that she is a radical satirical mouthpiece. The things Folly praises are
not absurd, unless they are actually absurd; she cannot make them
absurd on her own. Of course, the work can be read as more sharp-
edged. The above passage comes from the early sections of the work

when the code of how to read Folly's words is being established. Only in the second half of the work does she turn to matters of Christian doctrine and practice. So in the references to Gryllus and Pythagoras we are meant to see that she is misinterpreting (especially Homer in a humorous and inventive way) and praising positions that are indeed foolish. However, even within this example there are problems: the superiority of man over animals is a doctrinal matter, so this is not simply an innocent absurdity. The Erasmian Gryllus is easily recruited to Folly's cause, with a telling modification that he chooses the life of a pig for its simplicity and freedom from danger. Nevertheless temperance is an issue in this passage. A note of theriophily is again deployed for a comic purpose, but one with serious satirical force.[27] In this context Gryllus is a character who amuses rather than appalls, and who is able to cast some light on the false pretensions of humans: a rather different mood from the truncated appearance in *The Faerie Queene*.

Alongside Plutarch and Erasmus, Montaigne is the third member of a weighty triumvirate that represents the tolerant, serio-comic strand of theriophily. With all three aligned it becomes easier to favor that dynamic in possible interpretations of the story that tends against the swift conclusions of Guyon and the Palmer. Montaigne takes many things from Plutarch—both in the matter and the manner of his philosophy.[28] In one of the most important of the *Essais*, temperance is again a key part of a post-Plutarchan treatment of the virtues and vices of animals:

> Les cupiditez sont ou naturelles et necessaires, comme le boire et le manger; ou naturelles et non necessaires, comme l'accointance des femelles; ou elles ne sont ny naturelles ny necessaires: de cette derniere sorte sont quasi toutes celles des hommes: elles sont toutes superfluës et artificielles: Car c'est merveille combien peu il faut à nature pour se contenter, combien peu elle nous a laissé à desirer. . . . Les animaux sont beaucoup plus reglez que nous ne sommes, et se contiennent avec plus de moderation soubs les limites que nature nous a prescripts: Mais non pas si exactement, qu'ils n'ayent encore quelque convenance à nostre desbauche. Et tout ainsi comme il s'est trouvé des desirs furieux, qui ont poussé les hommes à l'amour des bestes, elles se trouvent aussi par fois esprises de nostre amour, et reçoivent des affections monstrueuses d'une espece à autre.[29]

Desires are either natural and necessary, like eating and drinking; natural and not necessary, such as mating with a female; or else neither natural nor necessary, like virtually all human ones, which are entirely superfluous and artificial. Nature needs wonderfully little to be satisfied and leaves little indeed for us to desire. . . . Animals obey the rules of Nature better than we do and remain more moderately within her prescribed limits—though not so punctiliously as to be without something akin to our debaucheries. Just as there have been mad desires driving humans to fall in love with beasts, so beasts have fallen in love with us, admitting monstrous passions across species.[30]

Montaigne cleverly overturns the taboo of bestiality, making it an animal aberration as well as a human one. His tolerance of animal character extends even to allowing them a few human lapses. Temperance, then, is not only the second of the crucial virtues of the gentleman Spenser hopes to fashion: it is also a key feature of the satirical promotion of animal over human virtues. Montaigne does not mention Gryllus here, but he is situating himself within a Plutarchan tradition of interest in animal virtue, to which he adds his own interest in primitivism. He handles this question not with the clear Christian perspective of Calvin or Holland, but with a nuanced and subtle resistance to clarity.[31] Géralde Nakam has it right when he says "le génie de Montaigne tient à sa haine des dogmatismes."[32] Like Erasmus, he does not introduce an animal perspective solely in order to condemn it.

Another book in this tradition, Gianbattista Gelli's *Circe* (1549), sees the eponymous goddess give various creatures the chance to address Ulysses with their opinions on their transformations. There is no Gryllus, no pig at all in fact, but as well as an oyster, a mole, a snake, a hare, a goat, a hind, a lion, a dog, and a calf, all of whom prefer animal form for their own reasons, there is a horse, who (in the English translation of Henry Iden), cites "temperaunce" in his reasoning:

E questo si è perché noi abbiamo molto più fortezza e più temperanza che non avete voi: con l'una delle quali noi raffreniamo quella parte dello appetito nostro la quale è chiamata da voi irascibile, che ella non tema troppo le cose paurose, e non si confidi troppo in quelle che ella ha; e con l'altra la concupiscibile, onde ella non segua troppo quelle che le arrecano diletto,

o non fugga troppo quelle che le porgono dolore. E così, avendo
in noi più moderate queste passioni, vegnamo a operare molto
più facilmente quello che appartiene a la natura nostra, che non
fate voi quel che si conviene a la vostra.[33]

We have farre more fortitude, and more temperaunce then you
have: with thone of the which we refraine that part of our
appetite, the which you call ireful, that the same fereth no
fearful thinges to much, nor trusteth to much in those thinges
that it hath. And with the other, the concupiscence, wherby it
foloweth not overmuch those thinges that bringe delite, nor
flyeth those to muche that bringe it sorowe. And so haveinge
these passions more moderate in us, we must doo farre more
easlyer that that apperteyneth unto our nature, than you do that
that belongeth to yours.[34]

The superior performance of instinctive actions ("that that apperteyneth unto our nature") need not be a meagre boast, since in theory
it is human nature to worship God, and many other higher activities.
However, the horse's argument, like those of the other animals, is
eventually overcome by that of the elephant. A philosopher in his
human life, the last animal to speak accepts Odysseus' argument that
only human beings have true knowledge and free will, and that therefore their state is to be approved. The final outcome favors humans,
but Gelli's horse can join the chorus that Gryllus echoes because so
much of the argument in *Circe* inclines in favor of animals, even if it
is rehearsed ironically in order to prepare the way for the elephant's
all-important clinching point. A further point derived from Gelli
comes in Marilyn Migiel's illuminating account of the "Dignity of
Man." She points out the feminine adjectives and pronouns associated
(and not always through obvious linguistic causes) with those who
resist Odysseus' arguments. In a feminist reading of Gelli, she argues
that Circe has a lesson for Ulysses and for the reader, which is that
the misogynistic ideology behind ideas of man's dignity needs to
be recognized.[35]
　　Guyon and the Palmer are clear about the meaning of Grille, but
the other texts evoked by the character are not. They illustrate the
extraordinary capacity of the poem but they hamper its clarity—a
reader might feel that these intertexts are not quite stifled, despite
(but also because of) the brevity of the episode. Some versions of
Grille/Gryllus imply conclusions different from those asserted by Guyon and the Palmer, and this complex figure is testimony to the

difficulty of sustaining a moral allegory while also writing an "endlesse worke" intersecting richly with tradition. Commentaries and criticism struggle to capture the texture of the many nuances surrounding Grille, shifting and elusive as they are. Indeed, this example reveals the value of one aspect of Leah Marcus's proposed "Unediting" of the Renaissance. Alongside her defence of "bad" quartos, and other aberrant texts marginalized by editorial tradition, she asserts the potentially debilitating effect of exhaustive commentary. Marcus cites Shakespeare's description of Sycorax in *The Tempest* as a "blew ey'd hag" as an instance of how the critical tradition can obscure and distort meaning.[36] The apparatus that now accompanies the phrase struggles to explain it and thereby inhibits its powerful, meaningful ambiguity. With all the scholarship removed, the feisty pig in the Bower of Bliss may be able to mean more things more easily, except that Spenser's inclusion of a very clear definition within the text makes analysis more necessary. Commentators have no option but to set out the corroboration for Guyon and his guide, and they may also, and perhaps should, include the case against. It is important for Spenser's allegory that Book II ends in a disciplined fashion, but it is just as important to the poem that there is a degree of resistance to that discipline.

New Hall, University of Cambridge

NOTES

1. See *The Spenser Encyclopedia*, ed. A.C. Hamilton et al. (Toronto: University of Toronto Press, 1990), *The Faerie Queene*, ed. A. C. Hamilton (London: Longman, 1977), and James Nohrnberg, *The Analogy of the "Faerie Queene"* (Princeton: Princeton University Press, 1976), 370–71, 500–502. This weighty company makes this an opportune moment to acknowledge the help of the *Spenser Studies* readers, Andrew Zurcher, Paul Alpers, and Helen Cooper, the latter two having heard the paper at the 2001 Spenser Society conference in Cambridge. Merritt Hughes, "Spenser's Acrasia and the Circe of the Renaissance," *Journal of the History of Ideas* 4 (1943): 381–98 covers some of the same territory as this article, though like the prevailing mood in commentary it lines up with the condemnation of Grille.

2. Quoted from *The Works of Edmund Spenser: A Variorum Edition*, ed. Edwin Greenlaw et al., 10 vols (Baltimore: Johns Hopkins University Press, 1949).

3. Stephen Greenblatt, *Renaissance Self-Fashioning* (Chicago: University of Chicago Press, 1980), 184, classes Grille with "such creatures [as] give a local habitation and a name to those vague feelings of longing and complicity that permeate accounts of a sensuous life that must be rejected and destroyed." While this recognizes a nagging strength, it also places Grille clearly within a moral scheme.

4. Nohrnberg, *Analogy,* p. 501.

5. Harry Berger, Jr, *The Allegorical Temper: Vision and Reality in Book II of Spenser's "Faerie Queene"* (New Haven: Yale University Press, 1957), 240, finishes with a brilliant passage depicting the downbeat mood of the end of Book II; but Grille, as I see him, may lighten things.

6. Pierre de Coustau [Costalius], *Le Pegme de Pierre Coustau* (Lyon, 1560; New York: Garland, 1979), 224; translation by Lantôme de Romieu of the Latin *Pegma* (Lyon, 1550).

7. Mason Tung, "Spenser's Graces and Costalius' *Pegma*", *English Miscellany* 23 (1992): 9–14. See also Irene Bergal, "Pierre Coustau's *Pegma*: From Emblem to Essay," in *Lapidary Inscriptions: Renaissance Essays for Donald A. Stone, Jr,* ed. Barbara C. Bowen and Jerry C. Nash (Lexington, Kentucky: French Forum Publishers, 1991), esp. 115–17 on sources in Erasmus's *Adagia* and Plutarch's *Moralia,* and 118–22, on its relationship to Montaigne and the essay form.

8. Natalis Comes, *Mythologiae* (Venice, 1567; New York, Garland, 1976), 175^r, amending "deseratur" to "deferatur."

9. Plotinus, *Enneads,* ed. and trans. A. H. Armstrong, 7 vols. (London: William Heinemann, 1966–1988), 1.6.6.

10. John Calvin, *Institutes of the Christian Religion 1539,* ed. Richard Wevers, 4 vols. (Grand Rapids: Meeter Center for Calvin Studies, 1988), I, 5. The *Institutio Christianae Religionis* was first published in Basel, 1536.

11. Plutarch, *Moralia,* Loeb Classical Library, 15 vols., vol. xii trans. Harold Cherniss and William C. Helmbold (London: William Heinemann; Cambridge, Mass.: Harvard University Press, 1957), 498–99.

12. *Moralia,* xii. 508–09.

13. See for example *Plutarchi Chaeronensis Philosophorum et Historicorum Principis Varia Scripta, Quae Moralia Vulgo Dicuntur* (Basel: Eusebius Episcopius, 1574), 241; the notes and editing by Guilielmus Xylander. *Plutarchi Chaeronensis Quae Exstant Omnia* (Frankfurt: Andreas Wechelus, 1599) is a folio with a Latin translation and the commentaries of Cruserius, and others, as well as Xylander, but even here the amount of interpretive detail is minimal; most of the notes are textual.

14. See Stephen T. Newmyer, "Plutarch on Justice toward Animals: Ancient Insights on a Modern Debate," *Scholia* n.s. 1 (1992): 38–50, and also his "Speaking of Beasts: The Stoics and Plutarch on Animal Reason and the Modern Case against Animals," *Quaderni Urbinati di Cultura Classica* 63 (1999): 100–110. See also G. Boas, *The Happy Beast* (Baltimore: Johns Hopkins University Press, 1933), and A.O. Lovejoy and G. Boas, *Primitivism and Related Ideals in Antiquity* (Baltimore: Johns Hopkins University Press, 1935).

15. *Moralia,* xii. 514–17.

16. *The Philosophie, Commonlie Called, The Morals Written by the Learned Philosopher Plutarch of Chaeronea* (London: Arnold Hatfield, 1603), 561–70: "That Brute Beastes Have Use of Reason, A discourse in maner of a dialogue, *named* Gryllus." The "Summarie" comes on pp. 561–62. There was no earlier English version of this dialogue, though other parts of the *Moralia* had been translated.

17. *The Philosophie,* trans. Holland, 562.

18. *The Philosophie,* trans. Holland, p. 564.

19. *Les Oeuvres Morales et Meslees de Plutarque*, trans. Jacques Amyot, 2 vols. (Paris: Michel de Vasconne, 1572; facsimile Wakefield: S.R. Publishers, 1971), I, 270ᵛ.

20. *Moralia* (Loeb), vol. v, trans. Frank Cole Babbitt (London: William Heinemann; Cambridge, Mass.: Harvard University Press, 1957), 156–57.

21. *Moralia*, v, 154–7.

22. D.A. Russell, *Plutarch* (London: Duckworth, 1972), 69.

23. See Erika Rummel, *Erasmus as a Translator of the Classics* (Toronto: University of Toronto Press, 1985), 71–88. The first *Moralia* versions were printed in London, 1513. Others appeared later in *Opuscula Plutarchi* (Basel, 1514), in *Libellus de non Irascendo et de Curiositate* (Basel, 1526), and in *Apophthegmata* (Basel, 1531). See also Lisa Jardine, *Erasmus, Man of Letters: The Construction of Charisma in Print* (Princeton: Princeton University Press, 1993), 182–87, on the printer Beatus Stephanus' planned collection uniting *Praise of Folly* with "Gryllus," Lucian's *Parasitica* and *Fly*, and other texts with a similarly irreverent tone.

24. Walter M. Gordon, *Humanist Play and Belief: The Seriousness of Desiderius Erasmus* (Toronto: University of Toronto Press, 1990) argues for the profundity of the comic elements in Erasmus. In his chapter on Greek sources, however, he includes Lucian, Aristophanes, and Plato, but omits Plutarch—whom he should perhaps have included. Rosalie Colie, *Paradoxia Epidemica: The Renaissance Tradition of Paradox* (Princeton: Princeton University Press, 1966), is the classic study of one mode in the light of which readers may have understood the various versions of Grille / Gryllus.

25. Desiderius Erasmus, *Moriae Encomium* (Paris, 1511), 50.

26. Erasmus, *The Praise of Folly*, in *The Collected Works of Erasmus*, vol. 27, ed. A.H.T. Levi (Toronto: University of Toronto Press, 1986), 77–153; 108. The translation is by Betty Radice.

27. Harry Berger Jr is one critic who depicts Erasmus as a writer deeply opposed to misanthropy, and hence perhaps inclined toward the same kind of tolerance as Plutarch's in the "Gryllus" dialogue. See Berger's "Utopian Folly: Erasmus and More on the Perils of Misanthropy," *English Literary Renaissance* 12 (1982): 271–90.

28. See Isabella Konstantinovic, *Montaigne et Plutarque*, Travaux d'humanisme et Renaissance, 231 (Geneva: Droz, 1989), esp. 291–334, and Yvonne Bellenger, "Montaigne Lecteur d'Amyot," in *Fortunes de Jacques Amyot: Actes du Colloque International (Melun 18–20 Avril 1985)*, ed. Michel Balard (Paris: Nizet, 1986), 297–311.

29. *Les Essais de Michel Seigneur de Montaigne*, "L'Apologie de Raimond Sebond" (Paris: Abel L'Angelier, 1595).

30. Michel de Montaigne, *The Complete Essays*, trans. M.A. Screech (Harmondsworth: Penguin, 1987), II. 12, "An Apology for Raymond Sebond," 526.

31. See Yvonne Bellenger, "L'intelligence des animaux: Montaigne et Du Bartas lecteurs de Plutarque," *Revue d'Histoire Littéraire de la France* 80 (1980): 523–39, esp. 535–7 on Montaigne's tone; Evelyne Meron, "L'animal est-il une personne?", *Bulletin de la Société des Amis de Montaigne* 39–40 (1995): 47–53; Floyd Gray, "Montaigne et le langage des animaux," in *Le Signe et le Texte: Études sur l'écriture au XVI* siècle en France, ed. Lawrence D. Kritzman (Lexington, Kentucky: French Forum Publishers, 1990), 149–59. See also William M. Hamlin, *The Image of America in Montaigne, Spenser, and Shakespeare: Renaissance Ethnography and Literary Reflection* (Houndmills: Macmillan, 1995), which has a distantly related focus on how different

writers saw the potential for civilization in New World peoples. Most important is his attempt to disprove that Spenser saw the truly "salvage" as entirely beyond redemption: Hamlin argues that he is more open-minded than that, which may bear on his brief appearance in the theriophily debate.

32.   Géralde Nakam, "Le Dieu de l'apologie de Raimond Sebond: De Plutarque à Montaigne," *Bulletin de la Société des Amis de Montaigne* 33–34 (1993): 131–48, quoting p. 144.

33.   Gian Battista Gelli, *Opere*, ed. Amelia Corona Alesina (Napoli: Fulvio Rossi, 1969), 347–48.

34.   *Circes of John Baptista Gello [Gelli], Florentine*, trans. Henry Iden (London: John Cawood, 1557), M5^r. On Iden, see Margherita Giulietti, "Il Gelli in Inghilterra: Due Dialoghi Fiorentini nel Rinascimento Inglese," *Studi di Letteratura Francese* 19 (1992): 265–78 (also on William Barker's translation of Gelli's *Cappricci*).

35.   Marilyn Migiel, "The Dignity of Man: A Feminist Perspective", in *Refiguring Women: Perspectives on Gender and the Italian Renaissance*, eds. Marilyn Migiel and Juliana Schiesari (Ithaca: Cornell University Press, 1991), 211–32. The Bower of Bliss episode could also be analysed with this gender-based approach.

36.   Leah Marcus, *Unediting the Renaissance: Shakespeare, Marlowe, Milton* (London: Routledge, 1996), 5–17.

ALEXANDRA BLOCK AND ERIC ROTHSTEIN

Argument and "Representation" in *The Faerie Queene*, Book III

Book III of *The Faerie Queene* is highly organized as to structure, so as to model and clarify the providential world it depicts. Through this formal architecture, it also sets forth an argument about its central virtue, chastity. The main division of the Book is into thirds: the first and last four-canto groupings (1–4, 9–12) feature Britomart, and the middle four-canto grouping, 5–8, is devoted to Belphoebe and Amoret, and to Florimell. In turn, analogies and contrasts organize each group. In the first group, for example, Britomart's victories over non-generative, loveless Malecasta and Marinell (promiscuity, fearful virginity) flank her coming to terms with her own love and future lineage. These formal devices often do cognitive and evaluative work, since through contrast and analogy within his structure, Spenser defines chastity situationally. Marinell's is the *in malo* form of virginity, juxtaposed with Belphoebe's *in bono* form (cantos 4, 5); Belphoebe's good, embowered virginity is juxtaposed with good, procreative sexuality in the Garden of Adonis (5, 6), then with the witch's bad procreation (her son, her hyena-like beast, Snowy Florimell) and virginal Florimell's frustrated love in 7 and 8. These dyads form a logical, Ramist kind of argument. In it, he uses two kinds of representation, not mutually exclusive, one being the embodying of a virtue or vice and the other, the championing of a virtue or vice. Such considerations elucidate the precise nature and ends of Spenser's allegory.

*W*E PROPOSE THAT THE narrative of Book III of *The Faerie Queene* embodies a comprehensive schema with a hermeneutic, heuristic, and mnemonic energy. The detailed formal architecture of the book comprises an argument that defines the virtue of chastity. In keeping with Ramist logic, the argument works through a matrix of binary figures, pairs of situated characters in Book III: they create who they are by acting as they do within a narrative.[1] For the reader the argument controls the errors of image and imagination—perception and conception—that plague the characters as they act.[2] The full import of the argument depends on Spenser's allegory, which, we propose, employs a double sense of "representation." One sense is "standing for," in the way that accounts, images, and symbols represent their referents. The other sense is "acting for," as a spokesperson represents a constituency. Each makes its representandum present in a different way.[3] For instance, Book III as a whole *represents* (stands for, depicts) a microcosm through its accounts and images; its argument *represents* (acts for, champions) chastity by using binaries to define and promote it. A single representational entity may, but need not, operate in both of these conceptually and practically discrete senses.

Argument and representation in Book III live within an architecture of formal repetitions and rearrangements of characters, events, and objects. Barriers at four-canto intervals—the armed knights at Malecasta's Castle Joyous (Canto 1), the ford that Timias must cross while the foresters assail him (Canto 5), and the barring of guests from Malbecco's castle (Canto 9)—culminate in the House of Busirane's encircling fire and locked doors (Canto 11). Again, Spenser at five-canto intervals (Cantos 2, 7, 12) employs circular containers, playing on the ideal of wholeness, to mark threats to the chastity of the three representatives of marital fidelity: Britomart's chastity becomes a theme when she sees first her own face, then Arthegall's, in a concave mirror; Florimell's chastity has the symbol of the golden girdle she wears and then loses; and Amoret's heart lies exposed in a silver basin until she is again "perfect hole" (xii.38). The architecture, which is rhetorical, of course includes the argument's binaries as formal elements, while as logical elements—logic is the Ramist complement to rhetoric—they aggregately provide and exemplify the proper working of reason.

Since Spenser criticism has not, so far as we know, plotted Book III in this way as to argument or representation, we want to chart our case as clearly as we can, often expanding and synthesizing others' readings and ways of reading.[4] Our analysis does not, however, pretend to be complete. The double sense of "representation" itself opens a space for further options. One might well choose to psychologize the characters, focus on allusions and genre, or stress gaps between what the narrator says and what the narration shows. Rather than explore these options, we will try to assemble a reading of Book III that's sufficiently coherent and reliable as to explain, though underdetermine, all the larger narrative events in the book.

1

Architecturally, the book falls into three sections: four cantos that star Britomart, four without her, and a final four where she reappears. We will call them Sections A, B, and C. In A, Spenser begins to define Britomart's role. At one end of A, Canto 1, she fends off the promiscuous Malecasta, who tries to seduce her—having mistaken her for a man—in a richly appointed castle; and at the other end, Canto 4, she nearly slays Malecasta's seeming opposite as to sex and sexual restraint, the virginal young man Marinell, who battles with her, mistaking her for a man, on a wealth-strewn shore. Whereas Malecasta refers her own present to the past, Marinell refers his present to the future. She authorizes and stokes her lust through myth, while a prophecy drives him, Marinell, to battle men and hate "wemans loue" (iv.27). Her tapestries of "*Venus* and her Paramoure," Adonis, show the "engored" youth transformed (into "a dainty flowre") by a woman (i. 34, 38); the youth Marinell hopes to avert death at a woman's hands, and when he is engored by one, Britomart, he enters the sea, not a flower garden. But morally, antipathy to love is the rule with both venereal, penetrable Malecasta and martial, fearful Marinell "in armour bright." He is "loues enimy," and she is "not to loue, but lust inclind" (iv.12, 26; i.49).

Between the encounters where Malecasta and Marinell dwell, and tallying with them, comes the story of Britomart's departing her home. Like Malecasta in Canto 1, Britomart in Canto 2 falls for a visual image, Arthegall's mirrored face. Frustrated longing for him drives her to envy some Ovidian sinners their physical satisfaction in incestuous and bestial sex, incest requiring an unnaturally close partner and bestiality, one unnaturally distant (ii.43). Through the direction given to her longings by Merlin's prophecy of fruitful marriage, she focuses them, and so can defeat the indiscriminate Malecasta in Castle Joyous. Cantos 2 and 3 retrospectively explain the end of Canto 1, just as Britomart's focusing her turbulent passions at the start of Canto 4, through recalling Merlin's prophecy, explains her defeat of Marinell.

As to her envying sinful lovers, her final exploit in Book III finally purges this lapse: in Canto 11, she terrifies the giant Ollyphant, guilty of sodomy and "beastly vse" as well as incest with his twin Argante, who has "suffred beastes her body to deflowre" (xi.4, vii.49). Within Section A, though, Britomart's lapses are partially remedied by her nurse, the *in bono* analogue to Marinell's solicitous mother —"Glauce" is the nurse's name, and the Nereids, such as Cymoent, Nereus's daughter and Marinell's mother, are in Statius (*Thebaid* 9.351) "glaucae sorores," sea-gray sisters.[5] As Canto 2 corresponds with Canto 1, so 3 corresponds with 4. Through Glauce, Britomart visits the prophet Merlin, whose lengthy vision of Britomart's line of legitimate royal offspring in Canto 3 contrasts with its Canto 4 analogue, Proteus's prophecy of truncation for Cymoent's bastard line, whether her fears come true (Marinell dies) or her hopes do (Marinell lives long, celibate). So completely does this armature of parallels and oppositions define Britomart's thematic role in Section A that Spenser can set her aside during Section B, while he develops the other plot lines of Book III.

When Britomart reappears in Section C, he reprises the architecture of A, through mirroring. The two narrative elements in A (Malecasta, Marinell) correspond, reversed, to the two in C (Malbecco, Busirane). Thus Cantos 9 and 10 look back to Cantos 3 and 4. Marinell's jealously guarded "*Rich strond*," with its "huge threasure" (iv.20, 22), recurs as Malbecco's castle and money in Canto 9. Cymoent and Marinell as possessive, older monitor and enforcedly chaste youth recur as jealous old Malbecco and the Hellenore he "mewes," of "far vnequall yeares" (ix.4–5). Proteus's prophecy of Marinell's death at a woman's hands recurs as the implied prophecy that the fatal Homeric Helen's legend provides for her namesake Hellenore, so that Marinell's demi-death via Britomart recurs in comic form in Malbecco's via Hellenore. A failed suicide, Malbecco withers amid "roring billowes" (x.58), reduced to his monomania, in a cave of a seaside cliff, as Marinell earlier, lifeless on the shore, has been borne to his mother's "watry chamber" (iv.42). Proteus connects them, since the person to whom Proteus prophesies in the *Odyssey* is Menelaus, Malbecco's Homeric parallel.[6] In the tallying of Sections A and C, constrainedly chaste Hellenore moves from a Marinell-like to a Malecasta-like position, servicing a troop of wildly virile satyrs, with no real moral alteration on her part. Finally, as the non-lineage of Marinell contrasts with Merlin's account of lineage from King Arthur through Elizabeth I, so the non-lineage of the Paridell, Hellenore, and Malbecco story six cantos later (iii.3 and iii.9) contrasts with the account there of British history from the fall of Troy to the Trojans' arrival in Britain.[7]

Just so, the second episode of Section C (Busirane) reworks the first of Section A (Malecasta). Britomart suffers wounds as victor in both the House of Busirane and its decorative and erotic precursor, Malecasta's castle. Her double role as the object and avenger of lust in Canto 1 merely splits in Canto 12. She punishes the evil desire of which Amoret is the unwilling object. Because she is more "male" than the powerless, distraught Scudamore in Canto 11, the gender muddling at the end of the book repeats that at the beginning, where Britomart and Malecasta "each believ[e] *the other* to be *a male.*"[8] Scudamore and Amoret then merge for a time into a kind of hermaphrodite (xii.46).[9] Just as Malecasta's knights wound Redcrosse, Britomart's succored partner in Canto 1, to make him "forgoe with fowle defame" his lady and cleave to Malecasta (i.27), Busirane tries to force wounded Amoret to love him rather than Scudamore. The parallel lets one read Redcrosse's holiness as a prolepsis, inverted, of Busirane's black magic. Venus, falsely represented on Malecasta's tapestries, bewailing her ever-bleeding Adonis (i.38), reappears as Venus's continuously bleeding foster daughter, Amoret, who resists being false. The pillar to which Amoret is bound may perhaps be a type of "the bloody Crosse" (i.64) on Redcrosse's shield, *scudo* of *amore divino*—like Christian martyrs, Amoret undergoes torture for her faith. Her forced march bearing the sign of her torture, her wound, and the "siluer basin" of blood (xii.21) reinforces the pillar's possible reminiscence of the cross.

At Malecasta's Castle Joyous, six knights with elegantly Italian names personify six stages in the onset of "love"—looking, talking, joking, kissing, reveling, and spending the night together (i.45).[10] Paridell and Hellenore exhibit these same behaviors in Cantos 9 and 10, but to see what Castle-Joyous love means and conceals, we through Britomart can look to Busirane's masque, with its plain-English, coupled complements: Fancy and Desyre, Doubt and Daunger, Feare and Hope, Dissemblance and Suspect, Griefe and Fury, Displeasure and Pleasance, and finally, Despight and Cruelty (xii.7–19). Cupid, who "kindled lustfull fyres" for Malecasta (i.39), reappears in the Busirane episode as idol and masquer (xi.46–48, xii.22–23), as does the fire. Finally, Sections A and C have hinges. In A the two-stage story of Britomart in Cantos 2 and 3 joins Malecasta and Marinell; and in C the comic captivity of Hellenore (Canto 9) and the tragic captivity of Amoret (Canto 12) articulate around the abjectness of two bereft men, Malbecco in Canto 10, Scudamore in Canto 11.

Even more elaborately, one may see how the linkage between Malbecco and Marinell, as discussed above, prepares us for linkage between Busirane and Merlin. Significant Marinell motifs have already been briefly "foretold" in the previous canto through the story of Merlin's perpetual imprisonment by the Lady of the Lake (iii.10–11): these include water, enclosure, death by a woman who pretends to be what she is not, and the failure of prophetic powers to be of help. If the story of old Malbecco in some sense transposes into the genre of fabliau a cluster of motifs set up by young Marinell, and the stories of Merlin and Busirane (the latter substituting fire for water) ring further changes on these motifs, Busirane appears architecturally as Merlin *in malo*. He evokes not a magnificent lineage but a doom of chaotic disaster, not a young woman's fulfilling her destiny with her true love but a young woman's alienation from what she was and is, with a false love. Within Section C, Spenser "foretells" this *in-malo* state in that Hellenore and Paridell—marital faithlessness linked to the bearer of lineage past (Trojan and hence British)—invert Britomart's and Arthegall's marital faith and a British lineage to come.

Between the mirroring Sections A and C, formal repetition also organizes Section B, so that by our method of analysis, its ground plan will be pretty clear. In Britomart's absence Spenser develops multiple actions involving three other paragons, Florimell, Belphoebe, and Amoret. Cantos 5 and 6, the first half of Section B, show Belphoebe's disinterested, constitutive virginity as countering Marinell's—she's virginity *in bono*—while the Garden of Adonis, equidistant in the poem from the mirroring Malecasta and Busirane episodes, reprises Malecasta's promiscuity *in bono*.[11] The transfer of Timias's wound from his body to his spirit in Canto 5 mediates between the mere bodily wound of Marinell in Canto 4 and the figure of once-wounded Adonis in Canto 6, where he and Venus preside over the garden of generative love (46–49). They revise their static, pictured selves on the walls of Malecasta's castle; their procreative love, faithful in and through change, "eterne in mutabilitie" (47), is embodied in Busirane's victim Amoret (vi.51–53). Malecasta and Marinell are complements; so are Amoret and Belphoebe, procreative and virgin chastity.

In the second half of Section B, Cantos 7 and 8 return to Florimell, who has appeared just prior to the Malecasta episode in Canto 1 and just after the Marinell episode in Canto 4. Florimell and her false twin, Snowy Florimell, reprise Amoret and Belphoebe, so that Canto 7 complements Canto 6, and Canto 8 complements Canto 5. That is, vulnerable, loving Florimell, who is to be Proteus's prey, parallels Amoret, who is Busirane's; Florimell's name suggests the garden that is Amoret's home. The snowiness of Snowy Florimell and her construction as an idol for the witch's brutish, lustful son parodies Belphoebe's virgin chastity and her construction, in Canto 5, as an idol in the mind of the squire, Timias, wounded by a figure of lust.[12]

To address the counterpoint of actions in Section B, we will start with a set piece, the witch's manufacture of Snowy Florimell in Canto 8. Trying to placate her lovelorn son after the real Florimell flees their cabin, the witch creates "an automatic sweetheart" that exactly impersonates Florimell's body.[13] She animates it with a male "wicked Spright yfraught with fawning guyle" (viii.8). In accord with alchemical principles, the witch constructs the body of snow, mercury, wax, vermilion, fire (burning lamps), silver, and gold (viii.6–7).[14] These elements, other than vermilion, include three metals (gold, silver, mercury) and three non-metals (fire, wax, and water—the snow) in three pairs of yellow and white, one each of solids, mutables, and fluids: gold/silver, wax/snow, and fire/mercury. If the burning lamps are taken as sulfur, Paracelsian fire, the yellow-and-white pattern of the fluid elements is clear. Furthermore, the pairing of mercury and sulfur, the two bases for alchemy, also explains vermilion, which was their product.[15] The apparent forms of wax and snow each may resemble any of three elements—water, earth, and air—when fused or evaporated by the fourth, fire. As Snowy Florimell is hermaphroditic, so are her components. Gold is Sol, masculine, and silver is Luna, feminine. Sulfur is masculine and mercury feminine.[16] But why yellow and white? The four colors crucial for alchemy, as for ancient painting, are white, yellow, red, and black.[17] To the pairs of white and yellow, the witch adds vermilion, red. The black appears in Stanza 8, which refers to the Spright's having fallen "with the Prince of Darkenes." Four elements, four colors, paired constituents to create a body as a microcosm—this is not pictorial bricolage but advanced lab work.

To Spenser's alchemy one can also trace the immediate career of Snowy Florimell, as she passes from the witch's son to Braggadocchio and thence to Ferraugh. Her body incorporates three of the seven metals, which are gold, silver, mercury, copper, iron, tin, and lead, and our notion of Spenser's logic should prod one to wonder if the other four—copper, iron, tin, and lead—might appear in her relational microcosm.[18] Ferraugh, who appears here for the only time in the 1590 books, provides the iron, *ferrum*. The other three appear, perhaps in the relationship among metals, life *ab extra*, and the creation of value. One finds this pattern, obviously, with the mineral manufacture of "Spright"-invested Snowy Florimell in Canto 8 and then in the next episode, where Malbecco loves his gold coins "as liuing breath" (x.2). Since a counterfeit knight, Braggadocchio, steals Snowy Florimell and has her stolen from him in Canto 8 (11–18), and then through his servant Trompart steals Malbecco's coins in Canto 10 (30, 54), Spenser may be carrying through an analogy with coinage and counterfeits. With such coins, Queen Elizabeth's stamped face conveyed a false promise. Copper, tin, and lead were the chief base constituents of counterfeit coinage, often silvered over or gilded, as with Snowy Florimell's gilded and silvered outside, and metaphorically with the fine show that Braggadocchio makes.[19] Counterfeiting: the ironic *discordia concors* of double-sexed and sexless Snowy Florimell provides the appropriate idea of impure mixture, as does the witch's other creation, the piebald hyena-like creature, whom she summons to pursue the real Florimell (vii.22). These stand opposed to the real *discordia concors* of the Garden of Adonis, Canto 6.[20]

From the structuring of Snowy Florimell stretches a web of connections. Thus, for example, the return of the witch's hyena, wearing Florimell's now torn golden girdle (viii.2), anticipates the creation of a sinister, hermaphroditic, mock-human double for Florimell. Because hyenas were thought to shift sex and to impregnate themselves, as well as to imitate human voices, the hermaphroditism of the witch's bestial hyena also differs from and complements that of the non-animal Snowy Florimell, who is at once sexless as an automaton and double-sexed in the manner detailed above.[21] The hyena's prey is Florimell's body, for which her devoured horse is the proxy; and Snowy Florimell incorporates Florimell's presence as a human being, consuming her, so to speak, by subsuming her.

As Snowy Florimell passes from the witch's son to Braggadocchio to Ferraugh, the real Florimell passes from the son to an old fisherman to Proteus, who woos her in changing shapes. The motif of a single enamored figure who changes shapes, paradoxically constant but unchaste, and of serial would-be seductions repeats in Canto 8 the seriality of the Squire of Dames in Canto 7, who seduces all the women he meets—they are no more chaste than he is. In turn, his lady Columbell's dominatrix chastity shares its virtueless violence with the lust of Argante (vii.50–51), a female serial rapist who imprisons her male victims in Canto 7 as male Proteus, with his series of shapes, imprisons female Florimell in Canto 8. Argante's seizing the Squire of Dames continues, not inaugurates, his life of captivity, as he trades one female controller for another. Argante's literal foe is also, fittingly, the riposte to Columbell's chilly cynicism—she is Palladine, a "faire virgin" female knight (vii.52), whose pursuit of Argante anticipates Britomart's of Ollyphant, Argante's brother (xi.3–6).[22] The Squire of Dames himself remains in the poem just long enough to meet Paridell, the failed defender of Florimell who takes over the Squire's seducer's role in Cantos 9 to 10.[23] In short, every action gets a poetic location and gains its meaning from its relationship to some other action or actions. Spenser's narrative stands opposite to the episodic structure one finds in contemporary prose romance.

As we have suggested, both an architecture and an argument appear in this account of the Snowy Florimell episode and its poetic surroundings. Formally, a number of components balance off against one another; conceptually, a definition of chastity grows through sequential binaries based on altering kinds of pairing—Florimell/Snowy Florimell, hyena/Snowy Florimell, Snowy Florimell/Columbell, Columbell/Argante, Argante/Palladine, Squire of Dames/Paridell, Amoret/Belphoebe, and so forth. Cold, imperious Columbell in Canto 7, who sends her lover on quests, also contrasts with the complementary Elizabeth figures, Queen Gloriana, dispatcher of knights, and the sexually inaccessible Belphoebe, of iv.54 and Canto 5 respectively. Other characters, such as Satyrane, articulate and staff the universe in which chastity functions.

The binaries into which Timias enters in Canto 5, beyond the ones with wounded Marinell in Canto 4 and wounded Adonis in Canto 6, provide another example. His rage at the forester who would have dishonored Florimell fits with his name, from Greek *timē*, honor or glory. So does Belphoebe's saving him from death, once he is wounded by the foresters, because she is the complement to Gloriana, with whom Timias's lord, Arthur, has just connected Florimell: Oft did he wish, that Lady faire mote bee/His faery Queene, for whom he did complaine:/Or that his Faery Queene were such, as shee" (iv.54). In desire, Arthur translates the ideal, inaccessible Gloriana—Elizabeth's public body, as the Proem to Book III announces—into the bodily, accessible Florimell, just as Timias translates the ideal, inaccessible Belphoebe—Elizabeth's private body—into an erotic object. Timias is saved from death and caused to lament by Belphoebe, whose name means "beautiful moon," just after Arthur complains about night, which in fact preserves him from possible disloyalty to Gloriana—he hopes to win "Most goodly meede, the fairest Dame alive" in Florimell (i.18). This parallel blemishes Arthur's continuously ideal image in the poem and gives location to Timias's mistake. Unable to discern what kind of love is due to whom, as his iconographic thigh wound warns, Timias longs for *eros* and exclusivity when he should rejoice in *agape*. Spenser himself, we presume, would insist that he loved his Savior Jesus and his queen, but neither love doomed him to pine away. Desperately ingenious,

Timias substitutes the order of poetry and of stanzaic argument for genuine order and reason, abasing himself in verse (v.45–47). So with his body, he substitutes sickness for health, keeping Belphoebe's attention. He abuses her *caritas*.

These elements recur in Cantos 11 and 12. Scudamore's impotent self-abasement and burning inner torment over his now inaccessible lover Amoret, Belphoebe's sister, parallel the love pains of Timias, who burns as from "percing leuin, which . . . calcineth" (xi.26–27, v.48). Belphoebe's double role as to wounds and healing devolves to Amoret and the armed maiden Britomart. Amoret's wounded, bleeding heart literalizes Timias's state, though it passes from the literal to the metaphorical when equal love merges her with Scudamore, "growne together quite"(xii.46). The elements of the order of poetry and misplaced *eros* from the Timias episode respectively recur in Busirane's allegorical parade and verbal charms, and depictions of tyrannical love. Timias and Belphoebe, figuring chastity as virginity in the first canto of Section B, point forward to the Busirane episode, figuring chastity as marital fidelity as the final episode of Section C. More centrally for the conceptual structure of Book III, the movement from lust to despair broached in the Timias episode recurs in Section C: the sins of the flesh and the world, given form in Hellenore and Malbecco respectively, have as their complement the sins of the devil, pride and despair. Accordingly, Scudamore lies in despair until Britomart rescues him; and until its ruin through Britomart, the House of Busirane emblazons pride and despair in its allegorical rooms and pageants. The diabolic sins there encompass the sins of the flesh and the world in images of lust and domination.

2

If chastity is not the most complex, it certainly was the most politically sensitive of *The Faerie Queene*'s virtues, now that Queen Elizabeth was beyond child-bearing years. To celebrate fruitful, married procreation as chaste while honoring his monarch's chosen virginity, Spenser needed to define chastity with exquisite care.[24] No method for this task would have allowed him more care, more apparent objectivity, than that of the dialectician and Protestant martyr Pierre de la Ramée, or Petrus Ramus (1515–72).[25] His choice of definition through binaries, such as we have been tracing, perhaps accordingly fits with the dichotomous Ramist analytic method.[26] Did Spenser

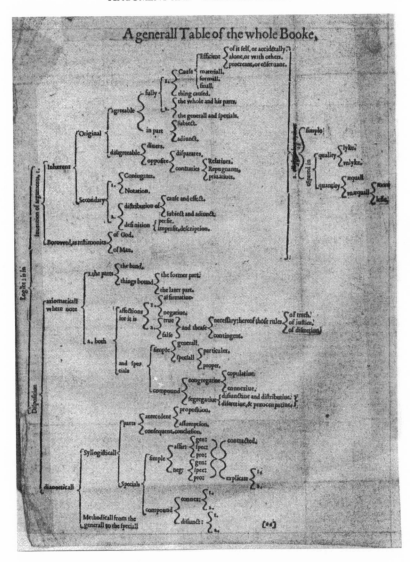

Fig. 1. "A Generall Table of the Whole Booke," from *The Lawiers Logike* (1588) by Abraham Fraunce. (Reproduced by courtesy of the Department of Special Collections, General Library System, University of Wisconsin—Madison.)

draw on Ramus directly? His close Cambridge ties to Gabriel Harvey, an apostle of Ramism in its English intellectual center, might imply that he did. Alternatively, he may simply have worked as seemed natural, given that Ramism came to dominate English logic and rhetoric from the late sixteenth through the seventeenth centuries. Whether Ramist logic is intended or not, Spenser's use of a logical method is vital. Analytic logic, a tool and expression of reason, supplies a patient *pis aller* to readers for the intuitive rational legibility of nature before the Fall.

Spenser begins deploying binary logic in the Proem to Book III, through the doctrine of the Queen's two bodies.[27] Elizabeth may agree

> In mirrours more then one her selfe to see,
> But either *Gloriana* let her chuse,
> Or in *Belphoebe* fashioned to bee:
> In th'one her rule, in th'other her rare chastitee.

Although, in accord with Spenser's *Letter to Ralegh*, Belphoebe's "rare chastitee" represents the Queen's private body, marital chastity in Book III must affect the public body, Gloriana. In bald political terms, Elizabeth's royal legitimacy depends on her lineage, and a legitimate lineage depends on chastity understood as women's marital fidelity.[28] Since her mother not only married Henry VIII unlawfully, some thought, but also died legally convicted of adultery and incest, issues of lineage had as much contemporary weight as those of virginity. Hence Britomart, although her name connects her to virginal Diana, Belphoebe's foster-mother, finds her love in "*Venus* looking glas," that of Amoret's foster-mother (i.8).[29] The mirror itself, prophetic Merlin's gift to Britomart's own royal begetter (ii.18–21), answers Elizabeth's two mirrors, as Gloriana or Belphoebe. It yields Britomart a vision that in the fiction of the poem will make possible both of the Queen's two bodies.

Britomart sees her husband-to-be, Arthegall (ii.22–25). Her own pubescent face will not yet do, and similarly Arthegall's in the vision is not that of Arthegall now, but of Arthegall as he will become. His savagery, transformed, must serve the virtue of justice, as her stirrings of sexual desire must serve the virtue of chastity. What she sees, then, pertains not to her present, as do Gloriana's and Belphoebe's representations of Elizabeth, but to a future. Their representations are images of what they are, whereas what she sees is shorthand for a narrative that Merlin's prophecy sets forth in its material form. So that Book III can dwell on the marital chastity that Britomart champions, the kind of chastity that enters into narrative, into historical progress, Spenser so to speak seals off chastity as virginity by limiting it to Cantos 4 and 5. Its *ne plus ultra*, Belphoebe, expresses all that needs to be expressed about it in Book III.[30]

Belphoebe and Gloriana (as Elizabeth's mirror images) logically do not represent chastity in the way that Britomart does. To return to our earlier categories of "representation," they exemplify chastity or stand for it (*Darstellung*, in Marxist criticism), while she acts in its name or champions it (Marx's *Vertretung*).[31] *Darstellung*, that is, represents by semiotic equivalence: the character Despayre in Book I *stands for* despair, and Malbecco in Book III comes to *stand for* jealousy. Despayre and Orgoglio in Book I are, as their names indicate, just *Darstellungen*, by contrast with Malbecco, who starts with a psyche and then reduces or purifies his nature to that of a *Darstellung* so that he "*Gelosy* is hight" (x.60). *Vertretung*, however, represents as the (Aristotelian) efficient cause for actions: an implicit allegiance to a delegated role guides one.[32] Britomart does not express an entity; she has a calling, a vocation to act in the name of chastity. Malbecco, unable to act and languishing in masochistic "painefulle pleasure [that] turnes to pleasing paine" (x.60), shows that standing-for bears on one's essence as a locus of one's actions. But Britomart's calling bears on what she does as logically prior to what she is. Similarly, while Belphoebe and her twin, Amoret, express the double ontological entity Chastity, Britomart serves, to use Spenser's language in his *Letter to Ralegh*, as its patron.[33] Her chastity is an active virtue. Nonetheless, because her practical knowledge is incomplete and fallible, her motivation at times jars with chastity the ontological entity. To distinguish *Vertretung* and *Darstellung* is to see how she may champion chastity without being its constant exemplar.

Vertreter and *Darstellung* are positions in the poem, germane to readers. They define a gamut of allegorical linkages between concrete and abstract entities. They also help one integrate a world in which the characters' actions are partly regulated by the characters' own different provenances, some in concepts (allegory, parable), some in the stock of semi-conceptual narrative forms (classical myths in which gods are gods of something that they represent), and some in goal-based narrative forms (romance, fabliau). *Vertreter* and *Darstellung* are not, however, roles in day-to-day Faeryland life. For readers, Britomart's actions must embody a fallible, practical knowledge of what chastity involves as she copes with practical situations. Readers need to be conscious of that calling as such. Britomart need not, however, recognize it, any more than do persons who are agents of God's providence in the real world (and aren't we all, for Spenser?). By having exemplarity to link actions with concepts, and *Vertretung* to link actions with practical knowledge keyed to those concepts, Spenser establishes a basic continuity from transcendent to everyday understanding in the narrative. Although fallen humans often botch their readings of life, they maintain access to the world of *intellectus* as they identify standings-for, and maintain access to moral behavior as they properly value actings-in-the-name-of. Such readerly skills underlie a grasp of the argument about chastity in Book III.[34]

Similar patterns hold for normative speech. Clearly, using ethical terms doesn't imply full, accurate knowledge of the concepts they represent. In *The Faerie Queene* the word "chastity" acts in the name of an ontological entity, but at any given moment it stands for some real-time, situated understanding. There are gaps here, which the act of definition in *The Faerie Queene* negotiates. Through learning, specifically through following Spenser's logic of definition, one can reduce the gaps, increase a continuity. Exemplifying something and championing it are perfectly compatible and, in practice, often difficult to tell apart. Taking them as discrete principles, however, clarifies why sharpening the reader's normative awareness should be a chief goal of Spenser's. Because words and characters can act in accord with a principled, destined role on behalf of a quality, though they fall short of its truth, the virtues of *The Faerie Queene* are always active but also always being more accurately defined. Spenser's cognitive terms are also ethical.

Britomart's normative practical consciousness—her sense of how to cope properly with circumstances—brings her closer to standing for the virtue that distinguishes her vocation. This is not to say that she learns, as though *The Faerie Queene* were a *Bildungsroman*.[35] Most of the definition of chastity in Book III takes place outside her experience, by Spenser's design. One never needs to infer that Britomart's personal knowledge grows as one's own does. Nonetheless, Spenser's reader can increasingly rely on a good fit between the ideal for chastity and what Britomart feels or does. When she first wills her chastity she has just reached puberty, an "vnguilty age." She knows no lust at the time she first sees Arthegall's face in the mirror (ii.23, 28). Her nurse is still her bedfellow. Spenser depicts her, therefore, as soon in her life as possible, dedicating her sexuality to fulfilling "the streight course of heuenly destiny" (iii.24). index in the process of defining "chastity."[36] Moreover, just as Britomart starts the genealogical line that leads to Elizabeth, paragon of chastity, so she creates the narrative line that defines "chastity." She precipitates all four current, non-retrospective actions in Sections A and C—Malecasta, Marinell, Malbecco, Busirane—and by her "slaying" Marinell in Canto 4, she prompts Florimell's flight, the spring of the main current actions in both halves of Section B.

Bad characters conceive egocentric narratives. They short-circuit the process of definition by imposing meaning on the people they meet: they represent (champion) themselves by misrepresenting (falsifying the standing-for of) others.[37] In the warped quasi-allegory of the bad characters, other humans stand for (*darstellen*) objects of their own desire or aversion. Malbecco sees his wife, Hellenore, as an exemplar of property. She's legally his property as an individual; she also, like his money, instances his property. When excessive heat (fire, lust) threatens both kinds of chattel, he agonizes which to save (x.14–15). In this reduced structure of representation, a *representans* takes on the power of its *representandum*, but it is also in principle fungible with whatever satisfies the same end, just as in a lexicon various synonyms are fungible as standings-for.

By reducing everything to ciphers and tools in his pursuit of avarice, Malbecco logically reduces himself as well. Self-reflexively. He too becomes a tool of desire. As insubstantial and deformed as a misrepresentation by nature should be, he comes to stand for, to exemplify, the *representandum* Jealousy. For her part, Hellenore accepts her ontological position from Malbecco—their marriage, however ill-assorted, allegorically levels them. But she chooses a different fungible, reductive option, a delightful sin of the flesh, lust, rather than a dreary sin of the world, avarice. Her glamorous lover, Paridell, mediates this change. As an object to be accumulated and a body to be used, Hellenore has a logic of identity—her karma as a Helen whore—that draws her to be the lover of a whole horde of ithyphallic, presumably interchangeable (fungible) satyrs.[38] Her hedonistic, self-regarding liberality, with its sexy, sleepless nights, counterpoises the equally self-regarding isolation of Malbecco or "Gelosy," with its own sleepless, turbulent nights. Although she revels and he shrivels, Hellenore and Malbecco represent—stand for—paired variants of reduction, an allegorical *leitmotiv* in Book III. As usual with Spenser, however, their resemblance draws attention to their differences as well: they're not fungible for us or absorbed into one another.

Since Spenser allegorizes figures in a poem he creates, and the bad characters perform reductive allegorizing of a sort upon human beings whom God creates, their allegorizing and his radically differ in moral and aesthetic criteria. As self-serving poachers, the bad characters cannot allegorize, like Spenser, *in bono*. For this reason, reading his poem and observing their reductions offers a double view of those characters who can be chaste. Such characters appear in themselves and also through the eyes of those who reduce them. As seen by the forester, the witch's son, the fisherman, and Proteus, Florimell stands for bodily lust. Fungible with Snowy Florimell, then, she's named for the sensory attractors *flower* and *honey*. But flower and honey, for Florimell as she should truly be perceived, evoke a harvest of natural sweetness, the flower and its honey offering the trajectory of a narrative. They suggest that her love and constancy of spirit arise spontaneously, naturally, letting one see why she flees, improvidently, to seek Marinell, unprotected. She pays for that improvidence by having to flee friend as well as foe. (Her precipitation contrasts with armed Britomart's prudence, and with Marinell's imprudence and false prudence. Chastity, which, because of lineage, is a public as well as a private virtue, demands true prudence.) Such binaries, an improper and a proper way of seeing an individual character, tend to be simple. They help ground the definition of chastity.

What is less simple comes through narrative binaries. Because of the gap between standing-for and acting-in-the-name-of, and the poem's representing chastity situationally, through characters and events, a logic in defining chastity becomes more necessary and more complex. Rather than a Ramist single principle that ramifies by division, Spenser's "chastity" emerges in sequential binaries that modify and enhance the definition. Orthodox Ramism invites one to see "a granular world," but Spenser, "a woven coherence," constantly "*mediating*—that is," maintaining a proportional or *balanced* relation—between the world of experience and the noetic realm."[39] Some unifying work done by Ramus's diagrams falls to the (diagrammatic) architecture of *The Faerie Queene*. Accordingly, the binaries of definition progress within the three four-canto groupings outlined above.

In the first third of Book III, Cantos 1 through 4 (our Section A), Spenser pairs Britomart directly with Malecasta and Marinell, who announce an Aristotelian pattern where virtue strikes a mean between two ugly extremes. Chastity cannot be the lolling, slavering lust of Malecasta or Marinell's rejection of sexuality and abstinence out of fearful self-interest. In accord with an Aristotelian pattern, chastity draws elements from both extremes, cleansed of self-interested motives. The cleansing allows for greater complexity in Section B, where Spenser translates the Aristotelian pattern into the Augustinian pattern we've invoked, of *malum* and *bonum*. Augustine's is an ontological version of the epistemological double view of individual characters that one derives from Spenser's and the bad characters' kinds of allegorizing. For Augustine, what is *in bono* recognizes the divine order in which it exists. What is *in malo* is a forgetting of that order, a misappropriation.

Given that the Anglican queen heads church and state, *The Faerie Queene* merges secular and divine order. We take an *in bono* action for Spenser to be attuned to this order and performed through a disposition to be attuned to it. Action and intention both count. At times, admittedly, Spenser relates them rather obliquely. Take procreative chastity, assuring orderly lineage. As Marinell is conceived *in malo* when Dumarin rapes sleeping Cymoent, so Amoret and Belphoebe are conceived *in bono* through the sun's shining into sleeping Chrysogone's womb, "the sacred throne / Of her chaste bodie" (iv.19, vi.5–7). In differentiating these actions, Spenser emphasizes that Dumarin finds Cymoent "by chaunce," while the sun is a universal agent of ongoing order:

> the fruitfull seades
> Of all things liuing, through impression
> Of the sunbeames in moyst complexion
> Doe life conceiue. (vi.8)

Furthermore, Dumarin and Cymoent are mismatched, he being "earthly" and human, and she a sea nymph. The sun's close kinship to Chrysogone is betokened by a symbol: the alchemical symbols for gold (*chrysos*) and the sun are identical, a circle with a dot in the center.[40] Amoret and Belphoebe's begetting is almost parthenogenetic.[41] Yet—and here is the intention necessary for an *in bono* action—Chrysogone is so shamefast that even her apparent loss of chastity makes her feel "shame and foule disgrace" (vi.9–10), reactions that Spenser does not show in Cymoent. The fact of chastity and the affect proper to it glorifies the birth of Amoret and Belphoebe. In turn, because Amoret and Belphoebe are *in bono*, readers believe in Chrysogone's chastity and accordingly adjust their ongoing criteria for *in bono* "chastity."

The sun radiantly fecundates the earth, Spenser says (vi.8); Typhoeus fathers the vile twins in Section B, Argante and Ollyphant, "of his owne mother Earth" (vii.47); Snowy Florimell's body comprises (sun-ripened) earthly ores; and richly fertile earth in the Garden of Adonis supports *natura naturans*.[42] Drawing on such analogies, Spenser fills Section B with *in bono* and *in malo* contrasts, as for instance the two Florimells. Similarly, the incestuous begetting of Argante and Ollyphant repeats *in malo* an earlier pseudo-incest, the union of two sames, gold and the sun, to beget Amoret and Belphoebe. What is natural to chastity, the implicit truth of like to like, lies close to what is unnatural, here and in the union of gold and sun parodied by the alchemical construction of Snowy Florimell. Florimell herself, with her name and golden girdle (the cestus of Amoret's foster-mother, Venus), obviously continues the Garden of Adonis *in bono* imagery; but in her, Spenser revises the constancy-through-flux of nature in the Garden. Her "flux," her fleeing, is a symptom of her steadfastness. All these distinctions and near paradoxes enter into defining chastity as a mode of human existence, with practical as well as ideal norms.

Numerous images of the union of likes—mirroring complements—color Book III. So do images of a paired motif, androgyny. When Britomart sees Arthegall's face (her complement) in the mirror, she sets out disguised as a male knight, like Arthegall. One might usefully connect these two motifs, mirroring complements and androgyny, with a starting point for Spenser, the two closely related aspects of royal chastity, faithful marriage and virginity, respectively. To do so is to see why these motifs should logically generate varied instances in the text. Snowy Florimell and the witch's hyena are the *in malo* limit-forms of androgyny or hermaphroditism. A kind of incest—the *in malo* limit-form of mirroring complements—lies in the planned union of two creatures of the witch's begetting, her son and Snowy Florimell. Amoret's love for Scudamore unifies complements *in bono*. His shield, as his name indicates, bears the image of Amoret's foster-brother, Amor, or Cupid, husband "in stedfast loue and happy state" (6.50) of her caretaker, Psyche.

These cognitive structures, expectedly, have epistemological consequences in a poem that so densely mediates "the world of experience and the noetic realm." The likeness of natural to unnatural, complements to androgynes, and *in bono* to *in malo* behavior, troubles the characters' discernment. Chastity's being an active virtue leaves it open to being misperceived. Plainly, for instance, the automatic sweetheart Snowy Florimell serves as the misperception of imprudent Florimell. Languorous in Malecasta's tapestry, woven Venus tempts one to sin and sentimentality, but the real Venus, not the fabricated one, embodies fruitful troth in the Garden of Adonis. Entrapped as they are by equivocal images and willful imaginations, characters naturally misread.[43] Spenser's audience, buoyed by *The Faerie Queene's* supplementary forms of reason, witnesses the figuration of reason's fallen state.

Spenser's mode of analogy sharpens the definition of chastity in two ways, besides the obvious one of presenting images of chastity and unchastity of various sorts. First, it contextualizes, letting chastity be an active virtue. Second, it hones the reader's skill to focus on discriminables. Binaries help do this. Marinell's selfish virginity *logically* produces wounds, others' and his own, that need healing. His integrity is false. *Per contra*, the nymph who teaches Belphoebe to heal wounds also *logically* brings her up "in perfect Maydenhed" (v.32, vi.28), while Timias counters her healing his wounds by effectively inflicting a wounded heart upon himself, unable to be whole in the "perfect loue" she manifests (v.54). In healing, Belphoebe's chastity implies *caritas*, the criterion, of course, for being *in bono*. It looks to the future not as Marinell and Cymoent do, but rather in moral terms, as Britomart's procreative chastity looks to the future, foreseen in Merlin's prophecy. Chrysogone and Belphoebe, though their two courses differ, show a natural chastity—that, one might say, of a sublunary sun and a superlunary moon respectively—both unlike the forced, angry asceticism of Marinell.

Such an argument prompts, but underdetermines, at least three kinds of variation in Book III: tonal, modal, and temporal. We cannot here describe these variations but we can indicate their range and emphasize its logical necessity. The range is logically necessary because Spenser contextualizes his analogies. Therefore, how one responds to examples of chastity will partly define what chastity means in practical terms. Each of the two elements of every binary in Section B, accordingly, receives a different tonal treatment: think of the different registers of reaction proper to Florimell and Snowy Florimell; to the ravening hyena and the sardonic Snowy Florimell as the witch's henchmen; to chilly Columbell and voracious Argante; to love-addled Timias with his poetical logic and the witch's son with his "soft sighes, and louely semblaunces" (vii.16); or to the semi-comic, hapless Squire of Dames, always on duty, and the off-duty knight Paridell, with his practiced swagger. Adding to his logic of discrimination, Spenser weaves several poetic modes into the poem, most visibly ekphrasis, elegy, courtly romance, Virgilian epic, Ovidian metamorphosis, and fabliau. The Malbecco-Hellenore episode combines the last four of these, with further allusion to Ariosto. Each poetic mode has a temporal syndrome proper to it: ekphrases, for example, describe in the present artworks made in the past. Spenser plays with these temporalities in the context of his own narrative, so as to vary the relations among, first, the literal order of events as they supposedly happen; second, the order in which we read his narration of them; third, allusions that implant his poem in our cultural experience; and fourth, the projected future of narrative trajectories, of our and the characters' learning, and of cyclic and perdurable phenomena.

Logically and structurally, the last stage in defining chastity comes in the House of Busirane, a new horror derived from familiar elements. This final episode follows naturally from the one right before it, Malbecco and Hellenore, as the fire around Busirane's House suggests: in Cantos 9 and 10 the threat of fire has forced open Malbecco's castle gate and fire has let Hellenore flee. Now in a new castle (xi.21), obsessive, possessive Busirane tries to make Amoret a Hellenore. Amoret's foster mother, Venus, connects the two women. In myth, Paris names Venus the most beautiful goddess so he may possess her human counterpart, Helen, the most beautiful woman. If Hellenore amid the satyrs parodies Venus in the garden, where "when euer that she will" she "possesseth" Adonis, then Amoret's "faithfull loue, t'abide for euermore" redeems her foster-mother's image (vi.46, 53). The lustful interpret Venus as lust: witness Malecasta's tapestries portraying smitten Venus's "sleights" so as to "steale [Adonis's] heedelesse hart away" (i.35–37). This ekphrastic Adonis forever dies in the static tapestry, transformed in the final scene to a flower whose dead unlikeness to the Garden's flora Spenser marks by jerking the reader out of the ekphrasis: "Him to a dainty flowre she did transmew,/Which in that cloth was wrought, as if it liuely grew" (i.38).[44] The ambiguity of Venus as real and as represented, as a type of Amoret and of Hellenore, helps explain Amoret's vulnerability to Busirane. Open to ambiguity, Amoret's endangerment inheres in her heritage, the complexities in the definition of chastity, and the vulnerability of the great, *ipsa natura*, to misrepresentation. Busirane's torture of Amoret, to make her misrepresent herself, implies peril even to the greatest, since Amoret is twin to a type of Spenser's own monarch.

Busirane would resolve all ambiguities by removing Amoret from her self. Her body, her "liuing bloud" as the ink he uses to write the charms "to make her him to loue" (xii.31), expresses his will. Not an extrinsic demon but her own mind, demonically altered by Busirane, would accomplish her abuse. Deprived of the capacity to be chaste, she'd lose what she *darstellt* and thus become a parody of herself, as Snowy Florimell parodies Florimell. The brazen (copper and lead or copper and tin) pillar, the iron bonds, the silver basin in which Amoret's heart lies[45] —these images in the last canto of Section C remind one of Snowy Florimell's creation in the last canto of Section B, just as the likening of Amoret and Scudamore to the "white marble" statue of Hermaphroditus (xii.46) exhibits, *contra* Snowy Florimell, the congruence of artifact and self. Similarly, the situation of the old man's imprisoning a chaste, loving young maiden reminds one of the real Florimell, trapped by Proteus as Snowy Florimell roams free. The line of continuity here passes from the binary of true and false Florimell (Canto 8), through that in which Hellenore's body extends Malbecco's avarice and then her lovers' lust (Cantos 9–10), to Busirane's attempt to commandeer Amoret's meaning.

Uncharmed, Amoret cannot love Busirane, her abuser. Charmed, she couldn't either, because instead of Amoret would smile a hermaphroditic creature, with self-loving Busirane's mind and will in Amoret's body. Bodies can be loci of lust, but they can't love: good love must be wedded to soul, *psychē*, as one is reminded by the allegory of Cupid and Psyche, spouses who appear just before the first mention of Amorets love for Scudamore,. From such a state of stedfast loue comes pleasure and procreation (vi.49–50, 53). Busirane, whose tapestries and masque represent a brutal Cupid, plays this brutal Cupid himself and for himself. His "deadly dart" in Amoret's breast (xii.21) is his imitation of those that Cupid lays aside in his love of Psyche. By practicing on Amoret's soul, he tries to manufacture for himself as a lover, Cupid, a false soul or Psyche, and for himself as a man, Busirane, a false Amoret.

Hermaphroditism, impersonation, division of the self from the self: Amoret's captivity has a variety of doublings. The metal pillar to which she is bound both expresses and ironizes her steadfastness. Exposing her heart both expresses and ironizes chastity's selfless love. Later, when she can represent herself truly, a defining binary to the pillar image appears, to which we alluded above, the marble statue of "faire *Hermaphrodite*," a sign of perduring union that Amoret's and Scudamore's embrace resembles (xii.45–46). The embrace re-presents *in bono* the upright and encircling image of the pillar and bonds, now incorporated into the body. As an emblem, then, the image of the temporary hermaphrodite "in long embracement" rebukes Busirane's emblems of maimed love in their own hypostatizing genre. True union is an ultimate reversal of false representations, Busirane's and those of the odd couples who promenade in the masque with which Canto 12 begins.[46] Since Hermaphroditus was half-brother to Eros or Amor, the image confirms the Amor on Scudamore's shield and returns Amoret to the family of Venus.[47] If the misdirected passion and despair of Scudamore in Canto 11 harked back to those of Timias in Canto 5, love's fulfillment in Canto 12 then tallies with that in Canto 6, the natural Garden of Adonis where Amoret first appears.

Britomart in the House of Busirane witnesses a denial of moral meaning by a denial of the natural order that undergirds moral meaning, including that of chastity. The first room shows the loves of the gods (xi.28–49). Jupiter's changes of shape, to Europa's bull, Leda's swan, and the like, mark the appropriate binaries from Cantos 8 and 10, Proteus's changes of shape in wooing Florimell and Hellenore's man-beast revel with satyrs. From this realm of brutish unchastity, the degrading of natural identity progressively leaves "Kings

Queenes, Lords Ladies, Knights and Damzels gent/ . . . heap'd together with the vulgar sort" before Cupid (xi.46). On Busirane's
walls, natural order collapses into universal lust and domination. Love
and war might be contraries; lust and domination aren't. They are *in
malo* expressions, in the flesh and the world respectively, of the room's
obsessively ubiquitous adjuration, "*Be bolde, be bolde*, and euery where
Be bold" (54).

The adjuration, a kind of caption, quotes the mental adjuration
that has driven figures in the room, male (Kings, Lords, Knights) or
female (Queens, Ladies, Damsels), in idolizing violent, random desire.
Tardily for those who are bold in "fowle Idolatree" (xi.49) comes
the rueful, single counter-adjuration, "*Be not too bold*," as the door
to the third room says. The procession emerging from it, from Fancy
and Desyre through to Despight and Cruelty with bleeding Amoret,
and then to a whole rout of maladies (7–26), acts as a gloss on the
inner conditions of the overbold. Overboldness accepts neither the
Aristotelian mean nor the opposition between *in bono* and *in malo*.
No principle of order has a place within the proto-Hobbesian state
of nature figured in rooms one and two. The logic of the sins of flesh
and world points to what the pageant shows, the diabolic sins, pride
and despair, that deny properly ordered action.[48]

Though she tries, Britomart cannot "construe" the slogans (54).
They pertain to an idea of nature and a kind of boldness that are not
hers. Because that idea of nature is Busirane's, though, she sees the
victim of his boldness, Amoret, led bleeding into the second room.
Amoret's reappearance in the innermost room, from which the
masque entered and to which it exited, brings the first two rooms'
logic into the core of Busirane's realm. Consequently, because his
representations pretend to universality, they begin to apply to him.
Like the enslaved lovers of the tapestries and masque, he passes from
executing his will to being forced to execute the will of another,
ending as a "captiue . . . led to wretchednesse and wo" (xii.41). After
undoing him, furthermore, his logic undoes itself. By saving Amoret,
Britomart does not merely remedy ills, as in the earlier parts of Book
III. Through a ritual of order—Busirane's backwards recitation of
his charms—she revokes an idea of nature in which love, virtue and
vice, good and evil, have no sense beyond the hedonic.[49] In such a
state, chastity as Spenser has defined it cannot exist. That is why
the Busirane episode caps Book III, reasserting Spenserian chastity
through the return of Amoret's self to herself as the encircling flame
and ornate rooms vanish utterly. Spenser in one way and Britomart
in another expose as a delusory superstition the normative space

that the House of Busirane doubly represents, standing for it and championing it.

3

We have proposed that Spenser built Book III as a dense network of double-associative elements: that is, each element has its place because of how it stands to other elements in regard to contiguity and resemblance, the two principles of mental association.[50] What we mean by resemblance will be clear from the examples in Parts 1 and 2 above. One kind of contiguity is juxtaposition in the poem. Timias's wounding and lament in Canto 5 repeats a pattern of wounding and lament from Britomart, wounded at Castle Joyous and lamenting on the shore, and Marinell, wounded by Britomart and lamented, and then, though he is not literally wounded, Arthur in "restlesse anguish and vnquiet paine"(iv.61). Another kind of contiguity is that of analogous standing within the architecture of Book III. Malecasta stands to Section A as Belphoebe to Section B as Malbecco's castle to Section C, each in the initial canto. It follows from our kind of analysis that they share elements. In each appears the onset of improper love, the theme of art (Malecasta's tapestries, Timias's poetizing, Paridell's rehearsing the matter of Troy), and an armed woman. Lustful foresters in the first two predict Paridell's role in the third, while Hellenore takes Malecasta's place and Britomart, Belphoebe's. Again, Sections A and B end with Marinell and Florimell respectively at the bottom of the sea (iv.42–43, viii.37–41); and Canto 12 provides the union of these lover's proxies, Amoret and Scudamore. Our analysis, we hope, establishes double-associative elements as objective phenomena in an architecture of contiguity and resemblance.

If Spenser gave Book III a dense structure not only of form but also of argument, conducted in accord with (the Protestant) Ramus's modern methods, then the book acts as a whole. Structure, when perceived, is not only aesthetic and hermeneutic. It is also mnemonic. Spenser devoted himself, consciously or intuitively, to shaping its parts so that one can recall Book III as a whole, multiple narrative "of Chastity," as he says in the first line of its Proem. Conceived as a whole, Book III enrolls themes of gender and problems of representation, for example, to serve the definition of chastity. Chastity emerges in the classical manner as a mean, in the hierarchical Augustinian manner of *bonum* and *malum*, and as the creator of a normative realm, that of Gloriana and Belphoebe, including a public legitimacy and a private self-rule. All the narrative elements also converge upon this definition. Chastity underdetermines what happens and how it is described, but no characters rest outside it. Although Elizabeth's virginity and dynastic position make Book III focus on female chastity, male chastity becomes paramount with Marinell and the intended sexual victims of Argante and Ollyphant (iv, vii, xi). Both sexes' chastity in love supplies Busirane with his mythological caricatures of both.

Similarly, although representation (*Vertretung* and *Darstellung*) and the poet's art are thematically complex in *The Faerie Queene*, they are like anything else in God's creation, abusable *in malo* and admirable *in bono*. The centrality of that moral fact (for Spenser) implies, as we have said, that his self-serving evildoers need not compromise his allegory. Spenser imparts the power of meaning to figments of a poem. The evildoers' reductive pathology, by contrast, drains power and meaning from fellow humans. Knowing, as he tells Ralegh, "how doubtfully all Allegories may be construed," Spenser *confirms* two forms of his own kind of allegory right before and during the Busirane cantos. First, Malbecco's transformation displays how Spenser's augmentative, *in bono* allegorizing of figments differs from a character's reductive, *in malo* allegorizing of a human being. As egoists, Malbecco and Hellenore reduce themselves so as to stay faithful to their base selves. Spenser locates this and them in raw nature, woods and shore, so that his allegory both uses and comments on theirs. So, next, does his use of Busirane's attempts to reduce Amoret; but now he stresses the unnatural, for Busirane's attempts vie with Amoret's true self. Black magic tries to naturalize the alteration of Amoret just as Busirane's tapestries and masque try to naturalize its moral ambiance. Whereas reduced Malbecco remains whole, despite a diet that "doth transfix the soule with deathes eternall dart" (x.59), reduced Amoret, Busirane's representation, seems riven, "transfixed with a cruell dart" (xii.31). Correspondingly, everything in the house around her exists in compartmentalized units, be they tapestries, rooms, or two-by-two promenaders. An allegory *in bono* rejects Busirane's reductions rather than, as with Malbecco and Hellenore, taking their logic forward. It faithfully heals divisions, so that the house is "vanisht vtterly, and cleane subuerst," and restores Amoret's nature as if "she were neuer hurt" (xii.38, 42).

If our analysis works well *grosso modo*, Spenser should have been extremely pleased with the integrity of the microcosm that he had *dargestellt* and the complex ideal of chastity of which Book III is the *Vertreter*. We are sure that he had much more reason to be pleased than we have been able to show. Our analysis is clearly incomplete.

Apart from any errors in it and apart from our paring away psycholog-ical readings that many critics have thought worthwhile, we recog-nize there are relevant issues we have omitted. We have not tried to address Spenser's use of language for structural effects, for example. We have slighted his allusions to Ovid, Ariosto, and Tasso. Nor have we tried to show how Book III relates to analogues in the books that precede it. We have shied from the remarkably different task, we think, of showing how it, published in 1590, relates to its seeming continuation in Book IV, published in 1596. Our analysis itself and our means of analysis, we hope, may provide tools for such inquiries.

University of Wisconsin—Madison

Notes

We are grateful to Heather Dubrow, Andrew Weiner, and Susanne Wofford for their careful reading of this essay and their invaluable suggestions for improving it.

1. Our use of binaries touches on but diverges from that in several earlier critical works. For Spenser criticizing and revising Platonic dualism, see Lauren Silberman, "Singing Unsung Heroines: Androgynous Discourse in Book 3 of *The Faerie Queene,*" in *Rewriting the Renaissance,* ed. Margaret W. Ferguson, Maureen Quilligan, and Nancy J. Vickers (Chicago: University of Chicago Press, 1986), 259–71. For a treatment of pairings of books, not binaries within books, see Ronald Arthur Horton, *The Unity of* The Faerie Queene (Athens: University of Georgia Press, 1978), chap-ters 5–6. For a powerful argument in favor of extraordinarily thorough structural control in Books I and II, at the level of stanzas and images as well as the level we treat, of narrative, see Maren-Sofie Røstvig, *Configurations: A Topomorphic Approach to Renaissance Poetry* (Oslo: Scandinavian University Press, 1994).

2. For a treatment of definition as central to allegory's analytic process, though in a vein different from ours, see Isabel G. MacCaffrey, *Spenser's Allegory: The Anat-omy of Imagination* (Princeton, NJ: Princeton University Press, 1976); Horton, chap-ters 8–9, explores the poem's "avatars" and "antitypes" quasi-definitionally.

3. For an analysis of these two types, see Hanna Fenichel Pitkin, *The Concept of Representation* (Berkeley: University of California Press, 1967). Pitkin differentiates but does not develop the German terms in "Representation," in *Political Innovation and Conceptual Change,* ed. Terence Ball, James Fair, and Russell L. Hanson (Cam-bridge: Cambridge University Press, 1989), 132–54. For a distinction between "imi-tation" and "emulation" of models, which also pertains here, see Harry Berger, Jr., "The Renaissance Imagination: Second World and Green World," in *Second World and Green World: Studies in Renaissance Fiction-Making* (Berkeley: University of Cali-fornia Press, 1988), 39.

4. In particular, we are profoundly indebted to A. C. Hamilton's notes in the first and second editions of his *Faerie Queene* (London: Longman, 2001). The latter

provides the text from which we quote, edited by Hiroshi Yamashita and Toshiyuki Suzuki. Two other works on which we have freely and gratefully drawn are Thomas P. Roche's pioneering *Kindly Flame* (Princeton: Princeton University Press, 1964) and James Nohrnberg's massively learned *Analogy of* The Faerie Queene (Princeton: Princeton University Press, 1980). A number of critics seek to account holistically for the relationships among Book III's structural elements. Besides Roche, many of whose fundamental premises we accept, we agree with Mark J. Bruhn, "Approaching Busyrane: Episodic Patterning in *The Faerie Queene,*" *Studies in Philology* 92 (1995): 275–90, and A. Bartlett Giamatti, *Play of Double Senses: Spenser's* Faerie Queene (Englewood Cliffs, NJ: Prentice-Hall, 1975), that the accumulating pattern of Book III's episodes conditions one's reading. Other holistic visions of Book III include Paul J. Alpers, *The Poetry of* The Faerie Queene (Columbia, MI: University of Missouri Press, 1982); Berger, "*The Faerie Queene,* Book III: A General Description," in *Essential Articles for the Study of Edmund Spenser,* ed. A. C. Hamilton (Hamden, CT: Archon, 1972), 395–424; Alastair Fowler, "Emanations of Glory: Neoplatonic Order in Spenser's *Faerie Queene,*" in *A Theatre for Spenserians,* ed. Judith M. Kennedy and James A. Reither (Toronto: University of Toronto Press, 1973), 53–82, and *Spenser and the Numbers of Time* (New York: Barnes and Noble, 1964); Northrup Frye, "The Structure of Imagery in *The Faerie Queene,*" in *Essential Articles for the Study of Edmund Spenser,* 153–70; Hamilton, *The Structure of Allegory in* The Faerie Queene (Oxford: Clarendon, 1961); William Nelson, *Poetry of Edmund Spenser: A Study* (New York: Columbia University Press, 1963); Silberman, *Transforming Desire: Erotic Knowledge in Books III and IV of* The Faerie Queene (Berkeley: University of California Press, 1995); and Kathleen Williams, "Venus and Diana: Some Uses of Myth in *The Faerie Queene,*" in *Spenser: A Collection of Critical Essays,* ed. Harry Berger, Jr. (Englewood Cliffs, NJ: Prentice-Hall, 1968), 97–114.

5.   The adjective *glaucus* "saepe maris ac fluviorum diis tribuitur" [is often attributed to the gods of the sea and rivers], Facciolatus, Jacobus, and Aegidius Forcellinus, eds., *Totius Latinitatis Lexicon* (2nd ed., Patavii, 1805), 1:383a. Glauce at first (ii.48–51) tries to fend off love from Britomart, as Cymoent tries to keep it from Marinell. Berger, *Revisionary Play: Studies in the Spenserian Dynamics* (Berkeley: University of California Press, 1988), 139, notes Glauce's alignment with Cymoent.

6.   Proteus appears in Herodotus, *The Histories,* trans. Robin Waterfield (Oxford: Oxford University Press, 1998), 2.112–20, as an Egyptian king who keeps Helen safe for Menelaus. Spenser's twist is that his Proteus unwillingly keeps Florimell safe for her destined husband, Marinell—this, at the end of Canto 8, directly precedes the story of the faux Menelaus, Malbecco, and his Hellenore. Though Spenser's Proteus is "with prophecy inspir'd" (iv.25), he can't foresee the ironies of his own action. By denying love to Marinell through "subtile sophisme" (iv.28) and by his own jealous, carnal love for Florimell, he in fact brings them together as lovers in Book 4. His blind, boomeranging infatuation aligns him with Merlin and Busirane.

7.   The sequence starts with an account in II.x.5–68, taking us from the arrival of the Trojans in Britain to the succession of Arthur's father, Uther Pendragon. The poetic space between it and Merlin's account in Book III is approximately the same length as the space between Merlin's account and that at Malbecco's dinner.

8.   Nohrnberg 445.

9. We focus on the 1590 text of Book III because it has its own narrative logic and closure, as a conclusion to what Spenser chose as the inaugural part of his poem. For the argument that to treat Books III and IV as a unit disturbs that original logic, see Helen Gardner, "Some Reflections on the House of Busyrane," *Review of English Studies* 34 (1983): 403–13.

10. For a detailed account of the parallels between the Malecasta and Malbecco episodes, see Alastair Fowler, "Six Knights at Castle Joyous," *Studies in Philology* 56 (1959): 583–99.

11. The *in bono/in malo* dichotomy originates with Augustine, who argues, for example in *Confessions*, Book 7, that all of God's creation is good, but is subject to misuse through the erring human will. MacCaffrey 270 notices Spenser's use of the dichotomy, and Røstvig recurs to it, chapter 6 passim.

12. Timias's role as balked lover of Belphoebe, one might note, is anticipated in Book II (iii.37–42) by Braggadocchio, who in Book III becomes one of Snowy Florimell's would-be lovers.

13. The wonderful phrase is William James's, quoted in Hilary Putnam, *The Three-fold Cord: Mind, Body, and World* (New York: Columbia University Press, 1999), 73.

14. Spenser has rarely figured in the numerous studies on alchemy in Renaissance literature. One exception is Roger W. Rouland, "Alchemical Transmutation in Spenser's *Fowre Hymnes*," *Cauda Pavonis: Studies in Hermeticism* 17 (1998): 1–8, which makes a detailed argument about the role of alchemical transformation and the quest for the philosopher's stone in *Fowre Hymnes*.

15. In alchemical theory, sulfur and mercury—generative principles, not the ordinary minerals—are thought to give rise to all metals and minerals within the earth, having themselves formed from the "exhalations" of water and earth when the sun shone upon them. See Lyndy Abraham, *A Dictionary of Alchemical Imagery* (Cambridge: Cambridge University Press, 1998), 192–94; Mark Haeffner, *The Dictionary of Alchemy: From Maria Prophetissa to Isaac Newton* (London: Aquarian, 1991), 175–77, 243–44; E. J. Holmyard, *Alchemy* (Middlesex: Penguin, 1957) 24, 75; John Read, *Prelude to Chemistry: An Outline of Alchemy, Its Literature and Relationships* (1936; reprint, Cambridge, MA: MIT, 1966), 17–21; and Gareth Roberts, *The Mirror of Alchemy: Alchemical Ideas and Images in Manuscripts and Books from Antiquity to the Seventeenth Century* (London: British Library, 1994), 50–51. As early Islamic alchemists discovered, heating a combination of mercury and sulfur yields mercuric sulfide (cinnabar), called vermilion for its red color. See Abraham 41; Haeffner 87–88; Holmyard 75.

16. See Abraham 193–94; Read 87–91, 101–05. Alchemy includes a complex awareness of male and female principles, which must be combined in creating the philosopher's stone. For alchemy and hermaphroditism, see Nicholas Flamel, *Nicholas Flamel: His Exposition of the Hieroglyphicall Figures (1624)*, ed. Laurinda Dixon (New York: Garland, 1994), 32–33; Abraham 35–9, 98–99; and Haeffner 141–42.

17. By the late Middle Ages, the progression of colors black-white-yellow-red was thought to mark the process of the creation of the philosopher's stone, though yellow tended to drop out of the sequence in the sixteenth and seventeenth centuries. See Abraham 44–45; Haeffner 88–89; and Read 13–17.

18. For the seven metals, see Haeffner 177–80.

19.   Counterfeit coins might contain zinc and bismuth, but these were assimilated into the seven metals mentioned; *OED*'s earliest reference to *zinc* is 1651, and *bismuth*, 1668. One might note that Elizabeth had restored English currency to its ancient standards of fineness, so that her portrait acted as a guarantor of value.

20.   For the roots of the *discordia concors* topos, see Edgar Wind, *Pagan Mysteries in the Renaissance* (revised ed., New York: Norton, 1968), chapter 5. For a treatment of it in *The Faerie Queene*, see Berger's *Revisionary Play* 19–35 passim.

21.   Though Aristotle, echoed in the mid-seventeenth century by Thomas Browne, denied that hyenas were hermaphrodites, the belief persisted that they changed sex annually and could impregnate themselves. See Lois E. Bueler, "Webster's Excellent Hyena," *Philological Quarterly* 59 (1980): 108. Also see Aristotle, *History of Animals* 579b and *Generation of Animals* 757a. *Generation of Animals, History of Animals,* and *Politics,* in *The Complete Works of Aristotle: The Revised Oxford Translation,* ed. Jonathan Barnes, 2 vols. (Princeton: Princeton University Press, 1984); Browne, *Sir Thomas Browne's* Pseudodoxia Epidemica, vol. 1, ed. Robin Robbins (Oxford: Clarendon, 1981), 3.17; Pliny, *Natural History,* vol. 3, trans. H. Rackham (Cambridge: Harvard University Press, 1956), 8.30; Ovid, *Shakespeare's Ovid: Being Arthur Golding's Translation of the* Metamorphoses, ed. W. H. D. Rouse, trans. Arthur Golding (London: De La More, 1904), 15.449–52; and Edward Topsell, *The History of Four-Footed Beasts, Taken Principally from the Historiæ Animalium of Conrad Gesner,* vol. 1 (1658; New York: Da Capo, 1967), 339–43, which is almost identical to Topsell's 1607 bestiary. Good summaries of the belief's history appear in Bueler; Marta Powell Harley, "Rosalind, the Hare, and the Hyena in Shakespeare's *As You Like It,*" *Shakespeare Quarterly* 36 (1985): 335–7; and Arnaud Zucker, "Raison Fausse et Fable Vraie: Sur le Sexe Ambigu de la Hyène," *Pallas: Revue d'Études Antiques* 41 (1994): 27–40.

22.   Why Palladine? Because the asexual birth of Pallas Athena, who sprang from the head of Zeus, contrasts with Argante's having been incestuously sired by Zeus's great foe, Typhoeus. Birth from a male god reprises the Book's theme of androgyny and complements the parthenogenesis of Amoret and Belphoebe in the previous canto. Further, because the dove, *columba,* is Venus's bird, the naming allows an allusive contrast between Columbell and Palladine, Venus and Minerva.

23.   We take "both" (ix.13–14) to mean Satyrane and Paridell, not the Squire of Dames. Paridell and Satyrane are fit for Britomart to challenge, unlike a "young Squire" (viii.52, ix.16), and they are the two significant male actors in the rest of the episode. As the mantle of promiscuity slips to Paridell, and Hellenore freshly embodies the female frailty the Squire exposes, the young man disappears from the poem.

24.   For a reading of Books III and IV as critical of Elizabeth, see Judith H. Anderson, " 'In liuing colours and right hew': The Queen of Spenser's Central Books" in *Critical Essays on Edmund Spenser,* ed. Mihoko Suzuki (New York: G. K. Hall, 1996), 168–82.

25.   Ramist dialectic has drawn limited attention from Spenser critics, though John Webster traces possible Ramism in Spenser's attitude toward the purpose of poetry in "Gabriel Harvey's *Ciceronianus*: An Emerging Renaissance Aesthetic," *Spenser at Kalamazoo* (1978): 2–19, and "Clarification and Reply," 29–34 in the same issue.

See Rosamund Tuve, *Elizabethan and Metaphysical Imagery: Renaissance Poetic and Twentieth-Century Critics* (Chicago: University of Chicago Press, 1947), and "Imagery and Logic: Ramus and Metaphysical Poetics" in *Renaissance Essays from the* Journal of the History of Ideas, ed. Paul Oskar Kristeller and Philip P. Wiener (New York: Harper, 1968), for Ramist influence on the construction of tropes and the rise of wit as fundamental to poetic images and metaphors.

26.   Ramus (1515–1572), a convert who died a victim of the St. Bartholomew's Day Massacre, proposed reforms for all the arts of the *trivium,* grammar, rhetoric, and dialectic (also called logic). These reforms came to dominate English universities—especially Cambridge—in the last quarter of the sixteenth century. See Wilbur Samuel Howell, *Logic and Rhetoric in England, 1500–1700* (New York: Russell, 1961), 178, 205–46. For Gabriel Harvey as a pioneer in Ramist rhetoric in the 1570s, see Howell 247–55. For explanations of pre-Ramist and Ramist logic and rhetoric, see Howell, chapters 2–4; Lisa Jardine, "The Place of Dialectic Teaching in Sixteenth-Century Cambridge," *Studies in the Renaissance* XXI (1974), 31–57; and Walter J. Ong, *Ramus, Method, and the Decay of Dialogue: From the Art of Discourse to the Art of Reason* (Cambridge: Harvard University Press, 1958), chapters 4–5. Dialectic—the formulation and judgment of propositions—interested Ramus most, and one aspect of his presentation became, for better or worse, a hallmark of the movement: dichotomies. As Howell points out, not all of Ramus's divisions are dichotomous, but Ramus's followers codified rigid dichotomies as the proper mode of division. In the Cantabridgean Marlowe's *Massacre at Paris*, ed. Edward J. Esche, *The Complete Works of Christopher Marlowe,* vol. 5 (Oxford: Clarendon, 1998), 288–405, the Duke of Guise labels Ramus a "flat decotamest" (9.29). Ong charts the course of the Ramists' increasingly exclusive reliance on dichotomies not only rhetorically but also visually, in their bracketed diagrams (see fig. 1). Some contemporary Ramist manuals are Gabriel Harvey, *Gabriel Harvey's Ciceronianus,* trans. Clarence A. Forbes (Lincoln: University of Nebraska Press, 1945); Peter Ramus, *The Artes of Logike and Rethorike,* trans. Dudley Fenner, in *Four Tudor Books on Education* (1584; Gainesville, FL: Scholars' Facsimiles, 1966); and *The Logike of the Moste Excellent Philosopher P. Ramus Martyr,* trans. M. Roll Makylmenæum [Roland MacIlmaine] (1574; Leeds: Scolar Press, 1966).

27.   For the idea of the monarch's public and private bodies, see Ernst H. Kantorowicz, *The King's Two Bodies: A Study in Mediaeval Political Theology* (1957; Princeton: Princeton University Press, 1997), who traces the evolution of the idea from its roots in the theology of the Incarnation. For an adaptation of this theory to a reading of the "two bodies" of *The Faerie Queene* itself, see David Lee Miller, *The Poem's Two Bodies: The Poetics of the 1590* Faerie Queene (Princeton: Princeton University Press, 1988), and "Spenser's Poetics: The Poem's Two Bodies," *PMLA* 101 (1986): 170–85.

28.   For a somewhat different reading of these lines and Elizabeth's larger figuration in Book III, see Bruce Thomas Boehrer, " 'Careless Modestee': Chastity as Politics in Book 3 of *The Faerie Queene,*" *ELH* 55 (1988): 555–73.

29.   See Roche 53–55.

30.   For Amoret and Belphoebe as helping to define Britomart, see MacCaffrey 285, 289. See also Berger's *Revisionary Play* 34–35.

31. MacCaffrey 271–291 *passim* differentiates between two types of characters—"paradigms" and "personifications." As modes of representation, her "personification" resembles our *Darstellung*, but her idea of the paradigmatic character diverges from our argument. See also John Erskine Hankins, *Source and Meaning in Spenser's Allegory: A Study of* The Faerie Queene (Oxford: Clarendon, 1971), 21–33, who distinguishes between "internal" and "external" allegory.

32. See *Physics, Complete Works*, ed. Barnes, 194b-195b.

33. We presume that for Spenser chastity *was* an ontological entity; whether in Platonic, Aristotelian, or other terms isn't for our purposes important. In other words, we take the ethics of *The Faerie Queene* to be based on a set of virtues, not on deontological or consequentialist grounds. For elaboration of these differences, see Christine McKinnon, *Character, Virtue Theories, and the Vices* (Peterborough, Ont.: Broadview, 1999).

34. MacCaffrey 37 argues that allegory attempts to bridge the postlapsarian gap between truth and human understanding by teaching readers how to read the fiction while they read it. Also see Giamatti 106–07.

35. For a recent incisive and nuanced discussion of Britomart's learning and her interiority in the context of Spenser's allegory more generally, see Theresa M. Kelley, *Reinventing Allegory* (Cambridge: Cambridge University Press, 1997), 32–38. Also MacCaffrey 39.

36. For calling our attention to Britomart's age and her role in all the current actions of Book III, including those where she does not appear, we are indebted to Andrew Weiner. Leo Steinberg, *The Sexuality of Christ in Renaissance Art and in Modern Oblivion* (New York: Pantheon 1983), emphasizes that chastity becomes possible as a virtue only when one can be unchaste. Thus, "the celebration of [Christ's] perpetual virginity . . . presuppose[s] sexuality as a *sine qua non*," and even the infant Christ occasionally exhibits "that physiological potency without which the chastity of the man would count for naught" (17, 79). However complex the idea of chastity turns out to be in *The Faerie Queene*, it necessarily starts from a common understanding. In the *Homilies*, "chastity and cleanness of life" refers either to strict monogamy or virginity, the latter in those with "a sufficiency and ability (through the working of God's spirit) to lead a sole and continent life." The prenubile are by definition not yet able to be monogamous, and they do not need the working of God's spirit to be continent. Britomart as patron of chastity could not therefore be younger, and if she were older she would less clearly dramatize a commitment to monogamy *ab initio*. We quote from "The Third Part of the Sermon against Adultery," *Certain Sermons or Homilies Appointed to Be Read in Churches in the Time of Queen Elizabeth* (London, 1713), 80–81.

37. For a related reading, centering largely on Cupid, see A. Leigh Deneef, "Spenser's *Amor Fuggitivo* and the Transfixed Heart," *ELH* 46 (1979): 1–20.

38. Fowler, "Six Knights" 585n., offers the same pun on "Hellenore."

39. We take these terms from the general discussion of analogy and allegory in Barbara Maria Stafford, *Visual Analogy: Consciousness as the Art of Connecting* (Cambridge, MA: MIT Press, 1999), 98–108.

40. See Holmyard 153 and Read 90.

41. See MacCaffrey 272 and Berger's *Revisionary Play* 139.

42. For the sun's role in the creation of metals and minerals, see n15 above.

43. For instance, see Fowler's "Emanations of Glory" 68–69 for the split between Cupid's positive "reality" and his evil representation at Busirane's hands.

44. For a slightly different reading of how Malecasta's tapestries pervert the Garden of Adonis, see Michael Baybak, Paul Delany, and A. Kent Hieatt, "Placement 'in the Middest' in *The Faerie Queene*," in *Essential Articles for the Study of Edmund Spenser*, 389–94.

45. Conceivably, even Cupid's lion belongs to this system of inter-canto parallels, since the lion corresponds in the order of animals to gold in the order of minerals. The lion is also the image, against a golden field, on Britomart's coat of arms (i.4), as on that of the Trojan Brute, her ancestor and Britain's founder. Cupid's dangerous lion in Busirane's pageant is the *in malo* version of the redemptive and progenitive lion that Britomart bears.

46. Nohrnberg 607 shows this merger invading the characters' names: "Scuda-moret, Britomartegall, . . . Paridellinore."

47. Detailed readings of the hermaphrodite metaphor as key to Spenser's allegorical approach in Book III appear in Lauren Silberman, "The Hermaphrodite and the Metamorphosis of Spenserian Allegory," *English Literary Renaissance* 17 (1987): 207–23, and *Transforming Desire*, Chapter 3. See also Berger's "General Description"; Donald Cheney, "Spenser's Hermaphrodite and the 1590 *Faerie Queene*," *PMLA* 87 (1972): 192–200; and Nelson 204–55.

48. For a reading of the injunctions on boldness as related to Petrarchan poetics, see Maureen Quilligan, "Words and Sex: The Language of Allegory in the *De planctu naturae*, the *Roman de la Rose*, and Book III of *The Faerie Queene*," *Allegorica* 2 (1977): 211.

49. As at the end of Book II Guyon destroys Acrasia's bower, in which human beings become beasts, so at the end of Book III Britomart destroys Busirane's house, in which the power of speech, intended, as Aristotle says, "to set forth . . . [humans'] sense of good and evil, of just and unjust, and the like," instead reduces these represented humans to a level of expressive ability no higher than animals': "pleasure and pain . . . and no further" (*Politics* 1253a). That is, Acrasia turns real people into real beasts, operating on the level of the flesh. Busirane turns represented people into effectual beasts through the abuse of speech. He operates on the level of reason and ethics; his representations present a world with no higher ethic than pleasure and pain.

50. As a standard mode of learning, with emotional validity, "the nervous system constructs [automatic associations] on the basis of temporal contiguity and resem-blance." James E. Alcock, "The Propensity to Believe," in *The Flight from Science and Reason*, ed. Paul R. Gross, Norman Levitt, and Martin W. Lewis (New York: New York Academy of Sciences, 1996), 66.

JASON GLECKMAN

Providential Love and Suffering in *The Faerie Queene*, Book III

This essay argues that Spenser is intrigued by the subtle yet significant difference between two kinds of human suffering: an unproductive self-generated discomfort (associated with such Church practices as hair shirts, fasting, and flagellation) and that ennobling, Job-like anguish that arises from harsh conditions imposed on the self from outside. In the Book of Chastity, Spenser uses the phenomenon of sexual desire as a way to examine these divine and debased components of human pain.

*I*N BOOK I, CANTO III OF *The Faerie Queene*, Spenser undertakes one of his epic's first inquiries into the nature of suffering. The book's heroine, Una, endures a continual, unsought, and unmerited pain with which the narrator empathizes but in a postlapsarian world can do nothing to prevent (I.iii.1–2).[1] In contrast, an old blind woman receives only mockery for her continual discomfort; neither sitting in ashes, fasting, wearing "rough sackcloth," or reciting "nine hundred *Pater nosters* euery day,/And thrise nine hundred *Aues*" (I.iii.13–14) can make any lasting impression on this figure whose "beads she did forget" (I.iii.14) at the first sign of danger. Spenser's theology in these passages is in tune with Reformation perspectives on the nature of suffering. The pain that comes from God is redemptive, but self-generated anguish—the pain of hair shirts, flagellation, fasting and other self-mortifying practices associated by the Reformers with the Church of Rome—is merely a form of spiritual "works" that attempts to secure God's favor by imitating rather than embodying the agonizingly cleansing spiritual fire of the true saint.[2]

In Book III of *The Faerie Queene*, Spenser embarks on a more thorough examination of the nature of true Protestant suffering by analogizing this condition to the experience of love, specifically chaste love of the sort embodied by Britomart, the Book's heroine and the champion of chastity. For Britomart, the process of falling in love with Artegall, her future husband, parallels the journey of the Christian saint as conceived by the Protestant church. While her experience begins in unsought, irresistible, and irremovable suffering, it is a redemptive pain that impels her forward to a providential future as a famous warrior and the initiator of a line of "Renowmed kings, and sacred Emperours" (III.iii.23). In illustrative contrast to Britomart, Book III also provides numerous histories of lovers who are not as chaste as she. Ranging from the virginal to the concupiscent, these figures are all characterized by a relationship to suffering that misconstrues its nature and significance in a Protestant world.

1

From its first articulation in the writings of Martin Luther, the Protestant religion is associated with suffering. The future true servant of God begins in a state of naive and over-confident faith that is suddenly transformed into tormented self-doubt, fear, and helplessness in the face of one's own incapacity for self-healing. Such despair is only transmuted into true, saving faith when the Christian experiences an inner awareness of that divine mercy which God offers freely to the undeserving believer. As John Calvin explains the process: "Thus confounded and amazed at his misery, [the sinner] is prostrated and humbled before God; and, casting away all self-confidence, groans as if given up to final perdition . . . the only haven of safety is in the mercy of God . . . ."[3]

For Spenser's Britomart, who exists in a world that expresses only the briefest intimations of Christianity, it is the movement towards love that symbolizes this path to election.[4]

Like the foolish and untested Christian, Britomart begins as a proud and fearless youth with no qualms about her future. She glances into the magic mirror in the same way that the overconfident Christian peruses the Bible, sure that when it speaks of salvation it speaks of hers. Yet, like that Christian, Britomart's gaze begins for her a process of psychological disintegration, beginning with the overthrow of her pride:

Thenceforth the feather in her loftie crest,

Ruffed of loue, gan lowly to auaile,
And her proud portance, and her princely gest,
With which she earst tryumphed, now did quaile

(III.ii.27)

The loss of pride is the least of Britomart's discomforts. As Luther notes, "once a man has thus been humbled by the law and brought to the knowledge of himself, then he becomes truly repentant; for true repentance begins with fear and with the judgment of God."[5] Britomart too proceeds from humility to fear:

Streight way with dreames, and with fantasticke sight
Of dreadfull things the same was put to flight,
That oft out of her bed she did astart,
As one with vew of ghastly feends affright

(III.2.29)

Ultimately, Britomart is literally driven into physical illness from the lack of another's love which she needs to be spiritually complete. However, like the Reformed Protestant, Britomart will eventually discover that her sickness of soul does not signal divine displeasure but divine redemption; her awareness of lack is the necessary first stage in a providential process of heroic growth that will propel her beyond spiritual adolescence into maturity. Although the progression of Britomart's love seems modelled to an extent upon Renaissance neoplatonism (the sight of the beloved being the first step that brings the lover of love onto God), the fruits of that love go well beyond neoplatonic enlightenment and reflect the goals of English Protestantism in the Elizabethan age. Britomart's love will eventually culminate in a chaste marriage whose long-term consequences explicitly include the triumph of a Protestant "royall virgin" over the "great Castle" of Catholic Spain (III.iii.49).

To these neoplatonic and Protestant conceptions of chastity, Spenser also contributes his own particular inflection of the virtue in question. As Spenserian temperance in Book II is surprisingly militant, so Spenserian chastity in Book III is considerably more erotic than might be suggested by neoplatonism, Christian theology, or the ideology promoted by a virgin queen.[6] Yet Britomart is initially compelled to her destiny neither by intellectual nor spiritual longings. Instead she is driven by the "fire" and "rage" (III.ii.37) of love's "dread darts" (III.iii.3), an unquenchable physical desire that propels her onward to her beloved and will eventually unite their "two loynes" (III.iii.3) in productive matrimony.

Valorizing the erotic, even lustful, dimension of his female heroine to this extraordinary extent allows Spenser to resolve a problem that beset the Protestants of his day, who grudgingly acknowledged the place of erotic desire within marriage but also feared (in good Christian and neoplatonic fashion) that excessive eroticism would constitute too great a pleasure and hence distract the lover from God.[7] Spenser responds to this cultural tension in a revolutionary manner, not only by taking the traditional recourse of controlling erotic pleasure by yoking it to marriage, but also by ennobling erotic desire by implanting within it the seeds of great pain as well as great joy. Hence the flesh and the spirit become one and the apparent immoderation of Britomart's eroticism ceases to signify a desire for excessive sexual pleasure, but rather the condition of one who has been touched by the divine spirit and perhaps endures the continuous throes of divine possession. It is her physical torment that gives Britomart, like any devout Protestant, the strength to become a warrior and surmount all obstacles that stand between her and the object of her love.[8] By connecting Britomart's erotic responses so directly to her noble destiny Spenser allows this heroine to represent both the triumphs and tribulations of her English Protestant descendants. Like Britomart, the elect who struggle towards faith endure conflicting emotions; they rejoice and hope but always remain painfully aware of the distance between them and the object of their devotion. Also, like Britomart, these suffering Protestants perceive their pains not simply in the mind but also viscerally, even in the flesh, as did Jesus himself.

Such providential pains are a source of strength and courage since their intensity makes all other pains relatively easier to bear. Hence, while Britomart is physically injured twice in Book III, in the first and last cantos, her injuries on both occasions are emphatically minor ("yet was the wound not deepe" [III.i.65], "Albe the wound were nothing deepe imprest" [III.xii.33]). This is because such literally superficial wounds cannot compete with the deeply instilled pains of love, placed within Britomart's *body* "through deepe impression of" the "secret might" of Cupid (III.iii.3). Love, for Britomart:

> hath infixed faster hold
> Within my bleeding bowels, and so sore
> Now ranckleth in this same fraile fleshly mould,
> That all mine entrailes flow with poysnous gore,
> And th'vlcer groweth daily more and more;
> Ne can my running sore find remedie,
> Other then my hard fortune to deplore,

And languish as the leafe falne from the tree,
Till death make one end of my dayes and miserie.

(III.ii.39)

The suffering that Britomart undergoes in love is akin to the suffering of the Protestant faithful in another significant way as well: such suffering continues even when its providential function is revealed. The Reformers insisted that the saved must endure the discomforts of life along with the nonelect, and the pain that takes hold of Britomart likewise persists even after its purpose is explained by the poet-surrogate Merlin. Merlin in fact makes sure that Britomart will understand the inescapability of suffering by pointedly reminding her, even before she has seen her husband's face, of his untimely death (III.iii.28). To the extent that we can conceive of Britomart as a developing character, she learns Merlin's lesson well, sadly repeating it to Scudamore in the eleventh canto before her climactic battle with Busirane: "For who nill bide the burden of distresse,/Must not here thinke to liue: for life is wretchednesse" (III.xi.14).

Of course, for Spenser as an epic poet and as a Christian, the balance between suffering and joy can never ultimately favor the former. Although Britomart reminds the self-pitying Scudamore that life must include pain, she also emphasizes that "all the sorrow in the world is lesse,/Then vertues might, and values confidence" (III. xi.14). The young heroine is referencing herself here; it is she who embodies the virtuous might and confidence that cannot eradicate or conceal suffering but which give it purpose in the Spenserian cosmos. Hence, Britomart's rousing speech to Scudamore foreshadows her victory over Busirane as well as the difficulties she will have to endure in achieving that victory; her speech also harkens back to Merlin's earlier wisdom.

The necessity of suffering in the world of *The Faerie Queene* has recently been given more attention as a dominant theme of the epic. Susanne Wofford has argued that the willingness of human beings to suffer is a prime measure of Spenserian heroism: "the heroic life as Spenser pictures it requires the strength to undertake one's quest without any certainty of what it means or where it will lead."[9] Spenser can even deliberately withhold from a character information that would mitigate such suffering. The virgin huntress Belphoebe, for example, has no knowledge either of her wondrous birth (her mother, Chrysogone, was impregnated by the sun and delivers her children in her sleep) or of her upbringing by the goddess Diana. As Wofford explains, these facts are withheld from Belphoebe in order to emphasize her "moral strength" in facing mortality.[10]

Spenser's position on the issue of suffering seems in fact to be so extreme that sensations which lack a dimension of suffering are radically excluded from the epic's narrative. Thus Chrysogone is abruptly excised from Book III when her newborn babies are stolen from her by the goddesses Venus and Diana (III.vi.27–28). Such apparently insensitive behavior on the part of these goddesses might, however, be comprehended in light of the lack of pain felt by Chrysogone during her particularly "miraculous" reproductive processes. Since the twins are virgin births, Chrysogone "bore withouten paine, that she conceiued/Withouten pleasure" (III.vi.27). Apparently, to escape the pains that accompany delivery Chrysogone must also sacrifice the pleasure that accompanies conception and even the pleasure that accompanies the raising of children: this virgin mother is deprived of the normal rights of motherhood because she has not suffered sufficiently. Correlatively, her offspring, produced without the pains that are all people's original sin, are too near the state of divinity to be raised by even a fairy being.

In contrast to Chrysogone, Britomart rises in stature as a result of her suffering. As Julia M. Walker notes, the discomforts she undergoes in the throes of young love are analogous to the symptoms of menstruation;[11] these pains foreshadow those she will later exhibit when losing her virginity and particularly in childbirth. On all three occasions, Britomart will endure suffering and specifically the loss of blood, but these pains must also be seen in the light of their continuously providential outcomes.[12] Such an intermingling of pleasure and pain in Britomart's own life history is recapitulated in the bloody history of England itself, its long-deferred "sacred Peace" (III.iii.49) attainable only after generations of war.[13]

One might argue in this context that Britomart is gendered female precisely to suggest the female body is the primary locus of joy and suffering in Spenser's Protestant world. To take such a position is to contest the naive opinions of figures like Glauce and the young Britomart who see in love's effects upon the female body only "wicked euill" (III.ii.32) the curse of defloration, the fruit, leaf, or flower "vntimely shed" (III.ii.31) or "falne from the tree" (III.ii.39). In contrast to these nostalgic longings for the perpetuation of childhood, Book III offers wiser figures like Venus and Merlin who see the onset of love not merely as a movement away from wholeness and into wounded desire, but also as a necessary entry into the real world.[14] Venus, after hearing a litany of complaints from court, city, and country about the actions of her son, Cupid, "did smile thereat" (III.vi.15), knowing that what seem to be love's cruelties will often appear later on to be love's blessings. In a similar vein, Merlin bawdily refers to the pains of Britomart's first love as merely "the hard begin, that meets thee in the dore" (III.iii.21).

Britomart's willingness to accept the implications of Merlin's comment and embark upon a sexually active life reflects not only the intensity of her desire but also her courage in undertaking the dangerous quest necessary to translate that desire into fulfilment. Similarly, Scudamore's climactic assessment of Britomart's worth before she goes to face her ultimate battle—"What huge heroicke magnanimity/ Dwels in thy bounteous brest!" (III.xi.19)—should not be read merely as erotic hyperbole but also as an indication of the witty confidence with which Spenser proceeds to transform the Ariostan heroine into the Protestant saint.

2

The contours of Spenserian chastity involve both the continuous presence of physical and psychological torment as well as an increasing awareness of the providentiality of these conditions. As in all six books of *The Faerie Queene*, however, the paradigmatic view of a given legend's virtue is elucidated not only positively (particularly through the climactic action of the hero or heroine), but also negatively, by contrast with a variety of misguided and even villainous conceptions of that virtue. Since chastity necessarily involves suffering, the competing views of it often hinge on the effort to negate such suffering; a mild version of such formulation is seen in a behavioral pattern that Spenser interestingly applies primarily to women: that of martial virginity.

As part of her effort to authorize herself as the virgin queen, Queen Elizabeth promulgated a version of chastity which viewed "her body as inviolable—virginal, unassaulted, sanctified."[15] Like other Protestants of his day, however, Spenser resisted his sovereign's effort to define chastity as self-sufficiency and instead promoted a humanist-based conception of the chaste body as one characterized by premarital virginity and marital fidelity.[16] Hence, the carefully constructed history of Britomart's descendants, constructed by Merlin, comes to a pointed and abrupt end when the "royall virgin" Elizabeth takes the throne (III.iii.49); Britomart's fruitful womb is contrasted to Queen Elizabeth's barren one.

Spenser also offers another, and less often explicated, argument for the rejection of chastity as virginity, one which involves its relationship to suffering. While Britomart is affected by various types of

physical and emotional distress as a result of her erotic desire for
Artegall—the pains involved in interacting with the world and the
anguish of unsatisfied longing—the martial virgins of Book III, particularly Diana and, to a lesser extent, her adopted daughter Belphoebe (the explicit figure of Queen Elizabeth within the epic),[17]
assiduously attempt to practice a variety of chastity that removes these
elements from their lives. Not only do they eschew heterosexual
encounters but also they seek to avoid the violence of the male gaze,
a painful element of life that, in *The Faerie Queene*, can only be
dispensed with at the cost of isolation from the social world.

The extreme approach taken by Belphoebe and Diana reflects not
only the care with which Queen Elizabeth determined the conditions
under which she would be seen,[18] but also the tremendous violence
associated with the male gaze. The extent of this aggression is revealed through a central encounter of Book III, when Britomart
battles the knights defending Malecasta (III.i.63–66) and is injured
by one Gardante, or the function of sight.[19] It is not only Gardante,
however, who is implicated in this incident because the male narrator
and poet are complicit in rendering such violence, as is the male
reader in responding to it. Spenser's insistence on marking this moment as an important instance of voyeurism is apparent in the uncom-
fortably detailed manner in which the narrator lingers upon it (a
tendency that has been often noted):

> . . . against the virgin sheene:
> The mortall steele stayd not, till it was seene
> To gore her side, yet was the wound not deepe,
> But lightly rased her soft silken skin,
> That drops of purple blood thereout did weepe,
> Which did her lilly smock with staines of vermeil steepe.
>
> (III.i.65)

The violence done to Britomart by Gardante's blade (i.e., his sight
of her) is linked to the erotic violence Britomart suffers by having
her sexual injuries made the center of the narrator's, and consequently
the reader's, scopophilic attention.

Yet, although Spenser, by equating violence with vision, suggests
the dangers of the male gaze, he also creates situations where that
danger is mitigated and even productive. For instance, when Diana
and her retinue bathe so discreetly in the wood, not intending to be
spied upon, much less lusted after, the narrative nonetheless describes
their actions in deliberately provocative terms, the goddess the most
erotic figure of all: "[She] had vnlaste/Her siluer buskins from her

nimble thigh,/And her lancke loynes vngirt, and brests vnbratse,/ After her heat the breathing cold to taste" (III.vi.18). The reader at this point might register a degree of voyeuristic unease, particularly since these particular objects of the gaze specifically wish to avoid being so, but such distress is notably distinct from, albeit aligned with, the discomfort associated with reading of Britomart's encounter with Gardante. That encounter reminded us that we are allured by the violence done to women, but spying on Diana and her nymphs enjoying their bath suggests a different order of violence—one which damages its victims but might nonetheless be termed "erotic" rather than "pornographic." As Teresa Krier suggests in her discussion of this scene, the fact that its primary voyeur is Venus marks "the shift of the perceived threat from masculine invasion to feminine interruption."[20] Consequently, the sight of the naked goddess becomes the occasion for an embarrassing social situation rather than a sexual violation. The reader can be aroused by Diana yet simultaneously permit her a certain degree of freedom to be "perfectly present" only to herself.[21]

As Krier's arguments imply, a crucial component of the gaze within *The Faerie Queene* is its unavoidability; those in Spenser's world or in his poem who would interact with others simply cannot help but be looked at, often in distasteful ways, and with consequent necessary discomfort, even pain. Thus, while the desire of virginal figures like Diana, Belphoebe, or Britomart (or Queen Elizabeth) to be purified of the lurid component of the gaze is understandable, it is nonetheless an impossible desire akin to other efforts in *The Faerie Queene* to mitigate the suffering essential to human existence. The only viable way to reduce the indignity of lustful gazes is, as Krier suggests, to live in a world where people, especially men, try to gaze differently—grateful for an inspirational glimpse but also embarrassed and abashed, sensitive to what Krier terms the "social habit that veils the private enclosed territory and secrecy of interiority."[22]

To demonstrate this point, Spenser offers subtle criticisms of powerful females who are determined to retain their autonomy through the traditional recourse of virgin chastity. Judith H. Anderson observes that Belphoebe is described as "dead" in a manner suggesting unfruitfulness (III.v.54) and David Lee Miller suggests she is cruel to refuse to her Timias "that soueraigne salue, in secret store" that would save his life (III.v.50–51).[23]

Like Belphoebe, Britomart also attempts to withdraw herself from social interaction, dressing as a knight not only to do battle but also to escape gender identification and consequent lustful gazes. Yet this

tactic is not noticeably successful. Britomart's chief nemesis, Busirane, apparently recognizes her true sex (III.xii.32.1) and a villain
like Malecasta is drawn to Britomart precisely *because* of her disguise
(III.i.47). Most importantly, in Book IV, Britomart's masquerade almost causes Artegall to kill her ("That seemed nought but death mote
be her destinie" [IV.vi.18]). She is saved only by the timely revelation
of her gender—an occasion that transforms Artegall's accidental
glimpse of her into a providential gaze indeed.

3

This powerful moment at the center of Book IV of *The Faerie Queene*
emphasizes that Britomart, like her fellow knights of virtue, functions
not only to exemplify a particular virtue but also to be the means by
which that virtue is transmitted to others. What Britomart provides
in this capacity is, as Sheila Cavanagh astutely notes, not the actual
protection of chaste females,[24] but rather a reminder of the inextricability of chastity and suffering in life. This is the lesson Britomart has
learned from Gardante's and Cupid's arrows and which she imparts to
other figures in the epic, such as Marinell, an especially foolish virgin
who, by virtue of his gender, is more readily subject to Spenserian
criticism than Queen Elizabeth herself or her fictional surrogate,
Belphoebe. Marinell too hopes to avoid the pain of intergender encounters, but, humbled by Britomart, he begins the path to redemption that will end in his own happy marriage in Book IV.

Britomart's role as an agent of fate allies her with the classical gods
of *The Faerie Queene*. Their role, as in Virgil's *Aeneid*, is to serve as
the executors of fate's judgments; and in Book III, an important
element of this job description is to initiate the redemptive processes
of love that will eventually unite figures like Britomart and Artegall,
Florimell and Marinell or, at the end of the 1590 *Faerie Queene*,
Scudamore and Amoret. Britomart's own emotion of love is begun
by Cupid and by Venus, in whose looking glass (III.i.8) she first spies
Artegall. Yet Venus and Cupid are not the only gods who act as
emissaries of love in Book III. Apollo too generates life in the wombs
of Liagore (III.iv.41) and Chrysogone (III.vi). In all these cases, however, the fruits of love are beneficial, producing children who do
credit to their parents and themselves. The gods who originate these
acts of generation are furthermore, in *The Faerie Queene*, portrayed
as agents of a greater divine power, as Merlin explains to Britomart:

> "It was not, *Britomart*, thy wandring eye,
> Glauncing vnwares in charmed looking glas,
> But the streight course of heauenly destiny,
> Led with eternall prouidence, that has
> Guided thy glaunce, to bring his will to pas
>
> (III.iii.24)

Ultimately the referent of "his" in this passage is neither Cupid nor Apollo nor even Jove but the Christian God himself, aligned with the force of love: a "sacred fire, that burnest mightily/In liuing brests, ykindled first aboue,/Emongst th'eternall spheres and lamping sky,/And thence pourd into men" (III.iii.1). Such love is a phenomenon affecting "the gentlest harts" (III.ii.23) so as "to order them . . . And all their actions to direct aright" (III.iii.2), again reiterating the role of the gods in serving the divine.

In this light, the actions of the gods in Book III of *The Faerie Queene* take on a deeper significance that is, like other elements of this book, simultaneously Christian and erotic, with the inevitable hints of abusive violence. The description of Apollo's transformation of the womb of Chrysogone, for example, suggests both a rape like those illustrated in Busirane's castle, but also the pregnancy of the virgin Mary.[25] After Chrysogone "in a fresh fountaine . . . bath'd her brest, the boyling heat t'allay" (III.vi.6), she lies down "naked bare":

> The sunne-beames bright vpon her body playd,
> Being through former bathing mollifide,
> And pierst into her wombe, where they embayd
> With so sweete sence and secret power vnspide,
> That in her pregnant flesh they shortly fructifide.
>
> (III.vi.7)

The sensual references to heat, water, and bare flesh (similar to those used in the description of Diana) create an erotic atmosphere confirmed by the suggestion that Chrysogone is "pregnant" or ready to receive sexual impress even before she is made so by the fructifying beams of Apollo.[26] Nonetheless, this is a miraculous, nonsexual pregnancy that produces the chaste fruit of Belphoebe and Amoret. The means by which this insemination is described imply that even virginal conceptions (and conceptions of virginity) have their erotic elements and, correlatively, that erotic inseminations may likewise include qualities of purity, innocence, sweetness, and chastity traditionally associated with virginity.

4

As Spenserian chastity challenges the avoidance of suffering that
comes with insulation, so it also critiques the effort to minimize
suffering by transforming it instantly into pleasure. This is the phenomenon of lust or concupiscence, and while it is predominantly
female characters who treat chastity as celibate virginity, it is largely
the epic's male figures who display this vice of lust masquerading as
suffering, a delusion much akin to the self-mortification opposed
by Protestants.

The well-matched pair Paridell and Malecasta (the latter significantly endowed with a male name, as Harry Berger reminds us) both
act to minimize suffering by making it a mode of pleasure.[27] Paridell
responds to the first promptings of love with a ready weakness that
is the opposite of Britomart's resistance: "He from that deadly throw
made no defence,/But to the wound his weake hart opened wyde"
(III.ix.29). Paridell's boastful emblem, "the burning hart, which on
his brest/He bare" (III.viii.45) stresses his love of suffering and consequent neutralization of the divine purpose of pain.[28] Malecasta likewise reacts to lust by giving the full "bridle to her wanton will"
(III.i.48–50). And to emphasize the continuity of the two figures,
both climax their seductions with an identically hyperbolic threat:
that they "mote algates dye" if they cannot attain immediate relief
(III.i.53; III.x.7). Unlike Britomart, these discomfited lovers prefer
to impose an obligation on the reliever of their smart rather than
attempt to cure themselves.

Theatricalizing their pain is only one way that lustful figures attempt to reconfigure the relationship between suffering and pleasure
to make the former merely delicious foreplay to the latter. In addition, both Malecasta and Paridell construct narratives that compete
with Britomart's for authority within the epic. Since Book III is the
book of chastity, these alternate parodic epics particularly highlight
the role of the goddess Venus. The centerpiece of Malecasta's erotic
bower is an illustrated portrayal of the seduction of Adonis by Venus
(III.i.34–38), stressing the "sleights and sweet allurements" (III.i.35)
of Venus as well as her passing grief upon Adonis's death. Malecasta
apparently models her own seductive behaviors upon her readings of
Venus; yet as Thomas Roche notes, the love games at Castle Joyeous
are incommensurate with the real pain Britomart endures there, signified by the literal wounds she receives and bestows.[29]

Paridell for his part tells a tale of Troy that emphasizes the sensuous
and erotic elements of love while minimizing its suffering. For Paridell, the Trojan war is a fiery backdrop against which his ancestor,

Paris, beloved by the most beautiful goddess and the most beautiful woman in the world, performs his noble deeds. Even circumstances that might tend to devalue Paris's achievement ("by whome/That warre was kindled, which did *Troy* inflame,/And stately towres of *Ilion* whilome/Brought vnto balefull ruine" [III.ix.34]) are transformed, in Paridell's account, into further evidence of a matchless passion. The destruction of a civilization and the countless human deaths that so move Britomart upon the completion of this tale (III.ix.39) are to Paridell as easily minimized as the griefs of the lover in love.

Despite their fascination with Venus and their efforts to evoke her aid in authorizing their narratives, neither Malecasta nor Paridell recognize that, in Book III, the love displayed by Venus is not a matter of passing fancy or of lust, but instead of highly committed, even chaste, love. Venus's relationship with Adonis is depicted in canto vi not as a god's dalliance in the manner of Malecasta's (and later Busirane's) false representation, but as a pathos-laden eternal love for a mortal—again analogous to the love of a Christian God for sinful men and women. What in Malecasta's tapestry is false and dead—the flower into which Venus transformed Adonis ("in that cloth was wrought, *as if* it liuely grew" [III.i.38; emphasis added])—is restored to true life in Venus's garden. Adonis lives there, as does "euery sort of flowre,/To which sad louers were transformd of yore" (III.vi.45); the reason these flowers thrive is because the love that generated them, especially that of Venus for Adonis, lives too.

The Garden of Adonis is a particularly fitting site to elaborate the nature of chaste love since, amidst its pleasures, indeed at their very heart, is suffering: the ineradicable power of time and death (III.vi.39–40) which Spenser conjoins with the masculine potential of destructive lust. The boar that represents Adonis's tragic fate can also be read as a castrating sexual creature; a "bore" as Maureen Quilligan puts it.[30] In the Garden of Adonis, however, this boar is at once powerless to act ("that wilde Bore, the which him once annoyd,/ She firmely hath emprisoned for ay" [III.vi.48]) yet compellingly, eternally present, neither destroyed nor exiled, but always lurking directly beneath the garden—a testament to the limitations of any creaturely love, no matter how chaste or powerful, to exclude suffering from its purview. Particularly in the strange fortieth stanza of canto vi—where Spenser invokes the entire pantheon of classical gods, their great "pittie" for humanity, and the possibility of their divine mercy, only to reassert the powerlessness of all of these factors over time and death—the poet insists that, even in the Garden of

Adonis, the fortress of chaste love, there remains no "redresse" for Time's scythe, "For all that liues, is subiect to that law" (III.vi.40).[31]

Yet while "mortalitie" (III.vi.47) is inescapable even in the Garden of Adonis, Venus, or love, has the power to make it seem otherwise. By constantly renewing the cherished objects of its affections, love makes them "eterne in mutabilitie" (III.vi.47), creating the impression that they live eternally even if they do not. Chaste love is thus analogized to nature, which creates a similar impression of immortality with its endless proliferations of new life. Indeed, Venus's own "heavenly hous" is described as:

> The house of goodly formes and faire aspects,
> Whence all the world deriues the glorious
> Features of beautie, and all shapes select,
> With which high God his workmanship hath deckt
>
> (III.vi.12)

Venus in other words is the handmaiden to God; her love creates the forms of beauty, particularly the human form (perhaps as Adonis, the most important, or "Father of all formes" [III.vi.47]), but only God's love can endow that form with truly eternal life. The power of death hangs over Venus's garden, but pleasure and pain are so perfectly balanced here that the tragedy of death is kept at bay through the generative, and perhaps even the remembering, capacities of love.[32]

A love so generative, tender, and protective is also, in *The Faerie Queene*, a love that is motherly; thus in detailing the love of Venus in Book III, Spenser also carefully foregrounds her role as nurturing mother. Harry Berger has suggested that Spenser's motive in doing so is to portray eros in Book III as largely "primitive or regressive" in its blurring of erotic and maternal boundaries (97–98),[33] but I would propose that Spenser is emphasizing the desirability of incorporating elements of maternal love into any meaningful conception of chastity. It is not heroines like Britomart but crude lovers like Paridell who strive to separate mothering from eros. When Venus promises "kisses sweet, and sweeter things" to man, she offers them only to "the man" who will help her find her son Cupid (III.vi.12). But whatever motive Venus had for providing Paris with Helen is unspoken in *The Faerie Queene*, despite Paridell's belief that his ancestor was rewarded for "worthinesse" (III.ix.34). When Paridell recounts the fall of Troy he naturally stresses Venus's affection for Paris while pointedly ignoring her true son in the *Aeneid*: the pious Aeneas who prefigures Britomart by founding a nation out of which will eventually arise England. Paridell, acknowledging that Aeneas is "begot of *Venus* faire," still implies that Aeneas abandoned Troy, "out of the flames for safegard fled" (III.ix.41) while Paris remained to fight.

The importance Spenser attaches to motherhood, rather than "romance," as his model for love is also seen in the many representations of loving motherhood in Book III: Glauce's love for Britomart, Cymoent's love for Marinell, and even the witch for her churlish son. Britomart's own suffering love for Artegall is itself elaborated by comparison to motherhood:

> The louing mother, that nine monethes did beare,
> In the deare closet of her painefull side,
> Her tender babe, it seeing safe appeare,
> Doth not so much reioyce, as she reioyced theare
>
> (III.ii.11)

This paradigm is in stark contrast to the narratives of unchastity promoted by Malecasta and Paridell in which a pantheon of gods urge human beings on to sexual license and fulfilment of erotic desires. Suffering, in this view, is not a phenomenon that must be accepted, as in the mother or lover's constant fear for the beloved, but a sensation at once uncomfortable and exciting, to be eradicated temporarily in the self-obsessed intensity of lustful consummation.

5

The lustful behaviors practiced so grossly by Malecasta and Paridell take on even deeper significance to *The Faerie Queene* since they largely reproduce, in a more obvious key, the behaviors of most of the male knights within the epic. Like Malecasta and Paridell, many of the supposedly heroic figures who inhabit Book III—including Arthur, Guyon, and Timias—are also afflicted by lust. Yet, more aware of the sinfulness of this impulse than are Malecasta and Paridell, they go to more extreme lengths to disguise its effects, even from themselves. Hence, the phenomenon of lust in Book III often takes the *outward* form of heroic Britomartian love but without capturing love's essentially charitable, rather than selfish, essence.

At the root of these knightly efforts to present lust as love is the phenomenon of chivalry. Configured either in terms of courtly or

Petrarchan love, chivalry requires that the one afflicted by love serve the love object without bitterness or complaint and endure the torments of love without necessarily harboring any hope of reward. These values are clearly modelled on the virtues of Christian suffering which, as we have seen, is likewise unmerited, intense, incurable, and a noble sign of submission. The dart of Cupid strikes like the hand of God and forces its unwilling followers into a servitude that nonetheless inspires courage and determination. Yet since such suffering is almost entirely internal, even the suffering of saints is always slightly suspect and no one can accuse the lover of the bad faith of lust.

In Book III of *The Faerie Queene*, knights and lovers deliberately place themselves within chivalric paradigms to transform the suffering caused by their unsatisfied lust into something more nearly approaching Christian love. One of the best examples of this behavior is that of Arthur in Book III, canto iv; by using Arthur as the example of lust here, Spenser is suggesting the power of this subtle vice to affect and deceive lesser knights as well.

The occasion for lust in this canto is Arthur's invective against night, occasioned by his inability to continue chasing after Florimell, whom he would rescue from the depredations of others but who is ironically as "affraid of him, as feend of hell" (III.iv.47). In his despair, the night sky "that now with thousand starres was decked fayre" appears instead as "a lothfull sight" (III.iv.52), and Arthur, "euer hastie" (III.iv.54), delivers a melodramatic soliloquy cursing the existence of night for inhibiting his heroism and providing "protection" and shelter to evildoers (III.iv.58). Yet Spenser's unusually blatant irony here reveals Arthur himself to be the guilty knight; the darkness he condemns is in fact the "cover," or excuse, he draws upon to hide his own excesses, specifically his desire to have either Florimell or "his Faery Queene" for company that evening (III.iv.54). The ease with which these two female figures blend together in Arthur's semi-conscious "fancies" (III.iv.54) reveals the component of lust embedded within his desire to aid needy women. And it is no surprise when this frustrated desire quickly transforms itself into an anger fixated on night's female gender, as a "foule Mother," the sister of "heauie death" and the wife of "Blacke *Herebus*" (III.iv.55). When Arthur finally resorts to blaming God for having created night ("What had th'eternall Maker need of thee,/The world in his continuall course to keepe" [III.iv.56]), it is clear that his tirade is less reflective of his actual beliefs about the night than of the way in which all his emotions and judgments have become distorted through the operations of lust and its consequent misogyny.[34]

These qualities in Arthur are frequently noted in other male figures of *The Faerie Queene*, although numerous critics hesitate to accept their implications.[35] Yet Spenser is quite specific about the preponderantly base motives of his otherwise noble knights when it comes to the rescue and protection of desirable women. In such cases, drives such as "cruelty," "despiteous rage," and "burning fury" (III.viii.28) or "proud enuy, and indignant ire" (III.iv.47) play a substantial role—even while such knights believe themselves to be acting chivalrously in protecting female honor from the ravages of other males.[36]

The susceptibility of male knights to lust is surely another reason that the knight of chastity is gendered female by Spenser. It is not so much, as Sheila Cavanagh has argued, that chastity is only a female virtue for the poet,[37] but rather that this virtue is best represented by a female figure, a Britomart who, like Venus herself (IV.x.41), possesses both male and female qualities. That men as well as women are expected by Spenser to be chaste is clear from the announced purpose of *The Faerie Queene* ("to fashion a gentleman"),[38] indicating that the virtues of all six books are proper for males to emulate. Rather, making the knight of chastity female allows Spenser to draw more attention to the perpetual lust and loose sexual mores of male knights, resulting in a critique not only of their own weak chastity but also of the inattentiveness given to this virtue in the courtly tradition of love as a whole. In Spenser's rewrite of the tradition, distressed damsels like Florimell are equally fearful of the knights who would rescue them as of their original captors, male dalliances with evil women are as much the result of male lust as female sorcery, and the inability of a knight to rescue his beloved might well be the result of his own "greedy will, and enuious desire"—noted as factors in Scudamore's case (III.xi.26)—rather than simply the power of his villainous opponent.

6

The notorious difficulty of distinguishing love from lust in *The Faerie Queene* is seized upon by the most complex and challenging villain of Book III, Busirane. Like Malecasta and Paridell, Busirane attempts to portray love as an entirely unchaste phenomenon indistinguishable from lust, yet his tactics are more difficult for Britomart to resist. Paridell and Malecasta wished simply to create an image associating suffering with love while repressing or aestheticizing any actual pain;

these lesser villains had little effect on Britomart whose adventures led her to the opposite conclusion that suffering is inescapable in this world. Busirane in contrast seduces by adding the component of true suffering to the love/lust equation, thereby acknowledging the interaction of pain and pleasure in human life and particularly in love.

Busirane's tapestries, depicting the passions of the gods for mortals, and his masque, offering an allegory of the progress of love, both emphasize a configuration Britomart already understands: love produces true anguish in those who feel it. The gods of Busirane's tapestries feel an irresistible lust that carries the pleasurable anticipation of release at the same time as it is a "scalding smart" (III.xi.30), a humiliating and destructive physical compulsion. The boisterous rapes the gods enact in response to lust are likewise infused with pain since the moment of orgasm is short-lived and inevitably followed by the renewal of frustrated desire and the pursuit of further metamorphoses. The pageant or masque which succeeds the tapestries creates a similar effect by pairing up personifications of love's allure (hope, dissemblance, pleasance) with love's discomfort (fear, suspect, displeasure) to stress the inextricability of pain and pleasure in the narrative of love.

Britomart, seeing for the first time in Book III a rendering of love that conforms to her own experience, is emphatically enticed by Busirane's seductive artwork. She gazes in wonder at Busirane's tapestries, is fascinated by the paradoxical phrases he presents, and is much "dismayd" by the disappearance of the glorious art (III.xii.42). She is particularly captivated by the image that climaxes both the tapestries and the masque, a golden Cupid, the controller of love and consequently the master of both men and gods:

> That wondrous sight faire *Britomart* amazed,
> Ne seeing could her wonder satisfie,
> But euermore and more vpon it gazed,
> The whiles the passing brightnes her fraile sences dazed.
>   (III.xi.49)

Britomart's susceptibility to Busirane's charms reflects not only the masculine contours of her "warlike Mayde" constitution (III.xi.53), but her deep awareness of love as a combination of pain and pleasure. Since Britomart herself perceives the pleasure of loving Artegall as the pain of loving Artegall, Busirane's climactic depiction of a god suffering in love, that of Mars ("painted full of burning darts,/And many wide woundes launched through his inner parts" [III.xi.44]) might well remind Britomart of her own "bleeding bowels" and "entrailes" flowing "with poysnous gore" (III.ii.39). The connection between Britomart's love and Mars's lust is reinforced by the apparent presence of the dart of Cupid in both cases; the "thrill" of love and lust is difficult to disentangle.

Britomart is of course not the only female figure to be targeted by Busirane's artwork. Amoret too is meant to succumb to Busirane's powerful magic, although if Britomart is drawn to the powerful masculine aggression of the gods, Amoret is to be allured by the passive and objectified, yet desiring, female victims fabricated so beautifully by Busirane's commissioned artist. These skillfully wrought female victims share Amoret's predicament and are meant to teach her to enjoy it. Busirane's tapestries suggest that the women who are assaulted by the gods take pleasure in their distinction; Leda appears at first to be Jove's helpless victim, but the careful viewer of Busirane's art can see her smiling at his proud onslaught (III.xi.32). The reaction of the reader to Busirane's tapestries is surely meant to replicate Leda's admiration for male power and cleverness. The "wondrous delight" (III.xi.34) felt when viewing the skilled artist's work extends to admiration of Busirane's care in displaying his tapestries (III.xi.28) and ultimately to awe at the gods who, like Busirane and his commissioned artist, can masterfully elude all obstacles to achieve their desires. Through her exposure to (and eventually literal emplacement within) Busirane's narratives of infidelity, Amoret is presumably to learn that she can no more resist Busirane than Mars can resist Cupid, that Busirane's very power to command her love is proof that she should give it, that it is godlike to shift one's affections to different partners over time, and that, by coming to share Busirane's understanding of sexuality, her terror will finally be transformed into the rapture of the perfect victim.[39] At the same time, the particular conflation of pleasure and pain in Busirane's tapestries and his masque can seduce Amoret away from Scudamore in the belief that love is ugly and demeaning and hardly worth the pains of fidelity.

Despite Busirane's power over Britomart and Amoret, both women do in the end successfully resist his efforts to draw them into his worldview. There are, as Spenser points out, seams in the master's artwork, "seems" through which these spectators can pass. For instance, the reader can perceive that conditions which might otherwise suggest the greatness of love, or Christianity for that matter—its ability to make warriors peaceful (III.xi.52), to equalize men and women and rich and poor (III.xi.46), or to grant human beings an incomparable taste of the pain and pleasure essential to human existence—are instead presented by Busirane as signs "to shew the victors might and mercilesse intent" (III.xi,52), in other words, the horrible strength of love to move even the gods from their proper home in "heauens kingdome" (III.xi.30) into the mire. The narrator's pointed warning regarding Busirane's Cupid – "Ah man beware, how thou those darts behold" (III.xi.48)—serves, as A. Leigh Deneef notes, to keep readers on guard concerning the reliability of Busirane's crafty representations, "*so* liuely and *so* like" (III.xi.46; emphasis added), yet so wrongly insisting that love is a "long bloudy riuer" (III.xi.46), leading only to "*death* with infamie" (III.xii.25).[40]

The pointed question the narrator poses in the stanza wherein Britomart finally encounters Busirane (III.xii.31), "Ah who can loue the worker of her smart?" signals the double reading of pain and pleasure, love and lust upon which Britomart must act if she is not to be seduced into Busirane's world. One reading of these words reminds us that no one can love a person who causes one pain; in other words, Busirane, as Amoret's rapist, cannot also be the recipient of her desire. Despite his meticulously constructed tableaux and the extraordinary violence of his efforts to disattach Amoret's heart from her body, Busirane, like Malecasta and Paridell before him, cannot imitate the providential actions of the gods but only mimic their outward behaviors in grotesque parody. Not even a "thousand charmes" (III.xii.31) can transfer Amoret's love from its rightful recipient, Scudamore, to Busirane.

The other meaning of this central question, however, complicates the nature of interpretation of this climactic scene, both from Britomart's perspective and the reader's. The words remind us that Spenser is aware of the connections that can be drawn between love and lust and between pleasure and pain but also that an interpretative space can be carved in which to interrogate rather than simply reiterate the connection.[41] The answer to the question, "who can love the worker of her smart?" is not only, as we have seen, "nobody," but also "everybody"—everybody who loves, in particular Amoret and Britomart who both love the men who cause them "consuming paine" (III.xii.21). Indeed, it is the nature of love in *The Faerie Queene* to cause pain and lovers are the primary cause of each other's pain, as Scudamore amply testifies in his grief over Amoret's condition (III.xi.11) and as Britomart reminds Amoret upon rescuing her (III.xii.40).

By posing this particularly difficult question, with its two contradictory answers, at this particular moment, Spenser stresses that the two very different answers to the question mark precisely the distinction between love and lust, seduction and rape, between Britomart's version of chastity and Busirane's, and even between poets like

Spenser (in his seductive *Amoretti*) and poets like Busirane (in his sadistic art). From the perspective of Britomart's and Amoret's chastity, the "smart" caused by Busirane's sadistic rape is not the same as that caused by the desire for one's future husband. Both Busirane and Amoret/Britomart emphasize the conjunction of pleasure and pain, but Busirane situates the source of desire in the male body and allows women to function only as approving objects to male lust. Britomart and Amoret's chastity, on the other hand, foregrounds female desire and suggests that Cupid's function is not to create erotic longing where none exists but to draw out latent desire and channel it into marriage and procreation. Thus, when Britomart conquers Busirane, she also "undoes" Amoret's rape and frees her to pursue her own desire, in other words, her own pain, rather than the pain Busirane has chosen for her. We should modify Paul J. Alpers's view that the closing of Amoret's wound signifies "that love, though apparently problematic and paradoxical, is ultimately harmonious and benign: it leaves no scars, exacts no consequences."[42]

Rather, as Maureen Quilligan proposes, Amoret's release allows her to return to the pains of chaste love, signified by the double-edged "blesse" that Amoret and Scudamore enjoy and which Britomart envies at the close of the 1590 *Faerie Queene* (III.xii.46; 1590); "blesse" is French for wound as well as English for joy, and Britomart envies not Amoret's release from pain but her opportunity to experience the pain that is proper to her.[43] In contrast, the "rape" that Busirane commits upon Amoret is not a wound that pertains to Spenserian chastity. Rejecting rigid definitions of this state that condemn women for being violated, the conclusion of Book III maintains that a victim of sexual assault can remain chaste—hence, Amoret is "restor'd" to being "perfect hole" by Britomart despite Busirane's action (III.xii.38).

In *The Faerie Queene*, the subjective desire of figures like Amoret and Britomart not only marks the crucial difference between love and lust (and hence the very meaning of chastity), but is largely responsible for the very movement of the narrative. As both Linda Gregerson and Susanne Wofford have argued, *The Faerie Queene* constructs two alternative models of reading, one which Gregerson terms "idolatrous" and Wofford "allegoric," and which functions by attempting to firmly solidify meaning and control interpretation. The other, called "interpretive" by Gregerson and "errantry" by Wofford, is represented primarily by Britomart, and is a mode of reading that generates indeterminacy or narrative—for example, the endless generative activity of the Garden of Adonis at the heart of the Third Book.[44]

Busirane acts vehemently against this narrative drive, depicting love as a fixed force both in his massy gold cupid and in his only superficially ever-changing illustrations of the ever-lustful gods. Yet although Britomart's future chaste conceptions are the joyful opposite of the hellish and fruitless metamorphoses of the lustful, it remains quite difficult to separate these two potently erotic sensations. Hence, the hermeneutic strategies that James Kearney has recently explored in relation to Book I (where the greatest sin is an idle and thus idolatrous reading) might need to be modified for Book III.[45]

For example, when Britomart first sees the mysterious promptings on Busirane's castle walls—"be bold" (III.xi.50) and "be not too bold" (III.xi.54), she attempts, not unreasonably, to find the secret within these messages, to interpret these signs aright. Such a hermeneutic is perhaps authorized by Book I of the poem and is definitely encouraged by the tantalizing way that Britomart's efforts have induced similar efforts on the part of readers for centuries.[46] However, when Britomart sees the command "be bold," and "oft and oft it ouer-red" (III.xi.50), her over-reading response may be precisely the problem. Failing to discover the "sence" of the mysterious phrase renders Britomart senseless; in the stanza's first line, she is explicitly regressing, moving "*backward*" as her Busirane-influenced "busie eye," tries to generate a full reading of the scene, "to search each secret of that goodly sted" (III.xi.50). Happily, however, by the stanza's last line, Britomart has thrown off the debilitating, even paralyzing, task of interpretation; she instead proceeds "*forward*" (III.xi.50.9), her "*bold*" steps conforming to Busirane's command textually while perhaps contesting that command through her very ignorance of its purpose. Similarly, when Britomart encounters Busirane's second inscrutable prescription, "be not too bold," her "mind" may "bend" to it (III.xi.54), but her "welpointed weapons" (III.xi.55) remain more forcefully directed.

On such occasions, Spenser is apparently mocking his readers' efforts to comprehend poetic meaning, and urging them instead to temper their own decoding activities through Britomart's posture of aggressively focused desire. No "ridling skill, or commune wit" (III.xi.54) can decipher Busirane's obscure messages, but Britomart is "no whit" (III.xi.50) and so does not allow the mage's pennings to halt her inexorable advance. In this sense, she resembles Guyon, who, at the climax of Book II, severs "true" temperance, from its near-neighbor, excessive tolerance, not through rhetoric, logic, or oratory but via "pittilesse" violence (II.xii.83). Indeed, if the enticing phrases "*Be bold, be bold*" and "*Be not too bold*" (III.xi.54) can be read as C.S. Lewis would read them, as an inducement to taste the pleasures of sex while withdrawing from its responsibilities, Britomart is able to sever the connection between these two commands and experience the boldness of erotic pleasure without succumbing to the fear that she will be labelled as unchaste.[47]

Chinese University of Hong Kong

NOTES

1. All quotations from Edmund Spenser, *The Faerie Queene*, refer to the edition edited by A.C. Hamilton (London: Longman, 1977).

2. See Charles H. and Katherine George, *The Protestant Mind of the English Reformation 1570–1640* (Princeton: Princeton University Press, 1961), 111–12.

3. John Calvin, "Reply to Sandoleto," in *The Protestant Reformation*, ed. Hans J. Hillerbrand (New York: Harper and Row, 1968), 162.

4. On the relationship between Christianity and Spenserian allegory in *The Faerie Queene*, see Susanne Wofford, *The Choice of Achilles: The Ideology of Figure in the Epic* (Stanford: Stanford University Press, 1992).

5. Martin Luther, "The Argument of Saint Paul's Epistle to the Galatians," in Hillerbrand, 103.

6. Katherine Eggert's recent essay, "Spenser's Ravishment: Rape and Rapture in *The Faerie Queene*" (*Representations* 70 [Spring 2000]: 1–20) emphasizes the tensions between Spenser's own rapturous, sensuous verse and his allegiance to a Protestant aesthetic that views the physical body with suspicion. While Eggert rejects the efforts of critics like Stephen Greenblatt and Linda Gregerson to reconcile these tensions in Spenser by recourse to an aware reader who is capable, like Book II's Guyon, of experiencing sensuous rapture without being overwhelmed by it, her essay does not address the role suffering plays in the rapture and rape equation.

7. See Mary Beth Rose, *The Expense of Spirit: Love, Sexuality in English Renaissance Drama* (Ithaca: Cornell University Press, 1988), 129; Stephen Greenblatt, *Renaissance Self-Fashioning* (Chicago: University of Chicago Press, 1980), 241–42, 248–49; Lawrence Stone, *The Family, Sex and Marriage in England 1500–1800* (New York: Harper and Row, 1977), 498–99; Levin L. Schucking, *The Puritan Family*, Trans. Brian Battershaw (New York: Schocken Books, 1970), 25–28.

8. For similar attitudes on Luther's part, see his discussion of the passage, "I am sick of love," from Song of Solomon 2:5. Although Luther does not speak of erotic feeling, he might otherwise be referring to Britomart when he says that, "this love for something we long for, I say, is like hell, hard and strong, and in this God trains His elect in this life in wonderful ways" ("Lectures on Romans," *Collected Works* [St. Louis: Concordia Publishing House, 1955–1976], 25: 378). Luther also notes that "God is hidden in the flesh" (*Collected Works* 11: 156) and Spenser likewise describes the "topography" of Britomart's erotic pain to emphasize that, like all

admirable human feelings, it originates "first aboue" but is emplanted and felt deep within its human subjects, eventually erupting, like a hidden "spring," in "noble deeds and neuer dying fame" (III.iii.1). This reading of the passionate nature of Britomartian love and suffering differs from less literal and more "metaphoric" readings of these conditions; Maureen Quilligan, for instance, attributes Britomart's love pains to overexposure to Petrarchan poetry (*The Language of Allegory: Defining the Genre* [Ithaca: Cornell University Press, 1979]), 81.

9.   Wofford, 259.

10.   Wofford, 255.

11.   Julia Walker, *Medusa's Mirrors: Spenser, Shakespeare, Milton, and the Metamorphosis of the Female Self* (Cranbury, NJ: Associated University Presses, 1998), 83.

12.   For two readings of the phenomena of female bloodshed that stress its symbolic function in perpetuating imperial, patriarchal dynasty see Elizabeth Bellamy, *Translations of Power: Narcissism and the Unconscious in Epic History* (Ithaca: Cornell University Press, 1992) especially 197, and Margaret Olofson Thickstun, *Fictions of the Feminine: Puritan Doctrine and the Representation of Women* (Ithaca: Cornell University Press, 1988), 50.

13.   The extreme amount of suffering in the history of Britain is a point apparently so significant to Spenser that he presents it twice in the 1590 *Faerie Queene* and at considerable length on both occasions: in II.x.4–68 and III.iii.27–55.

14.   Bellamy offers a complex Lacanian reading of Britomart's gendered consciousness emphasizing that her "sexuality—a specifically 'ideological' or dynastic sexuality—can only be constituted through trauma," 208.

15.   Susan Frye, *Elizabeth I: The Competition for Representation* (Oxford University Press, 1993), 107.

16.   Frye contrasts Queen Elizabeth's conception of chastity to Spenser's, 36–40 and especially 98–120.

17.   At two separate points, in stanza five of the Proem to Book III and in the *Letter to Ralegh* [Hamilton, 737], Spenser cites only the virgin huntress Belphoebe, and not Britomart, as analogous to Queen Elizabeth.

18.   Frye, 107.

19.   See Allan H. Gilbert, "The Ladder of Lechery, *The Faerie Queene*, III, i, 45," *Modern Language Notes* 56 (1941): 594.

20.   Teresa Krier, *Gazing on Secret Sights: Spenser, Classical Imitation, and the Decorums of Vision* (Ithaca: Cornell University Press, 1990), 119.

21.   Krier, 136. Philippa Berry, *Of Chastity and Power: Elizabethan Literature and the Unmarried Queen* (London: Routledge, 1989) provides a similar analysis of a scene in Book II (II.3.21–31) where Belphoebe's spiritual and sensual attributes are jointly heightened "in a most unsettling way" (158). Berry notes that Belphoebe's ability to "reuiue the ded" (III.ii.22) simultaneously evokes both her affinity to Christ (whose mother also was a virgin) and her irresistible sexuality. We might say that one function served by *The Faerie Queene* is to eroticize the Christian metaphor, emphasized by Protestants, whereby the recalcitrant heart of stone is transformed into one of painful flesh.

22.   Krier, 136.

23.   Judith H. Anderson, " 'In liuing colours and right hew': The Queen of Spenser's Central Books," in *Poetic Traditions of the English Renaissance*, ed. Maynard Mack

and George deForest Lord (New Haven: Yale University Press, 1982), 56. Maureen Quilligan, *Milton's Spenser: The Politics of Reading* (Ithaca: Cornell University Press, 1983), also makes this point, 189–90. David Lee Miller, *The Poem's Two Bodies: The Poetics of the 1590 "Faerie Queene"* (Princeton: Princeton University Press, 1988), 227. Spenser's critique of Belphoebe/Queen Elizabeth is addressed at length in Mary Villeponteaux's essay, "Semper Eadem: Belphoebe's Denial of Desire" in *Renaissance Discourses of Desire*, ed. Claude J. Summers and Ted-Larry Pebworth (Columbia: University of Missouri Press, 1993), 29–45.

24.   Sheila Cavanagh, *Wanton Eyes and Chaste Desires: Female Sexuality in* The Faerie Queene (Bloomington: University of Indiana Press, 1994). Cavanagh points out that Britomart pointedly fails to protect either of the two other threatened chaste females of Book III (Florimell and Amoret) despite the ease with which she might have done so, 143–47.

25.   For the suggestion that this pregnancy is beneficent, see Miller, 235, and Thomas P. Roche, Jr., *The Kindly Flame: A Study of the Third and Fourth Books of Spenser's* Faerie Queene (Princeton: Princeton University Press, 1964), 108. For the idea that rape is suggested, see Cavanagh, 3.

26.   Krier also notes this point on 139, and examines this scene at length, 137–41. It might be noted that the virginal Belphoebe deliberately protects her own "dainty Rose" from "the Middayes scorching powre" (III.v.51), suggesting her heightened awareness of the dangerous (because so swiftly and literally personified) natural world she lives in.

27.   Harry Berger, *Revisionary Play: Studies in the Spenserian Dynamics* (Berkeley: University of California Press, 1988), 107.

28.   Paridell's reaction to love continuously emphasizes his immunity to the pain that love is supposed to provide:

> But nothing new to him was that same paine,
> Ne paine at all; for he so ofte had tryde
> The powre thereof, and lov'd so oft in vaine,
> That thing of course he counted love to entertaine.

(III.ix.29)

29.   Roche, 70. Paul J. Alpers, *The Poetry of* The Faerie Queene (Princeton: Princeton University Press, 1967), 377, develops Roche's interpretation of this scene to stress the difference between the pastoral and heroic modes. To Alpers, Malecasta's tapestries of Venus and Adonis propose a:

> resolution of erotic tragedy [that] is merely picturesque and hence valid only in a world of mythological pastoral. The sufferings of human love—we shall soon see them in Britomart as well as in Malecasta—are deeper and more vicious than Venus'. The image of their resolution must acknowledge the turbulence of human feeling and express more vigor than the dainty flower does.

30.   Quilligan, *Milton's Spenser*, 196.

31.   Thus Book III might be said to have two centers. The first, as Michael Baybak, Paul Delany, and A. Kent Hieatt note ("Placement 'In the Middest' in *The Faerie Queene*" [*Papers on Language and Literature* 5 (1969): 227) is the anatomical *mons Veneris*, signifying the centrality of the female body to Book III. The second is the "bore" signifying the dangerous male body. Both male and female bodies are loci of both pain and pleasure, but it is the male body that is most susceptible to lust, less likely to be chaste, and therefore in need of greater control.

32.   Since the soul is not eternal in the Garden of Adonis, the Adonis Venus loves one day may not have the same spirit as the Adonis she will love tomorrow. But Venus and Adonis are abstractions—a goddess and a flower—and a goddess may love in a form what a person must love in another.

33.   Berger, *Revisionary Play*, 97–98.

34.   For a similar reading of this scene, see Gordon Coggins, " 'Hideous Horror and Sad Trembling Sound;' Arthur's Pursuit of Florimell," *Spenser at Kalamazoo* (1983), ed. Francis G. Greco (Clarion: Clarion University of Pennsylvania, 1983), 164–81.

35.   See for example Roche who claims that "we cannot suppose that Spenser intends the reader to think ill of Arthur and Guyon," 14, cited approvingly by Quilligan, *Milton's Spenser*, 186–87.

36.   Cf. Cavanagh, 16, 22–24. Harry Berger, " 'Kidnapped Romance': Discourse in *The Faerie Queene*" in *Unfolded Tales: Essays on Renaissance Romance*, ed. George M. Logan and Gordon Teskey (Ithaca: Cornell University Press, 1989), 208–56, makes a similar argument (223–28).

37.   Cavanagh, 25.

38.   Spenser (*Letter to Ralegh*), in Hamilton, 737.

39.   Cf. Berger who calls Busirane's art "a model of infinite desire which conditions the mind to view as hostile, perhaps even 'unnatural,' any recalcitrance, delay, or refusal on the part of the object of desire," *Revisionary Play*, 178. It should be noted that much of the excellent recent work on Busirane emphasizes his affinities with the figure of Scudamore from whom Busirane has stolen Amoret. Although Scuda-more plays the role of Amoret's "husband" to Busirane's "rapist," such textual features as Busirane's efforts to seduce Amoret and Scudamore's violent rapture of Amoret in Book IV, canto x, make the two figures shade into each other and thereby shed light on the problematic role of the wife as both equal and submissive partner in Protestant "companionate marriages" of the period. See especially Dorothy Stephens, "Into Other Arms: Amoret's Evasion," *ELH* 58 (1991): 523–44, and Elizabeth Bellamy, "Literary History as 'Symptom' in Spenser and Milton," *ELH* 64 (1997): 391–414.

40.   A. Leigh Deneef, "Spenser's *Amor Fuggitivo* and the Transfixed Heart," *ELH* 46 (1979): 14–15.

41.   One example of recent criticism that compels us to rethink Spenserian chastity but which does not do justice to Spenser's subtle distinctions between love and lust, seduction and rape, and by extension Busirane and Spenser, is that of Susan Frye. Frye (following David Lee Miller's more cautious expressions of these ideas) sees the two male figures as coextensive; both are poets and magicians who use art to control women and in fact desire to rape them as a punishment for their efforts at

independence. While Frye acutely identifies many points of similarity between the aggression of Busirane and that of frustrated Elizabethan courtiers such as Spenser, she makes little space for discriminating between these varieties of violence. Hence, intergender relations as complex as desire, seduction, manipulation, courtship, love, and marriage are all finally reduced to rape, while female sexual autonomy is consequently identified with virginity (128–35). Sheila Cavanagh's reading of *The Faerie Queene* is similar to Frye's; she sees the figure of "Leda's coyly smiling capitulation to Jove's sexual conquest" as "Spenser's own account" rather than Busirane's (5) and suggests that the pain women experience when loving men in the poem is a mode of patriarchal sadism (87). For a contrastive reading of *The Faerie Queene* that is attuned to the many varieties of the Spenserian gaze and their respective moral consequences, see Krier.

42. Alpers, 198.

43. Quilligan, *Milton's Spenser*, 199. Other elements of the passage's language confirm Quilligan's reading. The reunited Amoret and Scudamore engage one another in "sweet counteruayle," as "each other of loues bitter fruit despoile" (1590.II-I.xii.47). These two oxymoronic phrases epitomize the tension between pleasure and pain that has characterized Britomart's adventures; these lovers alleviate one another's bitterness only by taking that bitterness onto themselves.

44. Wofford, 220–24 and passim. Linda Gregerson, *The Reformation of the Subject: Spenser, Milton, and the English Protestant Epic* (Cambridge: Cambridge University Press, 1995), especially chapter 1. See also Silberman, 61. For a somewhat contradictory reading see Katherine Eggert, " 'Changing all that forme of common weale': Genre and the Repeal of Queenship in *The Faerie Queene*, Book 5," *English Literary Renaissance* 26 (1996): 259–90. Eggert sees Spenser's affirmation of open-ended, "female" modes of narrative wandering as highly troubled and anxious since such modes are at odds with the patriarchal, linear narrative necessities of the epic tradition that Spenser also upholds.

45. James Kearney, "Enshrining Idolatry in *The Faerie Queene*," *English Literary Renaissance* 32 (2002): 3–30.

46. As Susanne Wofford remarks ("Gendering Allegory: Spenser's Bold Reader and the Emergence of Character in *The Faerie Queene* III." *Criticism* 30 [1998]), "[Britomart's] exploring of the House of Busyrane is treated as textual space, furnished with a multiplicity of intertextual references . . . [Britomart's] imagined depth of character is represented in the text by means of the analogy established between her and the imagined figure of the reader whom she resembles," 10.

47. C.S. Lewis, *Spenser's Images of Life*, ed. Alastair Fowler (Cambridge: Cambridge University Press, 1967), 27–28.

GLEANINGS

FRANK ARDOLINO

Spenser's Allusion to the Defeat of the Spanish Armada in *Virgil's Gnat* (550–92)

*I*N "THE EFFECT OF THE DEFEAT of the Spanish Armada
on Spenser's *Complaints*," I argued that the visionary poems in this
collection contain imagery drawn from contemporary accounts of
England's naval victory in 1588.[1] Spenser uses images of storms
and ships wrecked in tempestuous seas, the defeat of large animals
by small ones, and the undermining and toppling of monumental
edifices by natural elements to allude to and celebrate the defeat
of Catholic Rome/Spain under Philip II, whose Babylonian pride
was humbled by little England with the help of the "winds of
God." Similarly, in *Virgil's Gnat*, the gnat's underworld account
of the ill-fated return home of the Greeks after their victory in
the Trojan war contains storm and shipwreck imagery, which
Spenser uses to depict, in small, the defeat and dispersal of the
Spanish Armada. I am not maintaining that Spenser's translation
of the pseudo-Virgilian *Culex* is as dominated by Armada imagery
as the visionary poems, but that the description of the storm and
its aftermath, which doubles the number of lines in Latin and is
original to Spenser for the most part, is influenced by the contemporary accounts of the scattering and destruction of the Spanish
fleet.

In the narrative of the storm in *Culex*, the Greeks are depicted
as paying penance for their brutal victory over Troy. When they
embarked, they were laden with the spoils of war, and all portents
were favorable for a safe return home. However, a doom followed
them, and, subsequently and inevitably, they were punished by
being drowned in the Hellespont:

> *reddidit, heu, Graius poenas tibi, Troia, ruenti,*
> *Hellespontiacis obiturus reddidit undis.*
> *illa vices hominum testata est copia quondam,*

ne quisquam propriae Fortunae munere dives
iret inevectus caelum super: omne propinquo
frangitur invidiae telo decus . . . .
cum seu caelesti fato seu sideris ortu
undique mutatur caeli nitor, omnia ventis,
omnia turbinibus sunt anxia.[2]

Their punishment is the result of a generalized sense of Nemesis.
Either by divine fate or some rising star or planetary influence, a
storm arose and all of nature erupted into a frenzied attack on the
fleet, whose defeat is the denouement of a Greek tragedy with the
triumphant heroes punished for their hubris.

By contrast, Spenser depicts a divine revenge tragedy in which
God uses the storm as punishment on the vaunted Armada, which
was defeated because of His championing Protestant England over
Catholic Spain. As in the visionary poems, Spenser politicizes his
source, "translating" the Greek context of the Latin poem to the
Protestant English context. The most obvious difference between the
two contexts is that whereas the Greeks were triumphant in the
Trojan war, Spain had failed in its attempt to invade England in 1588
and was further humiliated and demoralized by the long death march
home. In Spenser's translation, Spain is punished for its audacity in
attempting to invade England and reinstitute Catholicism.

Although Spenser begins with the same general notion about the
penance the victors must pay for their triumph—"Ah but the
Greekes . . . /To thee, o Troy, paid penaunce for thy fall"[3] —he
quickly emphasizes that their fall is due to overweening pride, which
caused them to claim a divine status:

Well may appeare, by proofe of their mischaunce,
The chaungfull turning of mens slipperie state,
That none, whom fortune freely doth advaunce,
Himself therefore to heaven should elevate:
For loftie type of honour, through the glaunce
Of envies dart, is downe in dust prostrate;
And all that vaunts in worldly vanitie shall fall through fortunes mu-
        tabilitie.

(553–60)

Spenser depicts the enactment of a fated vengeance through the con-
spiring of the heavenly and astrological powers to create the fatal
storm:

[I]n avengement of their bold attempt,
Both sun and starres and all the heavenly powres
Conspire in one to wreake their rash contempt,
And downe on them to fall from highest towres.

(577–80)

The seas and the sky engage in a war which parallels the battle the
gods are waging against the Greeks. The storm-tossed waves try "to
the heavens to reach,/ . . . th'heavens striving them for to impeach"
(575–76), that is, to punish their rebelliousness, which represents the
hubris of the Greeks/Spanish. The ships are attacked by death in
myriad ghastly forms on all sides, and they are rent, divided, and
scattered over the ocean, which is bestrewn with their treasures.

Some in the greedie flouds are sunke and drent:
Some on the rocks of Caphareus are throwne;
Some on th'Euboick cliffs in pieces rent;
Some scattred on the Hercaean shores unknowne;
And manie lost, of whom no moniment
Remaines, nor memorie is to be showne:
Whilst all the purchase of the Phrigian pray,
Tost on salt billowes, round about doth stray.

(585–92)

Implicit in the above lines—the storm falling down on them from
highest towres and the ships being scattered—is the dual image of
the destruction of the tower of Babel in Genesis 11 and the fall of
Babylon in Revelation 18. When the sons of the earth attempted to
build a tower that would reach to the heavens, God punished them
for their excessive pride and destroyed the tower and scattered them
over the earth, with each group speaking different languages: "So
the Lord scatred them from thence vpon all the earth, and they left
of to buylde the citie"(11.8).[4] An analogous scattering occurs after
the defeat of Babylon in Revelation: "For . . . so great riches are
come to desolation. And euerie shippe master, and all the people
that occupie shippes, and shipmen, and whosoeuer trauail on the
sea . . . " (18.17).

As S. F. Johnson has pointed out, in the sixteenth century Protestant apologists conflated the overthrow of the tower of Babel with
the fall of Babylon as a composite image of the inevitable destruction
of the confusion created by Catholicism.[5] Moreover, when the Spanish Armada was defeated in 1588, Protestant commentators saw its

destruction as the fulfillment of the Book of Revelation and the prophecies which had heralded 1588 as the *annus mirabilis*.[6] The victory was interpreted as the defeat of the Catholic Babylon by "the Lord himselfe [who] doth as it were sound the trumpet unto this battle against *Babel*."[7] Daniel Archdeacon compared Philip II to Nimrod, the builder of the ill-fated tower of Babylon, "who hath by hys ships, made like Babel towers, vaunted himselfe to make us afraid . . . ."[8] Elizabethan writers also saw the Armada defeat as a revenge tragedy in which God punished the Spanish for their overweening pride and greed. In *A True description of a straunge Monster*, James Lea depicts God as the unsleeping revenger who caused the fall of Babylon-Spain: "[H]e that keepeth Israel doeth neyther slumber nor sleepe. Babell is falling . . . . [T]he righteous God hath revenged our wronges on the proudest of our foes."[9] Thomas Nun extols God as the revenger who sends the destructive winds and actually participated in the battle: "Mightie was thine armie as was *Baracke*, but Jehovah would have the glorie as then hee had, his windes revenged thy quarel . . . . Jehovah . . . thou wast our man of warre in that day . . . ."[10]

The fated storm in *Virgil's Gnat* can be compared to the "winds of God" which were depicted as the cause of the defeat of the Spanish Armada. The winds that blew the Spanish ships astray and that caused the destruction of nearly half the Armada on its journey home, including shipwrecks off the coast of Ireland and Scotland, were associated with the role of England as the instrument of Providence favored by God in the climactic battle against the Catholic Whore of Babylon.[11] The sermon preached at St. Paul's on the day Elizabeth celebrated the victory was "Thou didst blow with thy winds, and they were scattered."[12] Coins were stamped displaying ships burning and scattered. In his celebratory poem *Ad serenissimam Elizabetham Angliae reginam* (1588), Théodore de Bèze describes how the winds and the waves humbled the inflated pride of the Spain and Philip II:

> But well have windes his proud blasts overblowen,
> And swelling waves alayd his swelling heart, . . .
> . . . O Queene, above all others blest,
> For whom both windes and waves are prest to fight.[13]

Similarly, in a hymn of thanksgiving composed by Queen Elizabeth, "he [God] made the wynds and waters rise / To scatter all myne enemyes."[14] In *The Spanish Masquerado* (1589), Greene declares that divine vengeance was exacted on Spain by the winds which destroyed the Armada: " . . . God . . . , to punish the enemies of his trueth, . . . let loose the windes . . . and threw a storme into the sea, that many of their shippes . . . perished on the Rockes: vsing the Sea for reuenge as he did against *Pharao* . . . ."[15] Richard Niccols depicts the same apocalyptic devastation as in *Virgil's Gnat* when he describes the scattered remains of the Armada:

> Then ceast the storme; then did the seas disclose
> The armes, the painted robes, and spoiles of Spaine,
> Which heere and there did flote vpon the maine,
> By England, Ireland, Norway . . . ,
> Where *Ioue* did act their fleets black tragedie.[16]

Finally, Thomas Brightman in *Revelation of the Revelation* celebrates the deflation and scattering of Spain's vaunted navy: "His [Philip's] inuincible Armye so called that was sent against vs the yeare 1588 . . . [h]ad deuored in hope ere it came, all our Country, lyues and goodes; but how nobly was it deceiued . . . beinge discoumfited, wrecked, and scattered vp and downe through all Seas . . . ."[17]

In his description of the storm that devastated the Greeks on their return home after defeating Troy, Spenser is alluding to the defeat of Spain in 1588, when sea storms and divine providence combined to overthrow the Catholic Babylon. The fact that he translates this passage from the pseudo-Virgilian *Culex* to the religio-political context of late sixteenth-century England demonstrates in small how large an influence the Protestant interpretation of the naval victory had on the imagery of the *Complaints*.

University of Hawaii

NOTES

1. Frank Ardolino, "The Effect of the Defeat of the Spanish Armada on Spenser's *Complaints*," *Spenser Studies* 16(2002):55–75.

2. Virgil, *Aeneid vii-xii and the Minor Poems*, trans. H. Rushton Fairclough, rev. ed. (Cambridge: Harvard University Press, 1946), 337–42, 47–49.

3. Edmund Spenser, *Complete Poetical Works of Spenser*, ed. R. E. Neill Dodge (Boston:Houghton Mifflin, 1936),550–51. All quotations of the *Complaints* are from this edition and will be cited within the text.

4. *The Geneva Bible: A Facsimile of the 1560 Edition*, ed. Lloyd Berry (Madison: University of Wisconsin Press, 1969).

5. S. F. Johnson, "*The Spanish Tragedy*, or Babylon Revisited,"in *Essays on Shakespeare and Elizabethan Drama in Honor of Hardin Craig*, ed. Richard Hosley (Columbia, MO: University of Missouri Press, 1962), 24–25.

6. Ardolino, "*Complaints*," 59–61.

7. George Gifford, *Sermons Upon the Whole Book of Revelation* (London, 1596), A3v.

8. Daniel Archdeacon, *A True Discourse of the Armie which the King of Spaine caused to bee assembled . . . in . . . 1588, against England* (London: John Wolfe, 1588), 8.

9. James Lea, *A True . . . description* (London: John Wolfe, 1590), 15.

10. Thomas Nun, *A Comfort Against the Spaniard* (Oxford, England: John Windet, 1596), C2r.

11. Elkin Wilson, *England's Eliza* (1939; rpt. N.Y.: Octagon, 1966), 279.

12. Ibid., 288.

13. Quoted in Wilson, 289.

14. Quoted in David Howarth, *The Voyage of the Armada: The Spanish Story* (N.Y.: Penguin, 1982), 240.

15. Robert Greene, *The Spanish Masquerado, The Life and Complete Works in Prose and Verse of Robert Greene*, ed. Alexander Grosart, 15 vols. (1881–86; rpt. New York: Russell and Russell, 1964), 5:275.

16. Richard Niccols, *Englands Eliza* (London,1610), 838.

17. Thomas Brightman, *A Revelation of the Revelation* (Amsterdam, 1615), 130.

THOMAS HERRON

Exotic Beasts: The Earl of Ormond and Nicholas Dawtry in *Mother Hubberds Tale?*

The satire of court corruption in the third episode of *Mother Hubberds Tale* has traditionally been read as referring allegorically to the English court. Certain signifiers have been overlooked, however, that turn our attention to intertwined Scottish and Irish politics as well. The poem would appear to sympathize with the travails of Nicholas Dawtry, the New English captain in Ireland and ambassador to the Scottish court. It may also condemn the "wilde" powers granted to the queen's cousin, Thomas Butler, earl of Ormond, whose coat-of-arms is found therein.

EDMUND SPENSER'S "Prosopopoia, or Mother Hubberds Tale," a politically daring poem included in his *Complaints* (pub. 1591), still holds a few surprises for those compulsively attracted to the nit-picking search for Elizabethan political allegories. We must for a moment turn our attention away from England, however, to understand the local particulars of its thickly veiled satire of the court.

The disjunctive plot is as follows. After a gloomy opening astrological description, the narrator relates a beast fable told by Old Mother Hubberd, which forms the basis of the poem. She recounts how two miscreants, a Fox and an Ape, disguise themselves to swindle individuals and institutions and finally to misrule the entire realm. Following a common medieval device, her tale includes four main parts that satirize different social estates: first the People, then the Church and then the Court and Monarchy come under scrutiny.[1] Critics have had great difficulty explaining the whole poem in terms of any other structural, thematic, or allegorical coherence.

The third episode (581–942) primarily interests us here. It involves a lengthy and sharp satire of the vanities and frustrations of life at court. The Ape and Fox follow the advice of a fat mule and go to court, where the Ape dresses as a gentleman and the Fox his groom. The traditional deceits, back-biting vices, and frivolous games of courtly life become glaringly apparent all around them and through their behavior until "justice seate" (921) discovers the foul activities of the Fox and banishes him from court; whereupon the Ape "want-ing his huckster man,/That wont provide his necessaries" (925–26) finds himself exposed as a fraud and must also leave.[2]

1. A Reference to Captain Nicholas Dawtry?

The criticisms of the court clearly have a general target. But two key lines in the third episode point toward a political allegory involving Scottish and Irish intrigues.[3] First, Mother Hubberd laments that the unsuccessful courtier "as a thistle-downe in th'ayre doth flie,/So vainly shalt thou too and fro be tost,/And loose thy labour and thy fruitles cost" (634–36). The thistle is the Scottish national symbol. The reference to "thistle-downe" could imply that the Scottish, not only the English, court frustrated the political hopes of individuals, courtiers. and ambassadors who sought favor and/or influence there: they shuttled back and forth as randomly as thistle-downs. A second meaning is implied in that the thistle-down, or wafting seed, corrupts the fields that it infiltrates from afar, rendering them "fruitles." The fruitless "cost" of this infiltration might then signify the damaging interference of the Scottish monarchy in the affairs of others: it plants the seeds of disaster, in part by spurning good courtiers and wasting their labor. Hence "thistle-down" should also remind us of *thistle crown*, a gold coin issued by James VI (*OED*; cf. also its companions, the "thistle dollar," "thistle merk" and "thistle noble"). The thistle was a standard emblem on Scottish coins in the sixteenth century and the thistle crown reminiscent of the head of a thistle (i.e., its "crown," from whence, naturally enough, comes the "down"). It shows a thistle on its reverse side. Spenser was himself a planter in Ireland: by stressing the "cost" to laborious fields of the thistle-down, the narrator of the poem thus appears to express a fear of Scottish corruptive influence abroad, numismatic or no; either the Scots sow tares directly or spurn virtuous visitors to their court.

Many lines later the narrator laments a similar phenomenon: he who "will to Court for shadowes vaine to seeke,/Or hope to gaine,

himself will a daw trie:/That curse God send unto mine enemie."
(911–13) [H]imself will a daw trie" (i.e., "will prove a fool") is a
suspiciously awkward phrase that could hint at someone real. One of
the most prominent captains fighting for the New English cause in
Ireland was Nicholas Dawtry. He is one of the interlocutors, with
Spenser and Lodowick Bryskett and others in Ireland, in Bryskett's
Discourse of Civill Life (c. 1582–85; pub. 1605). David Edwards places
him in the same pro-martial law camp as Spenser and the governor
of Connacht, Sir Richard Bingham. He advised Spenser's early patron, the militant Protestant Lord Grey, on military matters in Ireland
and wrote a lengthy policy paper, "A Booke of Questions and Answars Concerning The Warrs or Rebellions of the Kingdome of
Irelande" (1597), on the same.[4]

A Scottish court connection surfaces in that Dawtry served in
the administration of the heavily Scots-influenced Clandeboye, in
northeastern Ulster, in the late 1570s and 80s. In 1585 he traveled
to the Scottish court to persuade King James VI to help prevent
"redshanks," or Scottish mercenary soldiers, from continuing to
come into Ireland from the Western Isles of James's kingdom to fight
with their relations and/or for the highest bidder (often as enemies
of the English crown). Dawtry's mission obtained promises of com-
pliance from the king, but only the treaty of Berwick the next year,
as well as the massacre of over two thousand redshanks and family
members at Ardnaree (also in 1586) by Governor Bingham, stemmed
the Scottish tide into the country. Dawtry's embassade to Scotland,
in other words, arguably failed and left him looking like a foolish
bird (a tried daw); to borrow from the earlier image, Dawtry can be
said to have resembled "a thistle-down in th'ayre" among those shut-
tling back and forth on the heavy winds between both islands (with
a potential pun on "ayre" and *eire*, Irish for "Ireland").

If this reading holds, *Mother Hubberds Tale* invokes the specter of
Dawtry's tribulation with Irish-Scottish politics, in the context of
criticizing the vanities of the English court, and courts everywhere, in
order to wish such ill success upon an unnamed "enemie." The
politically minded Spenser could not have been unaware of Dawtry's
fruitless mission. Spenser had little reason to compliment the court
of James VI, whom the poet would later insult by portraying his
mother, Mary Stuart, as Duessa in Book V of *The Faerie Queene*
(1596).[5] Should James ascend to the English throne—an increasing
likelihood in the 1590s—and both favor Irish interests and exert
Scottish ones in Ireland, then Spenser's hard plantation "labour" in
Munster might also be turned to "fruitles cost" and himself become
the thistle-down made homeless by Scots-supported power. This

power could include a possible attack by Scottish mercenaries beholden to thistle crowns. Dawtry's mission at the Scottish court instead tried to promote a cause that Spenser (like Bingham) would
logically have supported.[6]

2. ORMOND AND THE WILD BEASTS

The description of the thistle-down follows hard upon a passage
describing the kind of courtiers one needed to woo in order to suc-
ceed, yet these courtiers are, again, untrustworthy. This passage, read
by many critics as an interpolation or "hasty revision"[7] in the poem,
has been read as a reference to the marriage woes of either Leicester
in 1579, or Essex in 1590, or the rivalry between Essex and Ralegh
in the late 1580s.[8] As the editors of the *Yale Edition of the Shorter
Poems* state, "Certainty in this case is impossible to come by but the
gossipy tone of this account of 'who's in, who's out' is unmistakable."[9] Partway through the third episode, a fat Mule advises the Ape
and Fox on how to ingratiate themselves at court:

> . . . the highest now in grace,
> Be the wilde beasts, that swiftest are in chase;
> For in their speedie course and nimble flight
> The Lyon now doth take the most delight:
> But chieflie, joyes on foote them to beholde,
> Enchaste with chaine and circulet of golde:
> So wilde a beast so tame ytaught to bee,
> And buxome to his bands is joy to see.
> So well his golden Circlet him beseemeth:
> But his late chayne his Liege unmeete esteemeth;
> For so brave beasts she loveth best to see,
> In the wilde forrest raunging fresh and free.
> Therefore if it fortune thee in Court to live,
> In case thou ever there wilt hope to thrive,
> To some of these thou must thy selfe apply.
>
> (619–33)

The animals, significant players at court, normally remain chained
and "enchaste" but have been let loose by their "Liege" ("she" of
line 629) into the "wilde forrest." In terms of English-Irish relations

this could easily refer to their release from London by Queen Elizabeth (also, presumably, the "Lyon" referred to here[10]) into the stereotypical "wilderness" of Ireland (or from Dublin to beyond the Pale), endangering both realms. These animals would include past or potential enemies such as the earls of Kildare, Clancarty and/or Desmond, who were all imprisoned in the Tower and released during their careers; or it could refer to powerful players, such as "Black Tom" Butler (1531–1614), the tenth earl of Ormond, whose ethnicity, close proximity to his cousin the queen, and more moderate views were distrusted by Spenser and his New English allies.[11]

More specifically, the above passage and its singular subject (cf. "his bands" in 626) could allude to the extended powers granted to Ormond over his palatinate of Tipperary (the "wilde forrest" where Ormond had total control), to the great dismay of Spenser and other hard-line Protestants. Ormond's inclusion in the poem as a feared (once unchained) wild animal would suit Spenser's fear of a reckless government in Ireland under Ormond's sway.[12]

Dense wordplay (as was typical of Spenser) points towards Ormond as the target of satire in the above passage. First, on a vague level, the description of the beasts as "on foote" may allude to his occupational surname, Butler (a name acquired thanks to the earl's traditional service as butler to the English monarch at ceremonial occasions, a post held in England by the Sidneys; this in turn entitled Butler to a generous tithe from all wine imported into Ireland). The image of a "buxome" tamed beast with a circle around his neck, halter-like, could allude to Elizabeth's pet name for him, "Lucas": the apostle Luke is traditionally figured as an ox.[13] The double mention of a "circulet of golde"/"golden Circlet" could also emphasize a pun on the French meaning of a (circular) *world* of *gold* in his title, Or-mond (originally from the Irish for "east Munster"). Finally, Ormond served much of his career as Lord Treasurer of Ireland; an association with gold and the (Elizabeth-conferred) chains of office would be an obvious one.

The Butler arms, beginning with Black Tom's, included two circlets (or *annulets*) of gold. Butler added a fourth quarter to his predecessor's coat as a means of including his claim to the lordship of Karryk (Carrick) mac Griffyn.[14] Its blazon is *argent, a lion rampant gules, on a chief of the last a swan close of the first between two annulets, or* [Fig. 1]. On this blazon, in other words, above a ramping lion stands a swan between two circlets of gold. Compare this image again to lines 620–27 ("wilde beasts . . . beseemeth"). What Spenser has described, in essence, is a picture of animals normally in "flight" brought (or slowed) down "on foote" and surrounded ("enchaste") with a chain and a circlet of gold; meanwhile a "Lyon" delights in seeing them. In the Karryk arms we see a bird of flight, the swan, on foot between two golden circlets and gazed upon from below by a lion. While the badge does not include a chain, its supporters were typically two chained griffins. This badge of wild animals chained or brought to earth could easily have inspired Spenser's description. Spenser's poem does not literally describe the grounded beasts as flanked by two circlets, but he does mention the circlet twice and their position in the stanza cleverly enchases the tamed "beast" within his verse.

Hampden-Sydney College

NOTES

1. Ruth Mohl, *The Three Estates in Medieval and Renaissance Literature*. (NY: Columbia University Press, 1933): chapters 5–7. Cited in Spenser, *The Minor Poems: Part Two. The Works of Edmund Spenser: A Variorum Edition*. Vols. 1–10. Eds. Edwin Greenlaw et al. (Baltimore: Johns Hopkins University Press, 1947) 8: 594–95.

2. "Prosopopoia. Or Mother Hubberds Tale." *The Yale Edition of the Shorter Poems of Edmund Spenser*. Eds. William Oram et al. (New Haven: Yale University Press, 1989), 327–79. All quotations from the poem herein are taken from this edition.

3. Note too the "old Scotch cap" worn by the Ape in the first episode (209): another link to Scottish politics?

4. For the little we know about Dawtry, see Willy Maley, *Salvaging Spenser: Colonialism, Culture and Identity*. (NY: MacMillan, 1997): 70–71, 161–62; Hiram Morgan ed., "A Booke of Questions and Answars Concerning the Warrs or Rebellions of the Kingdome of Irelande," by Nicholas Dawtry. *Analecta Hibernica* 36 (1995): 79–132, 82–86; David Edwards, "Ideology and experience: Spenser's *View* and martial law in Ireland." *Political Ideology in Ireland, 1541–1641*. Ed. Hiram Morgan. (Dublin: Four Courts Press, 1999), 127–57: 138–39.

5. Mark Eccles, "James I of England." *The Spenser Encyclopedia*. Ed. A.C. Hamilton. (Toronto: University of Toronto Press, 1990), 409. Eccles refers also to the "unsubstantiated" claim that the Ape in "Mother Hubberds Tale" allegorizes James. On James's Irish lineage and the fears among Spenser and the New English concerning his potential ascendancy, see Richard McCabe, *Spenser's Monstrous Regiment: Elizabethan Ireland and the Poetics of Difference*. (Oxford: Oxford University Press, 2002) 52–54.

6. For Spenser's sympathy with Bingham's hard-line Protestant policy, see Christopher Highley, *Shakespeare, Spenser and the Crisis in Ireland* (Cambridge: Cambridge University Press, 1997) 116–21.

7. W. L. Renwick, ed., *Complaints*. By Edmund Spenser. (London: Scholartis Press, 1928) 239.

8.   Spenser, *Minor Poems,* 363; Edwin Greenlaw, "Spenser and the Earl of Leicester." *PMLA* 25 (1910): 535–61, 551; Renwick, ed., *Complaints* 239; Percy Long, "Spenser and the Bishop of Rochester." *PMLA* 31 (1916): 713–35, 726; *Yale Edition.*355n; Charles Mounts, "The Ralegh-Essex Rivalry and *Mother Hubberds Tale." Modern Language Notes* 65 (1950): 509–13.

9.   *Yale Edition . . .* 355n.

10.   But see Greenlaw's comment that "the lion in the first incident [i.e., this episode of the chained beasts] is a courtier, in the second the king." Greenlaw, "Spenser" 548.

11.   Nicholas Canny, *Making Ireland British 1580–1650.* (Oxford: Oxford University Press, 2001): 125–28 passim.

12.   *cf.* the criticism of the feuding Butlers in Spenser, *A View of the Present State of Ireland. Spenser's Prose Works. The Works of Edmund Spenser: A Variorum Edition.* Vols. 1–10. Ed. Rudolf Gottfried. (Baltimore: Johns Hopkins University Press, 1949), 9: 39–231: 114–15.

13.   Cyril Falls, "Black Tom Ormonde." *Irish Sword* 5 (1961–62): 10–22, 12. States Falls, "Some jest must have been attached to [this pet name], but we cannot divine what it was." For more information on Ormond, see the *DNB*; Ciarán Brady, "Thomas Butler, earl of Ormond (1531–1614) and Reform in Tudor Ireland." *Worsted in the Game: Losers in Irish History.* Ed. Ciarán Brady. (Dublin: Lilliput Press, 1989), 49–60. David Edwards, *The Ormond Lordship in County Kilkenny, 1515–1642: The Rise and Fall of Butler Feudal Power.* (Dublin: Four Courts Press, 2003). See also McCabe, *Spenser's . . .* 28–30 passim.

14.   Butler's main seat was Kilkenny Castle, but Spenser could easily have had Butler's mansion at Carrick-on-Suir in mind when complimenting Butler's "braue mansion" in a dedicatory sonnet to Ormond in *The Faerie Queene* (1590). On this identification of the mansion and further discussion of Ormond in relation to Spenser, see Highley 28. For the Karryk arms and those of the Butler family, see Toby Butler, "Heraldry of the Butlers in Ireland." *Journal of the Butler Society* 2.1 (1980): 86–101. The Karryk arms can be seen above a chimney piece in a small room "at the top of the stair" of the Carrick mansion (Butler 90).

1a   1b

Fig 1a. The "Karryk Quarter" added as the fourth quarter to the shield of Thomas Butler, tenth earl of Ormond.

Fig 1b. The Ormond shield as it appears today. In the tenth earl's time the positions of the third and fourth quarters (the latter showing the Desmond quarter) would have been reversed.

(Source: Butler 90–91).

Index